Advance praise for *Best Ever Literacy Survival Tips: 72 Lessons You Can't Teach Without*

"This is my favorite resource even after teaching for many years. Each chapter includes eve you need to know on a specific topic, as well as teaching ideas from the include specific lesson plans. The topics include read-alouds, indeper assessment, grouping, fluency, nonfiction, and more."

—Mary Jo Barker, Reading Specialist and
Stanton Ele Missouri

"This is the survival guide that teachers have been craving. The format is easy to read, and the frequent headings enable the teacher to quickly review each strategy before implementation. Oczkus provides great student-friendly icons and language to engage students in the reading process. I now keep all of Lori's Top 5 Surefire Strategies within arm's length. The 20 bookmarks featured throughout are must-haves, too. My students and their parents love them! Oczkus's title speaks the truth: This book is a vital resource that I wouldn't want to teach without."

—Amanda Cleary, Second-Grade Teacher,
Jackson Elementary School, Valparaiso, Indiana

"Lori Oczkus knows how to give teachers exactly what they need to streamline their teaching. Each chapter of this book presents the essential theoretical considerations and relevant research on the topic in a completely accessible way, in just a few pages. Lori includes instructional strategies that are immediately applicable in the classroom. For new and experienced teachers alike, this book is a gem!"

—Tarie Lewis, Lecturer, Literacy Program, Elementary Education Department,
State University of New York at New Paltz

"*Best Ever Literacy Survival Tips* is more than a survival guide for reading teachers—it is a handbook that can guide teachers in making informed, effective, and creative instructional decisions to meet the literacy needs of their students. This is a book that should be on the desk of anyone who teaches reading in the elementary or middle grades. It is a wonderful example of the merging of the art and science of teaching reading."

—Timothy Rasinski, Professor, Kent State University, Ohio

"Lori Oczkus has done it again! Lori is often described as a teacher's teacher because she has an innate ability to dig into literacy research and translate it into practical tips, tools, and lessons. In this book, you will find hundreds of use-tomorrow teaching tips; a variety of literacy tools for helping students become engaged, proficient readers; and 72 lessons on diverse topics such as read-alouds, independent reading, comprehension, reciprocal teaching, assessment, grouping, fluency, phonics, and phonemic awareness. Lori calls this collection her 'greatest hits' and suggests that 'it's like putting all your favorite songs in one playlist.' Whether you are a beginning teacher or a veteran, a professional developer or university teacher educator, Lori's new book will provide you with the resources you need to reach your students, from pre-K through adult."

—MaryEllen Vogt, Professor Emerita, California State University, Long Beach
Past President, International Reading Association

Literacy Survival Tips

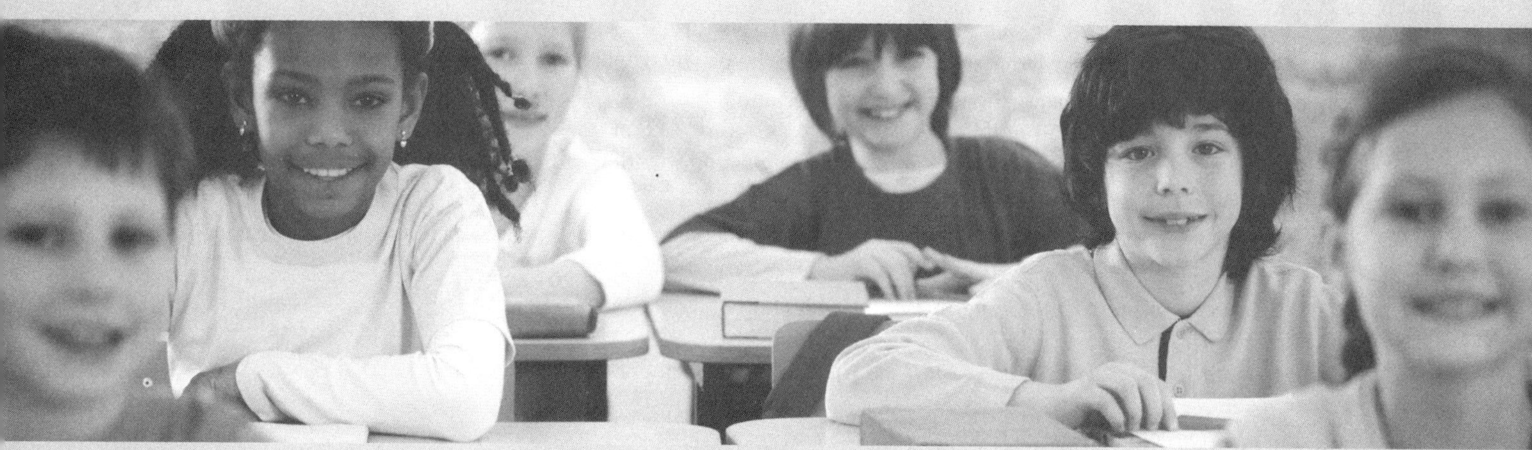

72 Lessons You Can't Teach Without

Lori D. Oczkus

Foreword by Timothy Rasinski

The International Reading Association attempts, through its publications, to provide a forum for a wide spectrum of opinions on reading. This policy permits divergent viewpoints without implying the endorsement of the Association.

Executive Editor, Publications Shannon Fortner
Managing Editor Christina M. Terranova
Editorial Associate Wendy Logan
Design and Composition Manager Anette Schuetz
Design and Composition Associate Lisa Kochel

Project Editor Renée Brosius

Cover Design: Frank Pessia; Front cover photos (from top): iStock/Joshua Hodge Photography, iStock/Kristian Sekulic, iStock/Mark Bowden; Back cover photo: Thinkstock.com

The publisher would appreciate notification where errors occur so that they may be corrected in subsequent printings and/or editions.

Library of Congress Cataloging-in-Publication Data
Oczkus, Lori D.
Best ever literacy survival tips : 72 lessons you can't teach without / Lori D. Oczkus.
p. cm.
Includes bibliographical references.
ISBN 978-0-87207-813-0
1. Language arts. 2. Lesson planning. 3. Motivation in education. I. Title.
LB1576.O297 2012
372.6--dc23

2012004791

Suggested APA Reference
Oczkus, L.D. (2012). *Best ever literacy survival tips: 72 lessons you can't teach without.* Newark, DE: International Reading Association.

To John Perata, a wonderful educator whose contagious enthusiasm, laughter, and passion for teaching have inspired thousands of teachers and students! I'm lucky to be one of them.

Contents

72 Lessons That Motivate, Engage, and Yield Results

In addition to the lessons featured here, you will find many more fantastic strategies throughout the chapters and in the online resources listed near the end of every chapter. Pick and choose the lessons that fit your teaching style, grade level, and students' needs.

20 Bookmarks

This book contains 20 bookmarks for you and your students to refer to all year long when reading and writing. A boldface **T** indicates the bookmarks that are designed for teacher use, and the rest are helpful tools for your students.

As you introduce each bookmark, refer to the lesson plan in the book. You may wish to run some of your favorite bookmarks in color, laminate them, or even put them on a ring for easy reference during lessons. You may also wish to put the teacher bookmarks on a ring for easy reference as you assess and coach students during instruction and practice.

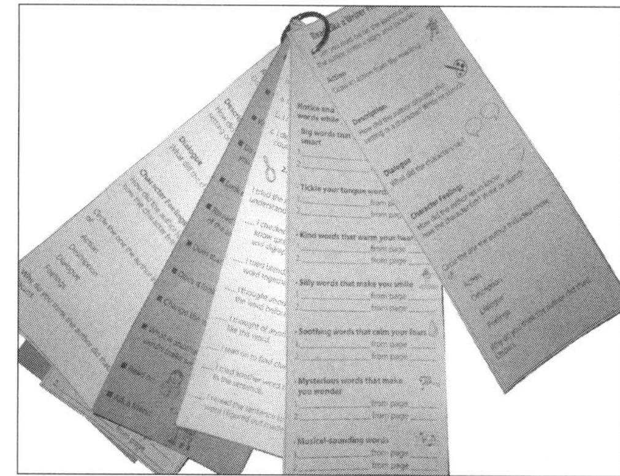

About the Author

LORI D. OCZKUS is a literacy coach, author, and popular speaker across the United States. Tens of thousands of teachers have attended her motivating, fast-paced workshops and read her practical, research-based professional books. Lori has extensive experience as a bilingual elementary teacher, intervention specialist working with struggling readers, staff developer, and literacy coach. She works regularly with students in classrooms and really knows the challenges that teachers face in teaching students to read! Lori was inducted into the California Reading Hall of Fame by the California Reading Association for her contributions to the field of reading in California and throughout the United States.

Lori recently published the second edition of the best-selling book *Reciprocal Teaching at Work: Powerful Strategies and Lessons for Improving Reading Comprehension* (International Reading Association, 2010). The *Reciprocal Teaching at Work* DVD (International Reading Association, 2005) won the prestigious Association of Educational Publishers Video of the Year award in 2006.

Her other popular titles include *Interactive Think-Aloud Lessons: 25 Surefire Ways to Engage Students and Improve Comprehension* (Scholastic and International Reading Association, 2009); *The Fabulous Four Reading Comprehension Puppets* (Primary Concepts, 2008); *Guided Writing: Practical Lessons, Powerful Results* (Heinemann, 2007); and *Super Six Comprehension Strategies: 35 Lessons and More for Reading Success* (Christopher-Gordon, 2004).

Lori resides in northern California with her husband, Mark, and their three children. She enjoys spending time with her family, traveling anywhere by any means, reading historical fiction, hiking and walking with friends, and occasionally scuba diving.

Author Information for Correspondence and Workshops

For feedback, questions, and information on professional development you can contact Lori through her website at www.lorioczkus.com.

Foreword

Over my many years in literacy education, I have found that the field of literacy is filled with ingenious researchers who are discovering how we learn to read. Similarly, literacy education is filled with dedicated teachers who help students acquire the ability to read and write. However, the link between what researchers find and what teachers do is sometimes missing. In short supply are those scholars who are able to take research and scholarly findings and translate them into practical and engaging strategies that can be implemented in classrooms and clinical settings. My friend and colleague Lori Oczkus is one of those rare and gifted scholars. Because she has the mind of a literacy scholar and the heart of a teacher, she has the ability to describe how literacy scholarship can be put into actual practice.

In *Best Ever Literacy Survival Tips*, Lori gives us another great example of her remarkable talents. This book is chock-full of lessons that address all the major issues in literacy education—from phonemic awareness to comprehension and everything in between. Each chapter provides readers with an evidence-based, yet readable, rationale and background for a particular literacy issue or instructional goal. It is followed with a set of creative and easy-to-implement lessons and strategies for achieving competence in that area. Every chapter offers a set of references that provide the scholarly foundation for the chapter and suggestions for further reading.

Lori was kind enough to describe my word ladders as a viable approach to phonics and phonemic awareness. Perhaps the best way, then, for me to summarize the content of Lori's book is with a word ladder. Here goes…

Start with BEST.

BEST Subtract a letter from BEST to make a word that means "to make a wager or to gamble."

BET Change a letter to make something that a baseball player might use to hit a ball.

BAT Change a letter to make a pet that is also called a feline.

CAT Change a letter to make a metal object in which food is often stored.

CAN Add a letter to make an object that might assist a person in walking or standing.

CANE Change a letter to make something that ice cream is sometimes served in.

CONE Change a letter to make a word that is a small bay or place of shelter.

COVE Add a letter to make what you do with your blanket in bed.

COVER Subtract a letter to make the opposite of *under*.

OVER Change a letter to make a word that, along with the first word, describes the strategies in this book.

EVER!

Truth be told, *Best Ever Literacy Survival Tips* is more than a survival guide for reading teachers—it is a handbook that can guide teachers in making informed, effective, and creative instructional decisions to meet the literacy needs of their students. This is a book that should be on the desk of anyone who teaches reading in the elementary or middle grades. It is a wonderful example of the merging of the art and science of teaching reading.

—Timothy V. Rasinski
Kent State University

Acknowledgments

Writing a book takes a leap of faith mixed in with a ton of work. Thanks to all the busy teachers, authors, and researchers who jumped in to generously share their favorite teaching tips. Thanks to Mary Jo Barker, Danny Brassell, Amanda Cleary, J. David Cooper, Nell Duke, Michael Ford, Linda Hoyt, Kathy Langham, Steven Layne, Judy Lynch, Rob Malling, Donalyn Miller, Tim Rasinski, Jenny Reilly, and Ray Reutzel. Special thanks to creative editors at IRA, Renée Brosius and Shannon Fortner, for maintaining my ideas and voice. It is a pleasure working with you!

I am especially grateful to those readers who gave me valuable feedback after reading my original online articles with graduate classes and in PD sessions in districts. Thanks go to fabulous educators Audrey Fong, Kathy Hannon, Tarie Lewis, Ellen Osmundson, Terry Thompson, and again Tim Rasinski.

First and foremost, thanks to my family: my husband, Mark, for all the cooking and support; my teenage daughters, Rachael and Rebecca, for cheering me on as a writer; and my college-age son, Bryan, for sage advice on reading. Oh, and thanks to Charley, our Maltipoo, who curled up adoringly at my feet while I wrote.

Introduction: Getting Started

The avalanche of critical information that educators must know to teach literacy today is overwhelming. If you purchased professional books for each of the hottest topics in literacy, you'd need a wheelbarrow to cart them to your car. (Not to mention several years to cover them all in professional development or learning communities!)

To teach our students to read and write effectively, teachers need to become "experts" on a wide range of important topics, including motivation, reading aloud, independent reading, assessments, grouping strategies for differentiating instruction, all aspects of comprehending both fiction and nonfiction texts, vocabulary strategies, phonics and phonemic awareness, effective writing techniques, and of course the new Common Core Standards (Common Core State Standards Initiative, 2010).

An Exciting New Resource Filled With "Greatest Hits"

Best Ever Literacy Survival Tips gives you the essential guidelines that every teacher *must know* about critical topics in literacy, plus more than 72 engaging lessons that yield results. In hundreds of school districts around the United States, I have witnessed schools struggling to find both the money and time for quality staff development. I developed this "greatest hits" collection to serve as a vehicle for covering hot topics in literacy quickly or in-depth as desired. It's like putting all your favorite songs in one playlist on your MP3 player, but occasionally choosing to play a particular album.

The idea is to provide an inviting format for covering some of the most important and salient information teachers need to know. The lively magazine-style layout makes the chapters appealing and easy to read. What began as a popular online article series available only to members of the International Reading Association now serves as a rich desktop reference and professional development tool with many useful added features, including

- A new piece on the topic of motivation
- Supplemental material for each topic, from "Best Ever Advice" you can use and a detailed staff development guide to new lessons with Common Core connections, assessment tips, bookmarks, and other reproducibles
- A wonderful bibliography of children's literature, provided by Booksource.com, organized by teaching topic for use with your students

Whether you've been teaching for decades or this is your first year, *Best Ever Literacy Survival Tips* is designed with you in mind. You can read it cover to cover or skip around to select lessons or topics. Study it on your own, in a professional development community, or as a staff during regularly scheduled meetings.

Organization of This Book

Each chapter in this collection addresses the importance of the topic and discusses problems that teachers and students encounter. There are engaging classroom scenarios and a wealth of evidence-based guidelines. Each chapter also has the following useful features:

- "Best Ever Advice" from literacy leaders and classroom teachers
- Lori's Top 5 Surefire Strategies
- A "Q&A" section
- Recommended online resources and professional books to study
- A before-, during-, and after-reading Professional Development Guide
- Scaffolded lesson plans for small groups or whole-class instruction, with Common Core connections
- Formative assessment tips
- Classroom-ready bookmarks and other reproducibles

Following is a chapter-by-chapter overview of the book.

Chapter 1: "Motivation Magic"

We possess the tools to teach any child to read, but can we teach children to love reading? What are the magic ingredients that when sprinkled into our classrooms and programs will win kids over to become lifelong readers? This chapter provides guidelines and practical tips for building a strong passion to read for a lifetime.

Chapter 2: "The Power of Reading Aloud to Your Students"

How can you effectively use read-alouds in your already busy school day? This chapter features a range of motivating strategies, from Laminack and Wadsworth's (2006) six types of read-alouds, to The Read-Aloud Challenge, to filling Mystery Literacy Boxes (Pearman, Camp, & Hurst, 2004). You'll also find a handy bookmark with discussion starters for partners to use when they turn and talk during an interactive read-aloud, as well as Lights, Camera, Listen, an engaging lesson on using senses during reading.

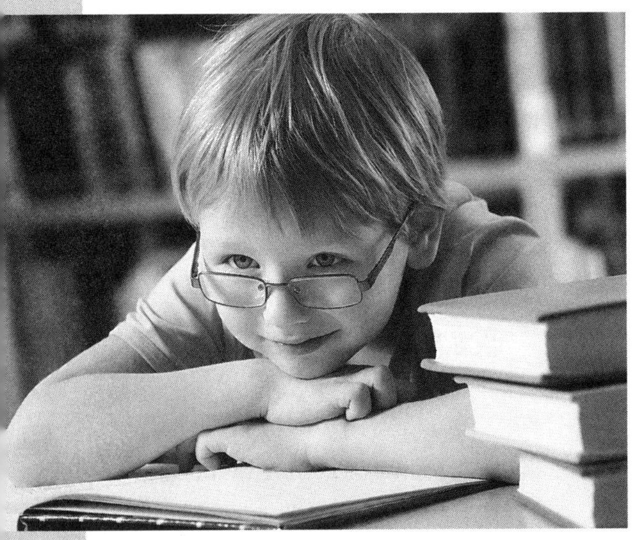

Chapter 3: "Super Practical Ways to Build an Independent Reading Program in Your Classroom"

Whether you call it SSR (Sustained Silent Reading) or ZYLAR (Zip Your Lip and Read), you know that independent reading time requires much more than simply providing time for kids to read silently. Make the most of this critical piece of the reading puzzle with suggestions from this chapter, including simple ideas for building a classroom library on a budget, conferring with students, and building comprehension. Support materials include a sample reading log, interest inventory, two independent reading bookmarks to promote comprehension and discussions, plus ideas for impromptu Buddy Circle discussions and a rubric to assess students on their independent reading behaviors.

Chapter 4: "Surefire Ways to Engage Students and Improve Comprehension"

Many of our students struggle with comprehension. This chapter is loaded with powerful new ways to yield results using familiar comprehension strategies (connect, predict, infer, question, monitor, clarify, summarize, synthesize, evaluate) and to motivate students to use the strategies on their own during reading! This chapter includes ways to make your think-alouds interactive and memorable so that learning sticks, with lessons like Connection Chains for building better connections and Pause to Clarify to promote rereading and decoding, a comprehension strategy bookmark your students will refer to daily, and a guide to free online lessons and suggestions for comprehension.

Chapter 5: "Reciprocal Teaching—The Reading Super Vitamin"

Do your students read and decode but often not deeply understand what they are reading? Reciprocal teaching or the Fab Four (Oczkus, 2010) is a research-based (Palinscar & Brown, 1986), interactive discussion technique that invites students to work cooperatively using four strategies: predict, question, clarify, and summarize. The promise of reciprocal teaching is that after just three months, student reading improves from one to three years! Even after just 15 days, you'll notice a difference in comprehension. This chapter provides guidelines for getting started with read-alouds and easy-to-implement lessons such as Fast Fab Four, Table Runners, and the ever popular Four Door to use for formative assessment. You'll find tools to help you implement reciprocal teaching, including a Fab Four bookmark, links to classroom footage showing reciprocal teaching in action, and a handy assessment rubric.

Chapter 6: "Navigating Nonfiction"

Today more than ever, our students need strategies to read nonfiction text well. Reading informational text is the key to success in school (Duke, 2000). The Common Core Standards (Common Core State Standards Initiative, 2010) and reading in the digital information age require that our students use critical thinking skills as they read and comprehend texts about the world around them—text that can include heavy vocabulary and concept loads. Creative ideas for teaching text structures and text features are included along with engaging lessons like Word Pop Prediction to predict informational text vocabulary, Flip It to promote deeper comprehension, and the wildly popular Hand Motion Summaries that students will beg for over and over again! Also add the Nonfiction Bookmark and Nonfiction Wonder lesson to your bag of informational teaching tricks.

Chapter 7: "Assessment Survival Tips"

You won't want to miss this chapter chock-full of super practical information for the teacher on assessment overload! Practical ways to use diagnostic, formative, and summative assessments are included. This chapter offers the following simple classroom assessment techniques that help keep you informed on student progress so you can adjust instruction or group students by need: Pile Sorting, tips for powerful reading conferences, and running record short cuts complete with handy teacher bookmarks to facilitate quick assessments of reading and retelling. The Ready, Set, Goal! student bookmark helps students set reading goals to stretch their reading habits, genres, and comprehension.

Chapter 8: "Grouping Survival Tips"

Grouping students in your classroom is a little bit like choreographing a delicate ballet dance number (or maybe a hip-hop number!) with students flowing in and out of whole-class formations complete with partnerships, to cooperative groups, to teacher-led groups and independent "smart" work. This grouping chapter provides many research-based suggestions, classroom scenarios, and powerful grouping options. A go-to bookmark for teachers with a template to guide small groups for fiction and informational text provides an engaging lesson plan. The coaching and think-aloud teacher bookmark gives you quality suggestions for coaching individual students or small groups. You might also try partnering students across reading levels with Partner Match-Up, practice reading with cross-age buddies, promote comprehension while writing Best Line Cooperative Reading Responses, or compare and contrast characters from different books using a Character Carousel. Formative assessment suggestions guide your instruction in any group setting. Suggestions are offered for keeping students actively engaged in independent work so you can meet with small groups.

Chapter 9: "Wonderful Words"

Turn your students into word wizards using the essentials on vocabulary instruction offered in this chapter. Learn exciting ways to reach all students, including your English learners, with lessons in a variety of modalities including art, music, dance, and other nonlinguistic representations (Marzano, 2004, 2010). Keep kids marinating in words with mentor texts, One-Word Prediction, a Key Word Dance, or the Wonderful Words Sorting Sheet. The chapter includes suggestions of online resources to extend vocabulary learning and helpful classroom assessments such as a vocabulary test for use before and after reading.

Chapter 10: "Phonics and Phonemic Awareness"

Most educators agree that students need phonics and phonemic awareness to read well, but questions form around when, how, how much, and under what circumstances phonics should be taught. This chapter puts at your fingertips in-a-nutshell discussions about the most popular types of phonics instruction along with research-based guidelines that really work. There is a useful selection of proven ideas you can incorporate into your routine for results, including Win at Wordo, Score With Word Sorts, and more. Two clarify bookmarks plus no-fuss teacher assessments provide students with the support they need.

Chapter 11: "Fluency Survival Tips"

Many of our students still struggle with poor reading fluency. Fluency is the bridge to comprehension and is much more than simply reading quickly. Fluency involves rate, accuracy, and prosody (Rasinski & Griffith, 2010). This chapter includes ways to increase fluency in any grade level. New exciting lessons for fluency include a paired reading bookmark and poster, Sing It Again Sam using popular music, Flash Mob Reading for joining in to read together, and a rich variety of online support lessons. You'll end up using the Quick Fluency Checks bookmarks constantly to help you informally assess reading fluency.

Chapter 12: "Guided Writing—The Missing Middle Piece"

Motivating students to write is a tough job! Help prevent "blank-page scares" by giving students guided writing experiences before setting them loose to write on their own. Dramatically improve the quality of writing in your classroom with super practical writing suggestions including mentor texts, Lori's "cool tools," drama to clarify during writing, Weekend Webs, Live Rubrics, and Daily Sentence "Make Overs." The Read Like a Writer fiction bookmark helps students make the reading–writing connection. Whether your students are learning to write paragraphs, personal narratives, or persuasive letters, the suggestions in this chapter provide support for your lessons.

Happy Reading!

Enjoy this set of guidelines and lessons on the hottest topics in literacy today, whether studying them alone or with a professional learning community. This array of proven, student-centered ideas is designed to yield results. I hope you find them useful and engaging for your students.

Please look for me on IRA's social media community, Engage (engage .reading.org), for discussions, more lessons, questions, and ongoing support for "The Best Ever Literacy...." Or check in to share some of your own favorite tips!

REFERENCES

Common Core State Standards Initiative. (2010). *Common Core State Standards for English language arts & literacy in history/social studies, science, and technical subjects*. Washington, DC: National Governors Association Center for Best Practices and the Council of Chief State School Officers.

Duke, N.K. (2000). 3.6 minutes per day: The scarcity of informational texts in first grade. *Reading Research Quarterly, 35*(2), 202–224.

Laminack, L.L., & Wadsworth, R.M. (2006). *Learning under the influence of language and literature: Making the most of read-alouds across the day*. Portsmouth, NH: Heinemann.

Marzano, R.J. (2004). *Building background knowledge for academic achievement: Research on what works in schools*. Alexandria, VA: Association for Supervision and Curriculum Development.

Marzano, R.J. (2010). *Teaching basic and advanced vocabulary: A framework for direct instruction*. Boston: Heinle.

Oczkus, L.D. (2010). *Reciprocal teaching at work: Powerful strategies and lessons for improving reading comprehension* (2nd ed.). Newark, DE: International Reading Association.

Palincsar, A.S., & Brown, A.L. (1986). Interactive teaching to promote independent learning from text. *The Reading Teacher, 39*(8), 771–777.

Pearman, C.J., Camp, D., & Hurst, B. (2004). Literacy mystery boxes. *The Reading Teacher, 57*(8), 766–768.

Rasinski, T.V., & Griffith, L. (2010). *Fluency through practice & performance*. Huntington Beach, CA: Shell Education.

CHAPTER 1

Motivation Magic: Guidelines and TOP 5 Strategies for Helping Kids Develop a Passion for Reading

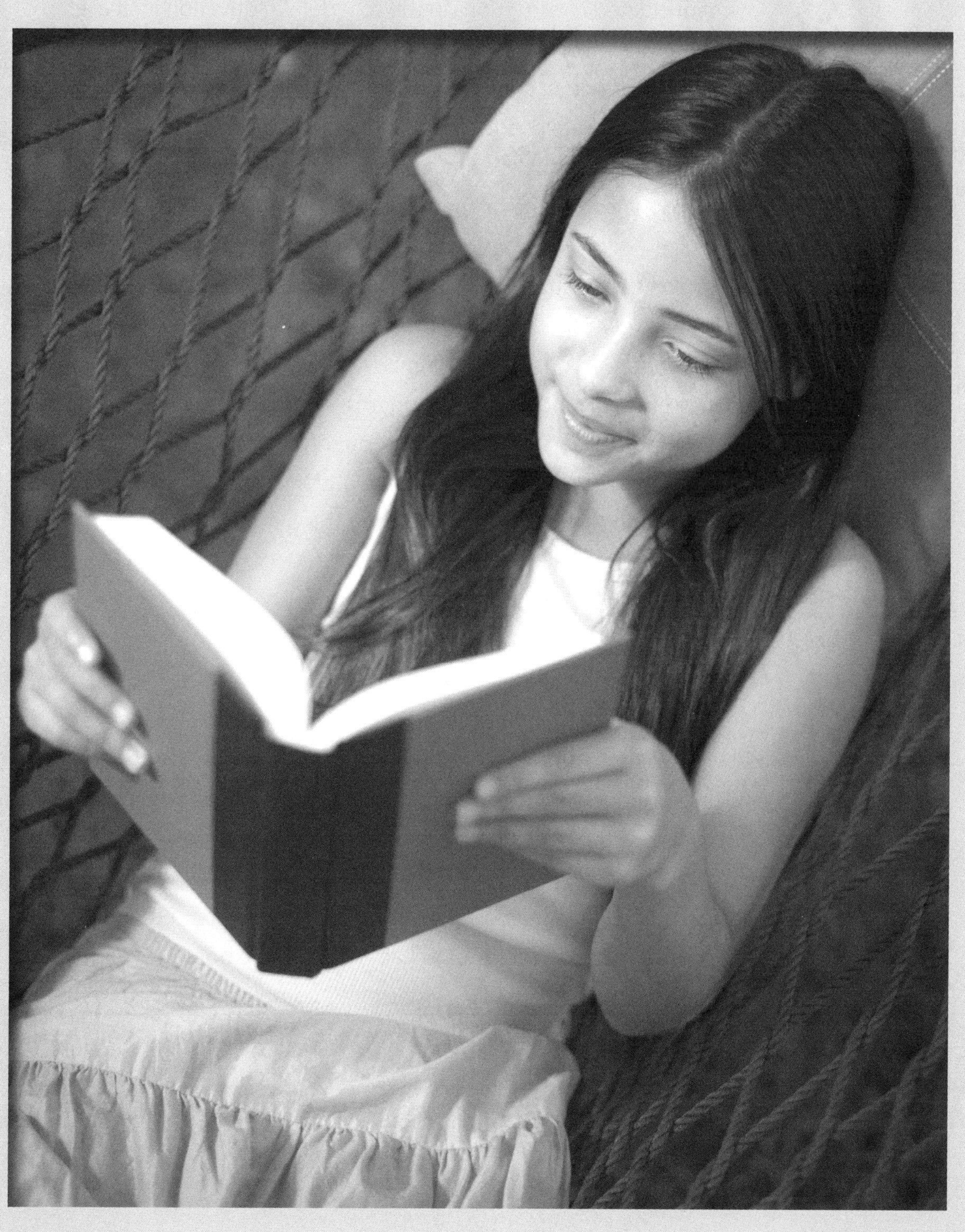

Best Ever Advice on... Motivation

My students, no matter the age or grade, have always loved unanticipated interruptions in the schedule! Motivation increases the minute we discover that routine is about to be broken. These days, for my graduate students, it's the sound of a bell resounding through the halls of our building, which heralds the arrival of our famous cookie trolley. That bell promises just-out-of-the-oven cookies and cold milk, along with a chance for my students to grab whatever material they'd like and read for a while. We call it "literacy café." Similarly, my elementary and middle school classes loved poetry breaks, when I would cease instruction in a manner that appeared completely impromptu and wildly yell something like "POETRY BREAK!" They were trained to know that this meant everyone was to grab any poetry book from my large collection, find a comfy spot, and read some poems—or grab a partner and read them aloud together. Treats weren't a must, but often a plate of something yummy magically appeared. When you see even eighth-grade boys whooping it up over poetry, you know you've discovered something motivating—and magical.

—Steven L. Layne, Author of *Igniting a Passion for Reading: Successful Strategies for Building Lifetime Readers* (Stenhouse, 2009)

Kids will love to read, reread, and reread again if you provide an audience. One way I provide an audience for my second graders is with Kindergarten Wow Reading. Students choose a book they think kindergarteners will enjoy and practice reading it aloud in a "WOW" way (with expression, accuracy, and character voices; by showing the pictures; etc.). Then on their special day, they sit in the teacher's chair and read the book to an entire kindergarten class. They even ask the kindergarteners comprehension questions. You would not believe how many times they choose to reread the book before their big day!

—Amanda Cleary, Second-Grade Teacher

What exactly does it mean to be motivated or to motivate? Motivation surrounds us every day in all aspects of our lives. Motivation causes you to lose weight and work out because you don't like the way you look in the photos from cousin Sally's wedding. Motivation drives the salesperson to call on more clients to try to clinch the winner's circle trip to Las Vegas. The motivated teenager works odd jobs to save up money to buy name-brand jeans to fit in at school. You decide to clean your closet or desk because you can't stand the mess for one more minute! Motivation, or the desire and willingness to do something, impacts all areas of our lives—including our reading habits.

What motivates our students to read and become readers? Jennie Nash, author of *Raising a Reader*, asks, "Can passion be passed along from parent to child? Can you in other words make someone love baseball, ballet, or books?" In this chapter we will explore the topic of motivation—what works, what doesn't—and present some solid action steps you can take to inspire your students to love reading.

When we ask students, "Do you like to read?" the responses often look something like this:

- "I like to read sometimes."
- "I hate to read."
- "I only read at school when I have to."
- "My mom reads to me."
- "I read if it is a book I like."
- "Reading is so boring!"

What we are really asking is, "Are you a reader?" Plenty of folks know how to read, and even like to read just fine, but they are not true readers. A reader is someone who enjoys the process of reading and reads often. A reader takes away *something* from all that he or she reads. A reader approaches reading with heated passion and talks about books with others, seeks out books, compares books, devours books for enjoyment and information, passes judgment on issues in books, and even selectively abandons books.

Readers know how to give each text the attention it deserves. They might read slowly and deliberately with curiosity, or thoughtfully with deep emotion, or frantically while skimming in search of answers to important questions. Readers carry their precious treasures with them in backpacks, purses, and tote bags, allowing the paper pages or digital devices to transport them at a moment's notice to different worlds. Readers' living spaces overflow with books as they joyfully wallow in them. The reader feels truly alive when surrounded by books and engaged in reading.

Unfortunately, many of today's students are not being encouraged to lose themselves in books and experience the joy of reading. Motivated students who spend more time reading become better readers. Reading motivation is directly linked to the development of lifelong readers (Morrow, 1992; Wang & Guthrie, 2004).

> "Read not to contradict and confute; nor to believe and take for granted; nor to find talk and discourse; but to weigh and consider. Some books are to be tasted, others to be swallowed, and some few to be chewed and digested: that is, some books are to be read only in parts, others to be read, but not curiously, and some few to be read wholly, and with diligence and attention."
>
> —Francis Bacon

When Did You Become a Reader?

Think about it. When did you first become a reader? Many people recall a particular book or situation that turned them into a reader. Although I knew how to read well, I didn't become an avid reader until the age of 26, when I married into a reading family whose dinner-table conversations turned into semi–book clubs, with rich discussions sparked by reading. To fit in, I began reading for enjoyment and in the process became hooked.

Coincidentally, both of my daughters treasure the same two magical books that transformed them into readers when they reached fourth grade. They loved *Because of Winn-Dixie* by Kate DiCamillo, the small-town friendship story turned hit movie about a mischievous dog, and *Esperanza Rising* by Pam Muñoz Ryan, the riches-to-rags tale of a Mexican girl who ends up as a migrant worker in the United States. We wept, we laughed, we stayed up too late reading both of these books.

For my son, it was most likely the hundreds of rereadings (he cried if we read anything else!) of the entire Curious George collection by Margaret and H.A. Rey that firmly secured his love of reading at age 2. Later, the Harry Potter series by J.K. Rowling and the Redwall series by Brian Jacques sealed the deal!

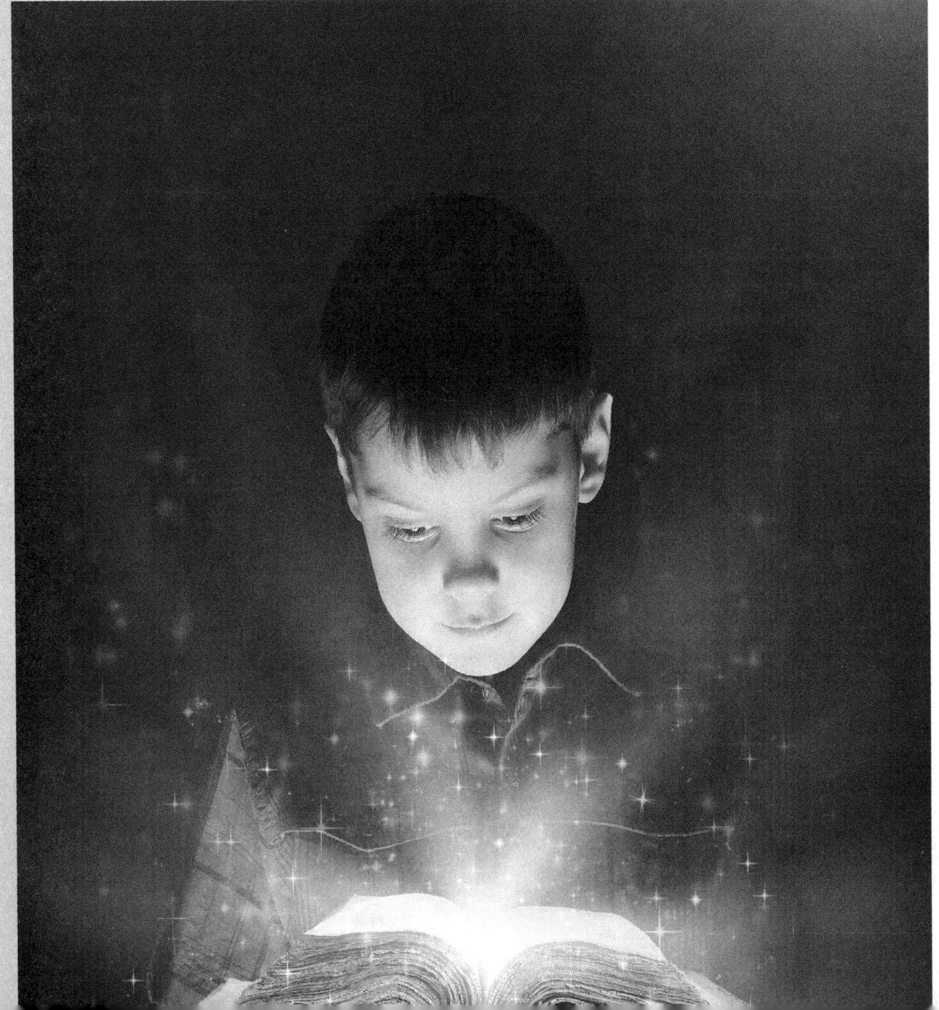

Encourage your students to reflect on those special books that inspired them to read. For students who are not yet readers, help them search for that one magical book, any book, that will turn them on to reading.

The Scary News—Everyone Is Reading Less

The National Endowment for the Arts (2007) study *To Read or Not to Read* concludes that Americans are reading a lot less. An increasing number of adults do not read even one book a year. Nearly half of all Americans ages 15 to 24 do not read for pleasure. The trend is similar for 9-year-olds, with only 54% claiming to read "for fun." American students are reading less for pleasure than in generations past. Our culture is losing interest in reading as people engage in other forms of entertainment, including up to two hours of television viewing for many adults. Are schools doing anything to contribute to or halt this decline in reading?

Are schools "killing" reading?

Kelly Gallagher (2009), in his landmark book *Readicide: How Schools Are Killing Reading and What You Can Do About It*, argues that schools are unintentionally killing reading through instructional practices and current priorities, including

- Placing value on test-taking over developing lifelong readers
- Teaching a mile wide but not deeply enough
- Throwing students into difficult texts without scaffolding or support
- Overteaching and overanalyzing books with "sticky note" mania
- Not setting recreational reading as a goal

Gallagher cites other factors, such as not enough time spent reading in school and at home and chopping up texts too much, which prevents what all good readers crave: getting lost in a book, or experiencing flow.

> "There are three things to remember about education. The first one is motivation. The second one is motivation. The third one is motivation."
>
> —Terrell H. Bell

Teach the will as well as the skill to read.

Our reading programs and testing pressures require that we spend time teaching students the critical skills of reading, such as phonics, fluency, comprehension, and vocabulary. But rarely do schools formally address other important aspects of reading including interest, attitude, motivation, and engagement (Layne, 2009). If we want our students to develop a lifelong love of reading, we need to find time in our school days to address this less tangible set of skills.

Steven Layne (2009), in his powerful book *Igniting a Passion for Reading: Successful Strategies for Building Lifetime Readers*, suggests many wonderful and practical ideas for promoting reading in the classroom and schoolwide. These include carefully selecting read-alouds; promoting books through book chats, in which the teacher talks about a title and entices students with inviting displays (picture a shelf spray-painted gold!); allowing student choice; organizing various "shopping for books to read" activities; and encouraging book referrals from peers. In an effort to promote a lifelong love of reading, the teachers in Community Consolidated School District 15 in Palatine, Illinois, took Layne's powerful suggestions to heart and have implemented a districtwide campaign called "Turn Up the Volume" (on reading) to ignite passion in reading.

Classroom Scenario: Life Books

All eyes are on Ivan as he perches on a stool in front of his sixth-grade classmates, ready to share his "Life Book," or the one book that has made a difference to him. The student running the video camera cues Ivan to begin. He takes a deep breath while holding up his treasured book and starts to speak.

"I choose *Charlotte's Web* by E.B. White, because it's a really good book. She saves the pig from dying. And it is the first book my dad read to me. It's an awesome book!"

Over a two-day period, the students in Patty Magro's classroom take turns sharing the one book that has made a difference in their lives. Inspired by Scholastic's Read Every Day campaign (www.scholastic.com/readeveryday), in which celebrities talk about reading and share their favorite books, the students decide to create a show of their own for the school website. The reasons for selecting their Life Books are as varied as the students themselves. Students share books because they are funny or scary, contain information about baseball or ballet, or were the first ones they read on their own. Some of the testimonials are moving. A hush spread across the room when Nancy, an orphan from Mexico, shared her connections to the characters in the Lemony Snicket Series of Unfortunate Events books. These testimonials about reading motivate students to read more, and the experience is priceless.

Guidelines for Motivating Students to Love Reading

Incorporate three ingredients kids need to read.

Gallagher (2009) notes that kids need three important ingredients to become readers:

1. Access to books
2. Time to read
3. A place to read

Access to books promotes an atmosphere of choice. Our classroom libraries need to be well stocked and organized to attract readers (see Chapter 3, "Super Practical Ways to Build an Independent Reading Program in Your Classroom"). Be sure to display your recommendations as well as those of students. I love encountering "staff picks" in bookstores. Those persuasive little summaries posted right there on the shelf, with the book facing out, inspire me and pique my curiosity. Why not adapt this idea for the classroom? Designate a specific time each day when students will read uninterrupted; if possible, allow them to move around to comfortable reading spots in the classroom.

Don't forget that kids need the same ingredients at home: access to books, time to read, and a place to read. You may need to send books home in book bags or create a check-out system. Encourage parents to take their children to the library. Children feel empowered when they have their own library cards from a young age. Jeannie Nash (2003) argues that children need to experience books in abundance. She says her children feel like they are getting away with something when they check out 10 books from the library for free. Even if they don't read them all, just the abundance makes a reader feel lucky to be surrounded by so many books that he or she has selected to read.

Practice reading with no strings attached.

Steve Krashen (2004) in *The Power of Reading: Insights on Research* calls the kind of reading that literate folks do all the time "free voluntary reading" (FVR). He suggests that we allow students to make time to read the books of their choice, without requiring book reports, dioramas, or questions. Krashen cautions us not to overrely on incentive programs but rather to use other means to inspire students to read.

Be careful with incentive programs.

My son, Bryan, a sophomore in college, called the afternoon I was writing this chapter. Because he is a reader, I invited him to weigh in on the motivation issue. Without hesitation, he offered sage advice:

> *Kids should* choose *what they read without any judgment. [Did I judge his reading when he went through his comic-book phase in middle school? Uh oh!] or without any rewards or punishment. The child should read for enjoyment, not something extrinsic but intrinsic. If you offer a reward, the kids will just read for the reward.*

Bryan hadn't read any of the research on the negative effects of reading incentives, yet he instinctively knew the truth about motivation: It comes from deep down and can't be bought! Whether it's baseball cards or pizza, incentive programs are not very effective in creating lifelong readers (Gambrell & Marinak, 1997; Kohen, 1993; Krashen, 2004; Marinak & Gambrell, 2008).

I tried incorporating incentives when my daughter Rachael was in second grade and found reading tedious and tiring. To entice her to read more during the summer, I set up a "stickers and rewards on Friday" program, in which she chose where we'd go for an ice cream treat. After about three weeks, she said: "Mom, you don't always have to give me the ice cream. I like to read more now." In the sixth-grade classroom of Donalyn Miller (author of *The Book Whisperer* [2009]), students set a goal to read 40 or more books during the year. The goal became incentive enough to move her students along in their love of reading.

Incorporate technology to motivate students.

Schools across the country vary in their use of technology and reading, depending upon funding. Our students, digital natives, are comfortable with and motivated by technology. Try allowing students to respond to reading using inexpensive video cameras, blogs, cameras, mp3 players, and computers. See the online resources at the end of this chapter for recommendations.

Build motivation using the ways students select books.

A great way to think about motivating students to read in your classroom and school is to design lessons, activities, and book displays around the ways they choose books. If you ask, "Why did you choose that book?" chances are students will answer with some of these reasons (Edmunds & Bauserman, 2006):

- "I like choosing what I want to read."

- "I dance and want to learn about ballet."
- "I like funny books and joke books."
- "I want to learn more about dinosaurs."
- "My best friend read that book and said it was good."

Choice: The entire third-grade class was quietly engaged in reading their self-selected books. I circulated to observe student choices and chat a bit about their books. Juan shared that he really likes his book. I asked why. He responded matter-of-factly: "Because I chose it." Choice is everything for readers. Even very young children enjoy selecting their own books to read. Choice is a powerful motivator. Model for students how to make a variety of choices based on different criteria, such as choosing books at your own level, choosing books whose topic interests you, choosing books because someone suggests them, and choosing books a little above your level because they encourage you to stretch.

Interests: Students' interests often drive their motivation to read. So, if a child hopes to get a dog for a pet or wants to learn about karate, then he or she may head for books on those topics. You can use interest inventories to help students target or find their interests (see page 35). Give the inventories several times per year as students' interests change. Incorporate the inventories into your conferences with students and use them to guide book recommendations and choices.

Characteristics of books: Sometimes readers are motivated to choose a book based on its characteristics. A student may

select a book because he or she enjoys funny, scary, or artistic books, thin or thick chapter books, or books with attractive covers. See which students give the characteristics of a book as the reason they selected it. You can then suggest more books based on those preferences.

Knowledge gained: Another way students select books is for the knowledge they will gain from it. When one student was about to become a dog owner, he said, "I want to learn about dog care." That was my entrée to suggest that he check out dog-care books from the library.

Referrals: A referral from a friend, librarian, teacher, or family member is often the best, most powerful way to inspire students to read. Think about your own responses to book suggestions from others. Most adult readers rely on referrals from friends, book reviews, or the media. Steven Layne (2009) has come up with a wonderful way to make referrals that motivate students. First, he suggests we select books based on students' interest inventories, goals, and reading habits. Next, he recommends saying to a student, "I thought of you...," and then handing the student a book or two to show how much you care. Try this approach with several students each week and watch their motivation increase.

Lori's Top 5 Surefire Strategies for Motivation

1 *Life Books*

This is an idea I created in response to Scholastic's Read Every Day Campaign (www.scholastic.com/readeveryday), in which celebrities share lists of their favorite books from their lives as readers. In this lesson, students focus on only one special book. You can add a video piece by recording each student.

- Ask students to reflect on that one special book they've read that has impacted their lives. Model the activity by sharing your own Life Book, explaining your reasons for selecting it.
- Students may share their Life Books in a variety of ways, including a videotape presentation, posters with explanations, or book talks.
- If you videotape the presentations, limit to about 1.5 minutes per student. You can invite one student per day to share a Life Book in class if you prefer to use only a few minutes per day. Or show the videos at an open house or on the school website.
- Have students share their selections with one another in a stroll line: Ask students to stand in two facing lines and share their books with the partner across from them. When you signal, one of the lines moves to the right to form new partnerships. Continue to signal for the line to shift until students have rotated through several new partners.

2 *Librarians Unleashed (Edmunds & Bauserman, 2006)*

- Collect all the independent-reading books students have read in the past month.
- Dump the books onto the floor.
- Invite students to become "little librarians" by creating any five categories they agree on, into which they will sort the books. Provide just five bins for students to use. Students label the book bins with the categories.
- Place the bins in the classroom library and allow students to check out the books.

3 *Book Talks*

Book talks may be simple, but they are really one of the best ways, if not the most effective way, to inspire students to read. Yet many teachers skip them. All year long, every day, promote titles to your class.

- Select a book to share with your class.
- Show the cover, front and back, and a few illustrations (if present).
- If it's a jacketed hardbound book, read aloud the inside flaps (Layne, 2009).
- Select a favorite passage to read aloud.
- Summarize the story, but don't reveal how it ends.
- Invite other students to give book talks also.
- Give book talks for titles found in your school library; during your talk, ask students to raise hands to show who would like to check out the book.

4 *Book Idol*

The sixth graders in Patty Magro's class came up with *Book Idol*, a mock television book-review show, complete with judges. Try videotaping the proceedings to improve student presentations.

- Select three volunteers to act as the judges. Judges should have distinctive personality profiles; work with the class to agree on these. Possibilities include a man or woman from London, a professor with glasses, and a skate boarder. Allow the class to come up with the profiles first and then vote on just three.
- Set up a table for the judges to sit at, and have them face the audience.
- Invite a fourth student to be the master or mistress of ceremonies.
- Use a video camera to record the show.
- Play the video at an open house or on the school website.

5 *Summer Book Bags (Allington & McGill-Franzen, 2003)*

The summer slump rears its ugly head every year when our students from low socioeconomic backgrounds skip out classroom doors only to skip reading all summer long. The result is disastrous: With a loss of as much as three months of reading achievement, these students return to school in worse shape than when they left. Contrast this situation with the three-month gains made by students from higher socioeconomic neighborhoods, whose parents tend to support their summer reading with trips to libraries and bookstores. As Richard Allington of the University of Tennessee notes, "The evidence is pretty clear that poor kids don't read during the summer, and middle-class kids do" ("Stopping summer slide," 2003, p. 1).

The difference between the two groups is access to books. To close this achievement gap, Allington developed an easy solution: Give books to the kids who need them. The results were astounding. Allington provided every student in 17 high-poverty schools with 12 books at the beginning of the summer; three years later, those in the program had significantly higher test scores and were motivated to read. The program cost only $50 per student!

- Provide 10–12 paperback books for students to take home over the summer.
- Allow students to choose their books, but be careful that struggling readers not choose too many books that are too difficult. Guide choices, but allow students to select titles they are really interested in.
- Over the summer, contact the readers who struggle most to ask about their reading.

Before Reading: Activate Prior Knowledge

- Discuss the quotes on pages 7 and 9. What does motivation mean to you in general? In regard to reading?
- Name some students in your classroom who are motivated. What are the characteristics of a motivated reader?
- Name some students who are not motivated to read. What do they have in common? What questions do you have about how to help them?

During Reading: Respond While Reading

- While reading this chapter, mark your text with self-stick notes. Use symbols to indicate questions (?), things you want to try (T), something you connect with (+), something interesting or surprising (!) (adapted from Hatt, n.d.).

After Reading: Think About and Discuss

- Do you think a passion for reading can be passed along? Explain.
- What are some obstacles to developing motivation? Why do you think people are reading less?
- Do you agree that schools are "killing" reading? Why or why not?
- Discuss the idea of teaching the skills to read as well as the will to read. What does this mean? What skills cultivate the will to read?
- What are some practical classroom suggestions for promoting a passion for reading? Discuss guidelines for motivating students to read.
- Why do you think incentive programs don't always work? Can they provide an initial incentive to read? Explain your ideas, thoughts.
- What types of technologies inspire and motivate your students to read?
- What are five ways students choose books, and how can you build on these to ignite a passion for reading?

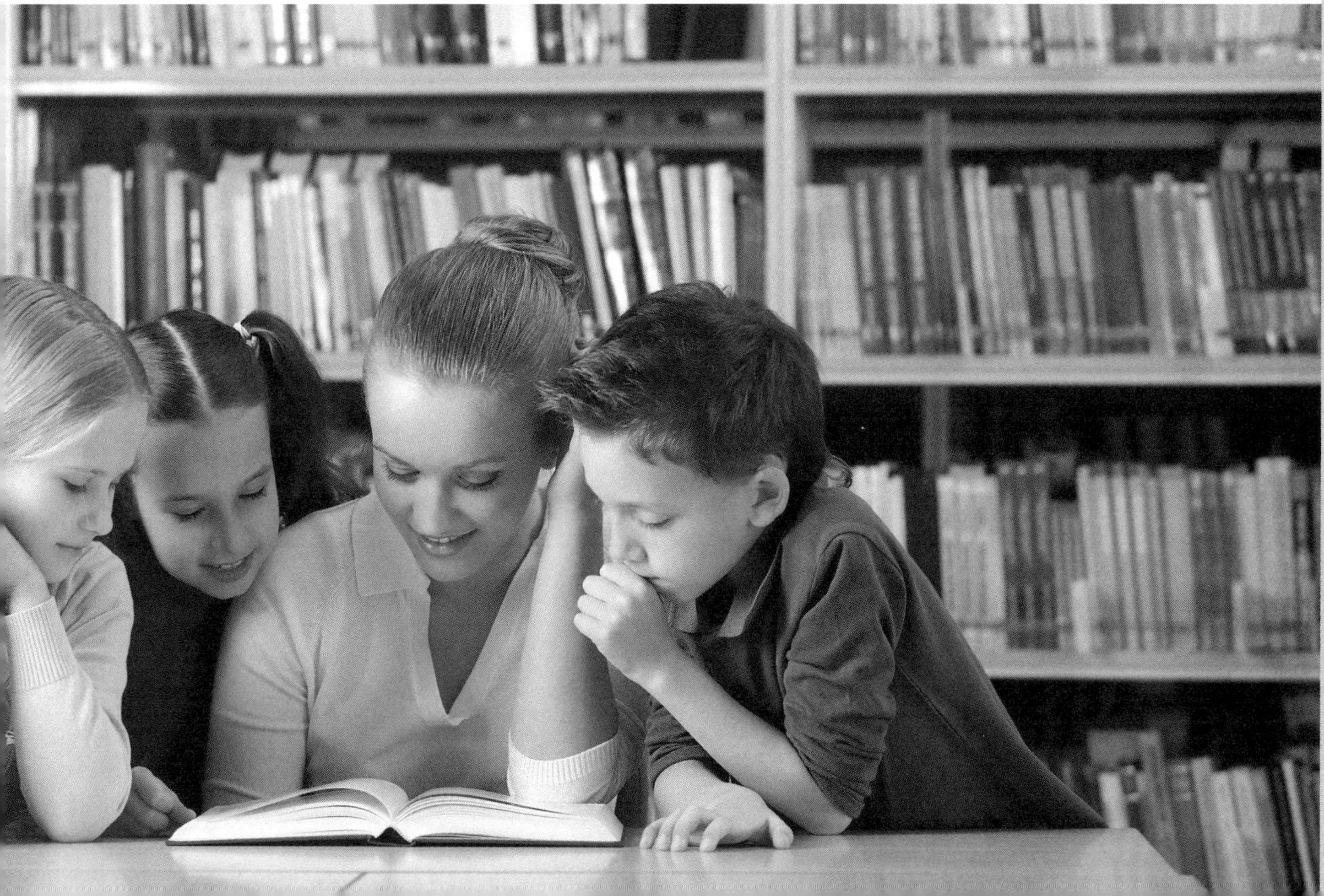

Putting Motivation Into Practice

Professional Development Breakout Groups

- Discuss ways your grade level or school can promote reading and motivate students.
- Reread the article and select the action steps you want to implement.
- Break into teams and select one of the ways students choose books: choice, interest, characteristics of books, knowledge, referrals. Make a chart and discuss practical ways to inspire kids to read.
- Discuss the importance of strong book chats. Choose a book and present it to the staff. How can we teach students to give better book testimonials, too?

Lesson Sharing

- Select one of Lori's Top 5 lessons. Bring student samples to discuss.
- Form interest groups based on the Top 5 lessons you wish to try. Bring student samples to share.
- Target struggling readers in your classroom. Come up with a specific plan to motivate them to read. Share and discuss with others.

Teacher as Reader

- Reflect on what motivated you to read as a child. Did you read a series? Race others to finish? Revisit what someone else read aloud to you? How did access to books impact your reading motivation?
- What motivates you to read as an adult? What do the factors that influence student motivation—choice, interest, characteristics of books, knowledge gained, and referrals—have to do with motivating you?

Before the Next Meeting

Read: Select the next chapter your group will read. Mark the text during reading.
Try: Try one of the lessons from the next chapter, or try something new from this chapter.
Observe: Visit a colleague's classroom to observe a motivation lesson, or record yourself teaching a lesson and share the video at a meeting.

Going Deeper With Motivation

- Try a book study using this resource loaded with strategies for motiving your students to read:

  Layne, S.L. (2009). *Igniting a passion for reading: Successful strategies for building lifetime readers*. Portland, ME: Stenhouse.

- Or consider studying the resources listed on page 16.

Observation Rubric of Reading Motivation

Directions: Use informal observations and interviews to help students become motivated to use different ways to choose books. Look at student book logs and other reflections to determine level of motivation. Use that information to help students select books.

Student Behavior	Exceeds Expectations 4	Meets Expectations 3	Needs Assistance 2	Struggles 1
Choice Chooses books and initiates choices **Ask: *How do you choose books?***	• Consistently selects own books to read	• Most of the time selects own books to read	• Needs prompting to select books to read	• Even with prompting, struggles to select books to read
Interests Chooses books based on interests **Ask: *What are some of your interests? Do you read books about those topics?***	• Consistently selects books based on identified interests	• Most of the time selects books based on identified interests • Needs some teacher prompting	• Needs lots of teacher prompting to identify interests and find books	• Even with prompting is unable to identify interests and is uninterested in books
Characteristics of Books Chooses books based on categories or genres: funny, scary, small, easy to read, pretty, etc. **Ask: *What kinds of books do you like to read?***	• Consistently selects books based on a variety of categories or genres	• Mostly selects books based on preferred categories	• Selects books based on one category • With prompting will try others	• Experiences difficulty selecting books based on any category • Resists prompting
Referrals Chooses books based on suggestions of others **Ask: *Who suggests books you can read? Do you suggest books to others?***	• Consistently reads books based on a variety of referrals from teachers, peers, family, or others • Refers books	• Sometimes selects books based on referrals from one or more sources • Sometimes refers books	• Once in a while selects books based on referrals from others • Rarely refers books without being prompted	• Rarely if ever reads suggested books • Never refers books without prompting

Interview:

- What do you like best about reading? What don't you like about it?
- How have you grown as a reader? Have you changed? How? What are you good at?
- How do you decide what to read next?
- How would you rate our reading time in class on a scale of 1–5, with 5 being the highest? Explain.

Note. Rubric created based on the categories and scales presented in "What Teachers Can Learn About Reading Motivation Through Conversations With Children" by K.M. Edmunds & K.L. Bauserman, 2006, *The Reading Teacher, 59*(5), 414–424.

Online Resources

- Use a safe blog or online forum like ClassPress (classpress.com) to discuss books.
- Use iPods and Garage Band to improve fluency at the Educational Technology website (www.eusd4kids.org/edtech).
- Find book suggestions for boys at Guys Read (www.guysread.com). Another helpful resource on this topic is the *Reading Today* article "Boys and Books" (www.reading.org/General/Publications/ReadingToday/RTY-0812-boys.aspx).
- Kid-Cast.com provides a resource for kids to post and listen to podcasts.
- ReadWriteThink (www.readwritethink.org) is a great resource for hundreds of free downloadable lessons, student interactives, and parent and after-school resources related to all aspects of reading. Try the wildly popular student interactive "Book Cover Creator" (Grades K–8) or the parent and after-school resources tip "Motivating Teen Readers" (Grades K–8) by Mary Patroulis.
- Scholastic Read Every Day, Lead a Better Life Global Literacy Campaign (www.scholastic.com/readeveryday) is full of ideas, celebrity testimonials, and more.
- Spaghetti Book Club (www.spaghettibookclub.org) features book reviews by kids for kids and is a great discussion forum for books.

Q&A

What can I do to motivate the older struggling readers who don't seem to like to read no matter what I do?

As Fielding and Roller (1992) point out, the key is to make difficult books accessible and easy books acceptable (see also Ivey, 1999). Recently, when I taught fifth grade, I directed a mixed group of students to read and discuss a novel together. When I asked around the table what books they liked to read, the students proudly shared their tastes, which ranged from Junie B. Jones to the Harry Potter series. Their teacher had established a safe environment for being honest and nonjudgmental about reading choices.

In a teacher-as-researcher project, Candace Barnes and Rachel Monroe (2011) developed some great interventions for motivating struggling readers, including

- Giving students choice
- Sharing books daily in a teacher book talk
- Encouraging students to share books with one another
- Administering a reading survey in which students rate reading on a scale of 1 to 4
- Building on student choices
- Allowing students to sit on Pilates balls while reading
- Offering reading on laptops
- Conferencing individually with students

"Our reading programs and testing pressures require that we spend time teaching students the critical skills of reading, such as phonics, fluency, comprehension, and vocabulary. But rarely do schools formally address other important aspects of reading including interest, attitude, motivation, and engagement (Layne, 2009). If we want our students to develop a lifelong love of reading, we need to find time in our school days to address this less tangible set of skills."

REFERENCES

Allington, R.L., & McGill-Franzen, A. (2003). The impact of summer setback on the reading achievement gap. *Phi Delta Kappan, 85*(1), 68–75.

Barnes, C., & Monroe, R. (2011). *Reading motivation strategies to motivate struggling readers K–8*. Retrieved January 20, 2012, from faculty.rcoe.appstate.edu/koppenhaverd/s11/5040/papers/candace&rachel.pdf.

Edmunds, K.M., & Bauserman, K.L. (2006). What teachers can learn about reading motivation through conversations with children. *The Reading Teacher, 59*(5), 414–424. doi:10.1598/RT.59.5.1

Fielding, L., & Roller, C. (1992). Making difficult books accessible and easy books acceptable. *The Reading Teacher, 45*(9), 678–685.

Gallagher, K. (2009). *Readicide: How schools are killing reading and what you can do about it*. Portland, ME: Stenhouse.

Gambrell, L.B., & Marinak, B.A. (1997). Incentives and intrinsic motivation to read. In J.T. Guthrie & A. Wigfield (Eds.), *Reading engagement: Motivating readers through integrated instruction* (pp. 205–217). Newark, DE: International Reading Association.

Hatt, C. (n.d.). *Better discussions in study groups*. Retrieved from www.choiceliteracy.com/public/796.cfm

Ivey, G. (1999). A multicase study in the middle school: Complexities among young adolescent readers. *Reading Research Quarterly, 34*(2), 172–192.

Kohen, A. (1993). *Punished by rewards*. Boston: Houghton Mifflin.

Krashen, S. (2004). *The power of reading: Insights from the research*. Portsmouth, NH: Heinemann.

Layne, S.L. (2009). *Igniting a passion for reading: Successful strategies for building lifetime readers*. Portland, ME: Stenhouse.

Marinak, B.A., & Gambrell, L.B. (2008). Intrinsic motivation and rewards: What sustains young children's engagement with text? *Literacy Research and Instruction, 47*(1), 9–26. doi:10.1080/19388070701749546

Miller, D. (2009). *The book whisperer*. San Francisco, CA: Jossey-Bass.

Morrow, L.M. (1992). The impact of a literature-based program on literacy achievement, use of literature, and attitudes of children from minority backgrounds. *Reading Research Quarterly, 27*(3), 250–275. doi:10.2307/747794

Nash, J. (2003). *Raising a reader: A mother's tale of desperation and delight*. New York: St. Martins Press.

National Endowment for the Arts. (2007). *To read or not to read: A question of national consequence*. Washington, DC: National Endowment for the Arts.

Stopping summer slide. (2010, June). *Reading Today, 27*(6), 1, 6, 7. Retrieved December 16, 2011, from www.reading.org/General/Publications/ReadingToday/RTy_June_2010/RTY_10Jun_summer_slide.aspx

Wang, J.H.-Y., & Guthrie, J.T. (2004). Modeling the effects of intrinsic motivation, extrinsic motivation, amount of reading, and past reading achievement on text comprehension between U.S. and Chinese students. *Reading Research Quarterly, 39*(2), 162–186. doi:10.1598/RRQ.39.2.2

CHAPTER 2

The Power of Reading Aloud to Your Students: Guidelines and Top 5 Read-Aloud Strategies

Best Ever Advice on... Reading Aloud

I believe that read-alouds reach their highest level of potency when they are based on a careful balance between fiction and nonfiction—exposing learners to the language forms and structures of the many different text types they need to control as a reader. The language of a set of directions, an informational poem, a Seymour Simon description, and a newspaper all differ dramatically from the language of a novel or picture book. If we are to empower students as readers of all the texts in their world, we must ensure they have ample opportunity to listen to and reflect upon the broadest possible range of text types. Read-aloud weaves a rich tapestry of wonder and thoughtful reflection that gains strength and momentum when built upon a wide range of subjects and differing text structures.

—Linda Hoyt, Author of the Interactive Read-Alouds: Linking Standards, Fluency, and Comprehension series (Heinemann)

Reading aloud every day to your students is a research-based, proven way to motivate your students to read on their own, model good reading, promote critical thinking, and create a sense of community in your classroom.

Perhaps you recall being read to as a child. Maybe you hold precious memories of a special adult at home sharing books with you every night for a bedtime story. Or maybe you remember filing into a classroom in elementary school after lunch recess, settling onto the rug or into your desk and chair, and losing yourself in a great book as the teacher's soothing voice transported you into the characters' lives and wove delicious stories that made read-aloud your favorite part of the school day.

When you read aloud to your class, perhaps for some of your students it will be the only time in their childhoods that someone reads aloud to them. You are helping all of your students develop a lifelong love of reading and providing them with memorable experiences with wonderful books!

Why Reading Aloud Is Your Secret Weapon for Inspiring Your Students to Read

The importance of reading aloud to children on a daily basis can't be overestimated. The U.S. Department of Education Commission on Reading took into account over 10,000 studies and found that the most important activity for building the skills and background for eventual success in reading is reading aloud to children (see Anderson, Hiebert, Scott, & Wilkinson, 1985). Children who are read to are usually the very best readers in the classroom, and they acquire large vocabularies, write well, and do better in other subject areas, as well.

Guidelines and Practical Tips for Great Read-Alouds

Select books YOU like to read aloud.

Be sure to choose books that you enjoy sharing with your class, and make sure to expose your students to modern classics as well as the old standbys. (See Suggestions for Read-Alouds as well as the Online Resources and References for recommendations.) When you are passionate about the read-aloud book, the students sense it and begin to share your enthusiasm for reading. If you begin reading a book and notice that your students are not enjoying it, abandon the book and explain that sometimes that is what readers do when they are not enjoying a particular title.

Set aside a consistent place and time slot of 15–20 minutes per day to read aloud.

Try never to give up your read-aloud time, even if some days you need to switch the timing of your read-aloud or even cut it short a bit. Make reading aloud such an ingrained habit in your classroom that the students beg you not to skip it. When my husband and I read aloud to our children when they were young (we still read aloud to the 12-year-old!), they simply could not fall asleep without their read-alouds and begged if we tried to skip reading to them.

Go under the spell of a good book.

Noted author and respected educator Lucy Calkins (1997), in *Raising Lifelong Learners: A Parent's Guide*, says that read-aloud is the time to go under the "spell" of a beautiful book and laugh, cry, and get lost in the flow of the story and the language.

Refer to your rich read-alouds artfully during reading and writing lessons.

In their book *Learning Under the Influence of Language and Literature*, Lester Laminack and Reba Wadsworth (2006) describe six types of read-alouds: books that (1) address standards, (2) build community, (3) demonstrate the craft of writing, (4) enrich vocabulary, (5) entice children to read independently, and (6) model fluent reading. For example,

- You may select a particular book to demonstrate a comprehension strategy from your district standards, such as making connections. When reading the short story "La Bamba" from Gary Soto's *Baseball in April and Other Stories* to fifth graders, we asked the students to watch for personal connections during the read-aloud. Afterward they discussed their connections to the story that included their experiences with talent shows.

- You might read aloud from a book like *Owl Moon* by Jane Yolen that is dripping with descriptive language, then refer to it again during a writing lesson to model rich vocabulary usage.
- The nonsense words from a Dr. Seuss read-aloud later seep into a phonics lesson when creating rhyming words.

Keep the read-aloud experience "pure" without too much direct instruction; however, it is quite natural to selectively draw on examples from your read-alouds during other reading and writing lessons.

Select books that cover some of the content.

You can choose books that take place during a time period in history that you are teaching about, or a particular topic in science.

Use good reading strategies before, during, and after reading.

Before reading, encourage students to help you predict what the day's reading may be about based on visual clues. Review the events that happened in the portion of text you read the day before. During reading, ask students to enjoy the book, but ask them to watch for something such as connections they make or clues to solve the problem in the story. After reading, students may wish to discuss points they wondered about or favorite parts of the text. Make the discussion feel as natural as a chat among friends rather than a teacher-directed "quiz"!

Break the rules.

As your students become hooked on your read-aloud time together, be sure to occasionally go over time and read more. You'll find that often when read-aloud is over, the students will whine and ask you to read on. Sometimes just do so! Your students will love it.

Lori's Top 5 Surefire Strategies for Reading Aloud

Try these proven read-aloud strategies and watch your students' interest in reading and comprehension soar!

1 *The Read-Aloud Challenge: Read 5–7 Times a Day*

This sounds like a crazy idea, but it really works and students absolutely love it. Try reading aloud 5–7 times per day and choose the amount of time that works for you.

- One of the read-aloud sessions is longer to build attention, comprehension, and stamina: around 10–15 minutes. The rest of the read-alouds are fast: 1- to 3-minute "quick reads" that you squeeze in at different times throughout the day.
- Open the day with a quick read-aloud, do one again right before recess and lunch, or read aloud as you transition between subjects or when students are lining up.
- Include poems, nonfiction, newspaper articles, how-to books or directions, jokes, menus, online material, and short stories. Keep a bin in which to store a variety of read-aloud materials.
- Assign a student the task of selecting the quick reads for the day and checking off the allotted number of read-aloud hits throughout the day.
- Ask students to turn to partners and discuss the reading by making up questions to quiz each other, or have them discuss what they are wondering by posing open-ended questions.

2 *Senses Alert (Oczkus, 2009)*

As your students listen during read-aloud, ask them to be on the lookout for sentences, words, and phrases that require them to use their senses to really experience and comprehend the book.

- Throughout the reading, ask questions like, Did you see that? Did you hear that? Can you taste that or feel that?
- Ask students to turn and talk to partners after you read a portion of text and give examples of one or more senses depending upon the text.
- Ask students to make movies of the book in their heads. Even when reading a picture book, the illustrator leaves some of the action up to the reader to formulate in his or her head.
- After a read-aloud session, students may quickly sketch a scene they imagined during the reading. Students share sketches with one another.
- Discuss how visualizing and using other senses helps good readers comprehend text.

3 *Partner Talk/Discussion Starters (Oczkus, 2009)*

Before and after reading aloud, to deepen student comprehension, allow students to quickly turn and talk to partners for just a minute or so about their questions, confusions, and ideas related to the text. You might try using discussion starters such as these to guide and direct the interactions (select one at a time for younger students or put this list on a chart and allow the students to select their own discussion starters):

- Something new I learned was....
- I liked the part where...because....
- I realize now that...because....
- This reminded me of...because....
- I was surprised by...because....

4 *Literacy Mystery Boxes (Pearman, Camp, & Hurst, 2004)*

This is a very clever idea that some educators developed and then shared in an article in *The Reading Teacher* journal. The authors suggest bringing in a box that holds several items that relate in some way to the story. So, for example, to help students predict what *Charlotte's Web* by E.B. White is about, the teacher pulls out of the box a plastic spider, a plastic rat or pig, a spider web, or a blue ribbon. For *The Very Hungry Caterpillar* by Eric Carle, the authors suggest bringing in a stuffed caterpillar, green leaf, apple, and lollipop. The possibilities for mystery boxes are endless, even for students in middle school and high school. Mystery boxes make reading aloud memorable for students and provide discussion prompts and opportunities for rich vocabulary instruction. Have students bring in mystery boxes to go with the books they are reading, as well.

5 *Interactive Engagement (Oczkus, 2009)*

You can easily make your read-alouds a bit more interactive by inviting students to turn and talk to partners before and after the reading. Discussion alone has been shown to deepen comprehension (Lapp, Flood, Ranck-Buhr, Van Dyke, & Spacek, 1997). Sometimes that is all it takes to grab your students and focus their attention. You may also choose from these interactive engagement ideas after a read-aloud:

- Drama—Ask students to make faces to demonstrate the emotions of the characters in various parts of the reading. Or ask volunteers to come forward and act out portions of the text. Students may also turn to a partner and "interview" each other, taking turns role-playing as characters.
- Art—Students can quickly sketch a favorite part or character, or what they've learned, and share with a partner.

Before Reading: Activate Prior Knowledge

- What do you remember about being read to as a child? How does that experience shape your approach to reading aloud to students in your classroom?
- What are some of your students' favorite read-alouds? What is hard about reading aloud to students? What is the best thing about reading aloud to students?

During Reading: Respond While Reading

- While reading this chapter, mark your text with self-stick notes. Use symbols to indicate questions (?), things you want to try (T), something you connect with (+), something interesting or surprising (!) (adapted from Hatt, n.d.).

After Reading: Think About and Discuss

- Justify reading aloud. Why does it matter? How can you make time for it?
- Should parents read aloud to students at your grade level? Explain.
- What age is "too old" for read-aloud? Review the Education Week article "Reading Aloud to Teens Gains Favor Among Teachers" (Zehr, 2010) and discuss.
- What are the six types of read-alouds suggested by Laminack and Wadsworth (2006)? Name some books you could use for each.
- Do you agree with the guidelines in this chapter? Why, or what else would you add? What guidelines have you found to be useful when reading aloud to students?
- Discuss ways to make your read-alouds more interactive and engaging. How can students turn and talk to a partner during your read-aloud? Which of the Top 5 would you like to try with your students?

Putting Read-Alouds Into Practice

Professional Development Breakout Groups

- Make a chart and list the problems you have experienced when reading aloud to your students (e.g., choice of books, attention span, fitting it into your schedule). What are some possible solutions?
- Work with team members to research books for reading aloud at your grade level. Share read-aloud ideas.

Lesson Sharing

- Try one of Lori's Top 5 lessons with your class. Be prepared to share. On a scale of 1–5, how did the lesson go? Explain. What do you want to try next?

Teacher as Reader

- Discuss in detail what you remember about someone at home or school reading aloud to you as a child. What did you like and dislike?
- Are you satisfied with the way you read aloud to your students? What could you do to improve your technique? Where in your life do you read aloud (e.g., in church or for another group, to your own children or an elderly parent, while listening to audible books)?

Before the Next Meeting

Read: Select the next chapter your group will read. Mark the text during reading.
Try: Try one of the lessons from the next chapter, or try something new from this chapter.
Observe: Visit a colleague's classroom to observe a lesson on reading aloud, or record yourself teaching a lesson and share the video at a meeting.

Going Deeper With Read-Alouds

- Try a book study using this practical resource loaded with fresh new takes on getting the most from reading aloud to your students:

  Laminack, L.L., & Wadsworth, R.M. (2006). *Learning under the influence of language and literature: Making the most of read-alouds across the day.* Portsmouth, NH: Heinemann.

- Or consider studying the resources listed on page 28.

Interactive Read-Aloud Bookmark Lesson

Objective: Provide students with a bookmark with prompts that they can use as they "turn and talk" to one another.

Common Core Connections: Students confirm their understanding of a text read aloud by asking and answering questions. Encourage students to compare and contrast the reading with other material they've read. They need to provide evidence from the text when explaining their thinking. Encourage students to use words and phrases from the read-aloud in discussions.

Teacher Modeling: Throughout a read-aloud session, pause periodically and model how to use one of the bookmark prompts. Conduct a think-aloud that starts something like this: "In this part here, I am thinking...."

Guided Practice: Ask students to turn to their partners and use the same prompt you just modeled. Eventually, give students choices among several prompts. Listen to the pairs and invite students to share with the whole class. Praise their efforts.

Independent Practice: Students may use the same prompts you used in your read-aloud lesson when they read their independent reading books. They can mark with self-stick notes those passages they wish to share with the group or a partner.

Wrap Up: Ask students how the discussion helped deepen their comprehension. Ask which of the prompts on the bookmark is their favorite or the most helpful and why.

Lights, Camera, Listen Lesson

Objective: Focus students' attention on sensory images during a read-aloud.

Common Core Connections: Ask students to share evidence from the text, plus their experiences, to infer visual images. Encourage students to use selection vocabulary.

Teacher Modeling: Pause periodically during and after a read-aloud to read from the text and think aloud as you demonstrate how good readers use sensory images to comprehend a text. Select specific portions of text to use as examples. Say, "During this part, I could see [or hear or feel]...."

Guided Practice: Invite students to turn to a partner or their tablemates and share the sensory images they see and experience. Students may sketch before or after discussing examples with a partner.

Independent Practice: Students hunt in their own independent reading books for other strong examples of sensory images and then sketch those as well.

Wrap Up: Invite students to tell partners and the class how sensory images help them comprehend as they read. Share favorite examples from the text.

Assessment Tips

During read-alouds, observe students and listen to their responses in class and partner discussions. Encourage students to use physical, verbal, and sometimes written responses to your read-alouds (e.g., thumbs-up, slates, make a face, dramatize, and partner talk). Keep a clipboard or student role sheet nearby to jot down quick notes and observations during or after the lesson.

Connect: Are students making logical connections to themselves, other books, and the world? Do they vary their connections?

Predict: Do students use the text plus text clues (e.g., text structure, previous events, headings) to help make sensible predictions? Do students change predictions during reading?

Question: Do students ask questions that go with the text? Are questions just literal or are they inferential, too? Do students question the author?

Inference: Do students use text clues to make inferences about character traits or feelings?

Monitor/Clarify: Do students identify words and ideas that are unclear? Do they identify multiple ways to figure out words and ideas? Do they use sensory descriptions during reading?

Summarize: Do students retell in their own words and in order? Do they use text structure to help organize a summary?

Synthesize: Do students identify new ideas from the reading or how they have been changed?

Evaluate: Do students evaluate and give reasons for opinions about the author's style, storyline, or characters' actions?

Interactive Read-Aloud Bookmark
Partner Turn & Talk Points

Listen carefully while your teacher reads aloud. Take turns discussing with your partner

Before Reading:

- I think this is about...because....
- Already this reminds me of...because....
- I think I will learn...because....

During and After Reading:

- It was confusing when....
- At first I thought..., then I realized....
- I was surprised by...because....
- So far...has happened....
- This reminds me of...because....
- Something new I learned was....
- I liked the part where...because....
- It was so (funny, sad, wild) when....
- I think the character...was very... because....
- The author probably wrote this because....

Interactive Read-Aloud Bookmark
Partner Turn & Talk Points

Listen carefully while your teacher reads aloud. Take turns discussing with your partner

Before Reading:

- I think this is about...because....
- Already this reminds me of...because....
- I think I will learn...because....

During and After Reading:

- It was confusing when....
- At first I thought..., then I realized....
- I was surprised by...because....
- So far...has happened....
- This reminds me of...because....
- Something new I learned was....
- I liked the part where...because....
- It was so (funny, sad, wild) when....
- I think the character...was very... because....
- The author probably wrote this because....

Best Ever Literacy Survival Tips: 72 Lessons You Can't Teach Without by Lori D. Oczkus.
© 2012 International Reading Association. May be copied for classroom use.

Lights, Camera, Listen

Scenes from (title) ________________________________ **by (author)** ________________________________

Listen as your teacher reads aloud.

Make a movie in your head. Use all your senses.

Sketch what you see.

Share with a partner. Choose a scene to act out, and classmates guess your scene.

Scene One ______________________	Scene Two ______________________
Scene Three ______________________	Scene Four ______________________

Suggestions for Read-Alouds

Picture Books

Amazing Grace by Mary Hoffman
Charlie Anderson by Barbara Abercrombie
The Great Kapok Tree: A Tale of the Amazon Rain Forest by Lynne Cherry
Mike Mulligan and His Steam Shovel by Virginia Lee Burton
Rikki-Tikki-Tavi by Rudyard Kipling
The Story of Ferdinand by Munro Leaf

Chapter Books

Because of Winn-Dixie by Kate DiCamillo
Charlie and the Chocolate Factory by Roald Dahl
Harriet the Spy by Louise Fitzhugh
The Lion, the Witch and the Wardrobe by C.S. Lewis
Stone Fox by John Reynolds Gardiner
Stuart Little by E.B. White
Winnie-the-Pooh by A.A. Milne

Q&A

Many of the teachers in my building skip reading aloud because our school is under fire to bring up test scores immediately. How do I justify taking the time to read aloud to my students?

You can't afford to *not* take the time to read aloud to your students. The benefits of read-aloud are many, as students develop background knowledge, comprehension, robust vocabularies, and critical thinking skills. If you throw in discussions about the read-aloud, students develop oral language and deeper understandings.

I am not sure what books make good read-alouds for my grade level. Any suggestions?

See the Suggestions for Read-Alouds, Online Resources, and References provided here, for a start. You do *not* need to purchase books to read aloud to your class. You can rely on your school librarian or public librarian for suggestions. One of my favorite online resources is a website sponsored by Jim Trelease, author of the best-selling book *The Read-Aloud Handbook* (2006). Pam Allyn (2009), teacher and staff developer, suggests books by ages and themes in *What to Read When: The Books and Stories to Read With Your Child—and All the Best Times to Read Them*. See also literacy specialist Nancy Anderson's *What Should I Read Aloud? A Guide to 200 Best-Selling Picture Books* (2007).

"Make reading aloud such an ingrained habit in your classroom that the students beg you not to skip it."

Online Resources

International Reading Association Choices Reading Lists: www.reading.org/resources/Booklists.aspx
Featuring annual Children's Choices, Teachers' Choices, and Young Adults' Choices reading lists.

Jim Trelease's Home Page: www.trelease-on-reading.com
Read-aloud expert Jim Trelease provides many suggestions for reading aloud to children of all ages.

Read Aloud America Recommended Books: readaloudamerica.org/booklist.htm
Suggested read-aloud titles for infants through high schoolers.

Storyline Online: www.storylineonline.net
Celebrities read children's books aloud.

References

Allyn, P. (2009). *What to read when: The books and stories to read with your child—and all the best times to read them.* New York: Penguin.

Anderson, N.A. (2007). *What should I read aloud? A guide to 200 best-selling picture books*. Newark, DE: International Reading Association.

Anderson, R.C., Hiebert, E.H., Scott, J.A., & Wilkinson, I.A.G. (1985). *Becoming a nation of readers: The report of the Commission on Reading*. Washington, DC: National Institute of Education.

Calkins, L. (with Bellino, L.). (1997). *Raising lifelong learners: A parent's guide.* Cambridge, MA: Perseus.

Hatt, C. (n.d.). *Better discussions in study groups*. Retrieved from www.choiceliteracy.com/public/796.cfm

Laminack, L.L., & Wadsworth, R.M. (2006). *Learning under the influence of language and literature: Making the most of read-alouds across the day.* Portsmouth, NH: Heinemann.

Lapp, D., Flood, J., Ranck-Buhr, W., Van Dyke, J., & Spacek, S. (1997). "Do you really just want us to talk about this book?": A closer look at book clubs as an instructional tool. In J.R. Paratore & R.L. McCormack (Eds.), *Peer talk in the classroom: Learning from research* (pp. 6–23). Newark, DE: International Reading Association.

Oczkus, L. (2009). *Interactive think-aloud lessons: 25 surefire ways to engage students and improve comprehension*. New York: Scholastic; Newark, DE: International Reading Association.

Pearman, C.J., Camp, D., & Hurst, B. (2004). Literacy mystery boxes. *The Reading Teacher, 57*(8), 766–768.

Trelease, J. (2006). *The read-aloud handbook* (6th ed.). New York: Penguin.

Zehr, M.A. (2010, January 6). Reading aloud to teens gains favor among teachers. *Education Week, 29*(16), 1, 12–13.

CHAPTER 3

Super Practical Ways to Build an Independent Reading Program in Your Classroom: Guidelines and TOP 5 Independent Reading Strategies

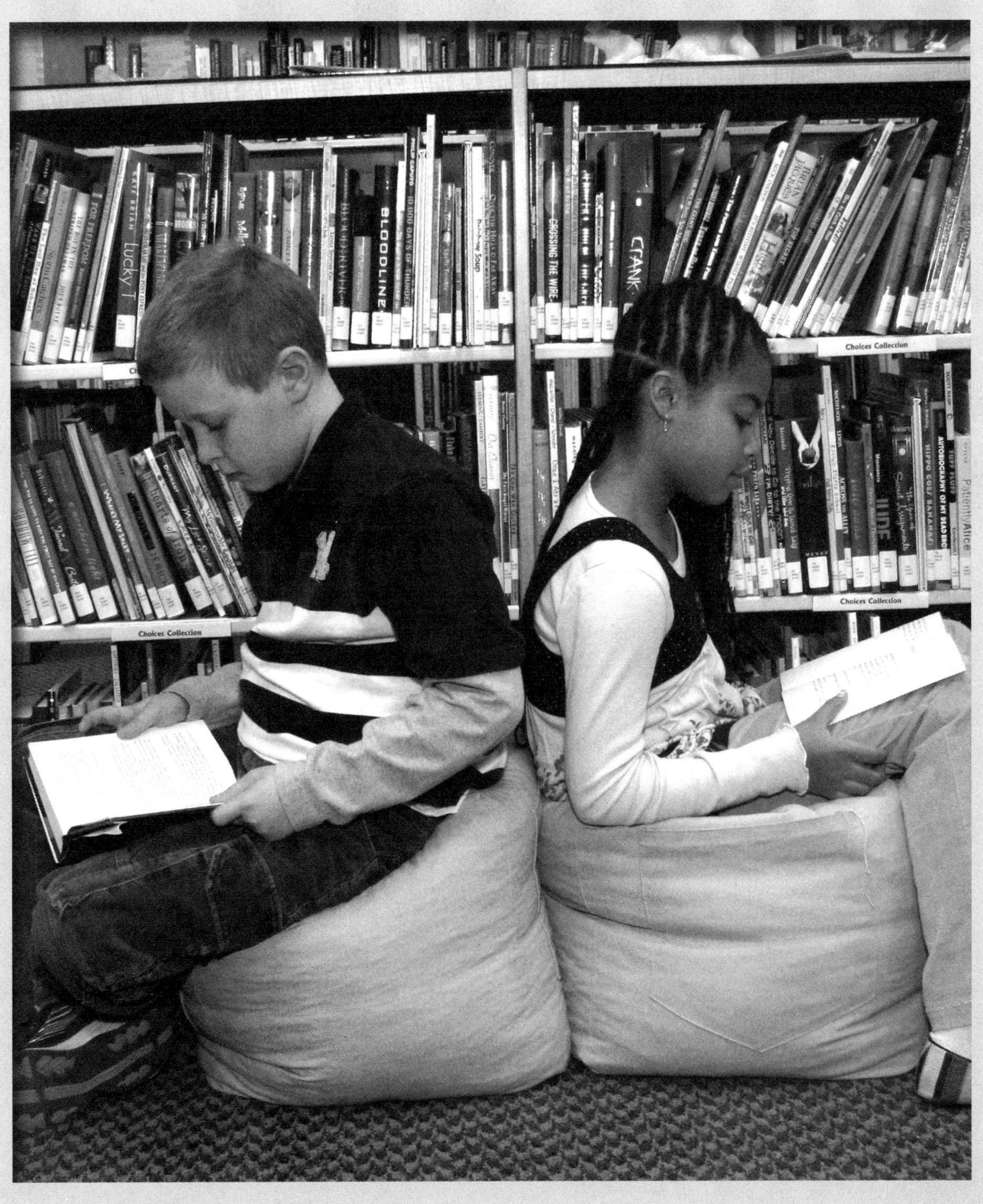

Best Ever Advice on... Independent Reading

Share your reading life with your students every day. Talk to them about your reading experiences—what you found interesting, appealing, or challenging about the books you read. Make recommendations and take their suggestions when offered. I find that creating a community of readers, which includes me, does more to engage and motivate my students to read than any other activity. They trust me as a reader, not just as their teacher.

Consider replacing your warm-up or bell-ringer with reading time instead. Look at dead spots in the day, like classroom interruptions. When a lesson runs shorter than you planned, recapture this time for independent reading.

Nothing motivates a child to read more than saying, "I just finished this book and while I was reading it, I knew you would like it."

—Donalyn Miller, Author of *The Book Whisperer: Awakening the Inner Reader in Every Child* (Jossey-Bass, 2009)

One effective practice for motivating students' independent reading is to provide them with choice. Choice of reading materials has often been thought of as "unconstrained" and relatively unguided, but that is unrealistic in most classrooms. All reading choices within classrooms are constrained and guided; the question is the degree of constraint and guidance. Typically, students in classrooms do not have the universe of books from which to choose at any time. So, what really works? Providing students with guided choices within an overall organizational structure has proven highly motivating (Fawson, Reutzel, Read, Smith, & Moore, 2009; Reutzel, Jones, Fawson, & Smith, 2008). To provide this guidance and structure for choice, try wide reading of books guided by the use of a genre wheel: Students choose a book from one slice, or genre, in the wheel. When they have completed reading a book from that genre, they color that slice of the genre wheel and then choose another slice. They continue to read widely, making choices from each uncolored slice until the entire wheel has been colored. At that point, they can select a new genre wheel containing a different set of selections.

Genre Wheel

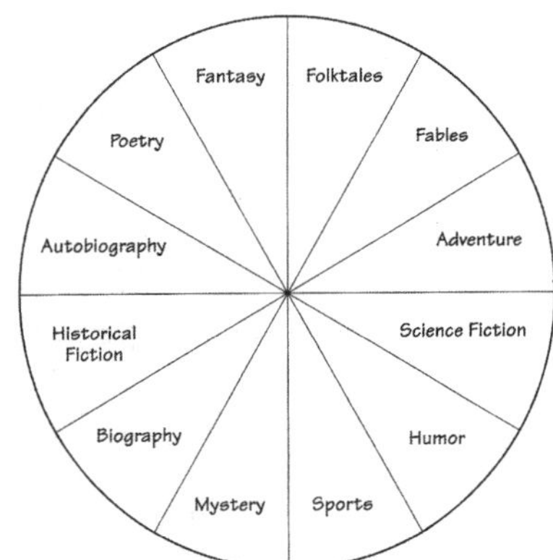

From *Your Classroom Library: New Ways to Give It More Teaching Power* by D.R. Reutzel & P.C. Fawson, 2002, New York: Scholastic. Reprinted with permission.

—D. Ray Reutzel, Coeditor of *Revisiting Silent Reading: New Directions for Teachers and Researchers* (International Reading Association, 2010)

Independent reading time, or sustained silent reading, is a critical component of a well-designed literacy program. When you provide time every day for your students to practice reading in a book they've selected, students not only grow their vocabulary, fluency, comprehension, word attack skills, and stamina, but they also develop a love of reading. Let's peek inside two elementary classrooms for a glimpse of students engaged in a successful independent reading block.

After lunch, the fifth-grade students file into the classroom sweaty, a bit tired, and anxious to settle on various perches for silent reading with their independent reading books. Students sprawl on the floor on pillows near the classroom meeting place, while more scatter around the room on rug samples. Colorful vinyl beanbag chairs house more eager readers. Many students relax comfortably at their desks as they devour their latest book choice. The teacher carries her clipboard around the room and jots quick notes as she asks a student to tell her about his most recent selection.

Across the hall in first grade, little beginning readers nestle into their chairs with books they've stashed in their personal book boxes. A few students make their way to the inviting, carpeted corner classroom library, which holds plastic bins of books organized by reading level, topic, and author. The noisy "silent" reading begins as students read alone and with partners. The teacher kneels next to a student to ask her to read aloud her favorite part and to suggest possible next titles.

Anticipate Problems With Independent Reading Time

Independent reading time sounds easy, right? Just provide books and invite students to read on their own quietly while you meet with individual students. Setting up independent reading time in your classroom isn't difficult, but if you don't take some common-sense steps to provide the right books and establish simple procedures, you'll most likely face the following pitfalls associated with independent reading time:

- Students experience difficulty selecting books, choosing books that are too difficult or too easy
- Students spend the entire time selecting books and never settle down to read
- Students fidget or stare at pages without actually reading

In this chapter, we explore some practical tips, suggestions, and important guidelines for establishing a successful independent reading time in your classroom.

What Is Independent Reading?

Independent reading is a 20- to 30-minute block of time per day in your classroom when students read from self-selected reading material while you confer with individuals and occasionally model reading strategies and procedures. Independent reading has lots of fun nicknames and acronyms:

SSR	Sustained Silent Reading
USSR	Uninterrupted Sustained Silent Reading
DIRT	Daily Independent Reading Time
SQUIRT	Super Quiet Uninterrupted Reading Time
DEAR	Drop Everything and Read
WEB	Wonderful Entertaining Books
GRAB	Go Read a Book
SURF	Silent Uninterrupted Reading Fun
OTTER	Our Time to Enjoy Reading

Here are some less common, rather comical names for independent reading that teachers of intermediate students created. Enlist your students for ideas and make up your own acronym for independent reading!

KBAR	Kick Back and Read
ZYLAR	Zip Your Lip and Read
BARF	Be a Reader Freak

Whatever you call it, independent reading is simply a time every day when your students read books they've selected with some guidance from you. Independent reading time should be an established routine that runs smoothly in your classroom so all of your students experience reading gains.

Why Is Independent Reading Important?

A principal at one of the schools where I've worked as a consultant reported an interesting finding when she analyzed the third-grade reading test scores: Although all the teachers had taught the same reading program, and done a good job with it, one teacher's students scored markedly higher on the standardized test in reading and comprehension. This teacher had done just one thing differently from the others: She added a 15- to 20-minute silent reading time to the daily schedule. (The other teachers didn't feel they had time for that and only had independent reading occasionally.) The payoff was noticeable, and the following year all the teachers added a consistent independent reading block to their schedules.

Research tells us that the time students spend in independent reading is one of the best predictors of reading achievement—in comprehension, decoding, fluency, and vocabulary (Anderson, Wilson, & Fielding, 1988). Students who spend the most time reading independently outperform others on standardized tests and other measures. Our best writers are also the students who read for pleasure, because they acquire a varied, rich vocabulary, background knowledge, and an understanding of how language works.

Practice is the key to proficiency at tennis, dance, cooking, or anything in life. Reading is no different. Your students need time to practice the reading strategies and skills they've learned in class to reach their reading potential. Opportunities to get lost in a book and lose track of time ultimately translate to finding reading pleasurable (Moss & Young, 2010).

Independent reading time doesn't replace the rich, explicit instruction your students receive during the other reading times in the day—students also read during shared reading, guided reading, and lessons with core literature, basals, leveled text, and content area texts. The key to reading success during the independent reading block is providing books that are at the students' level and offering the right amount of support.

Reading that students do on their own at home is also critical for them to practice their skills as readers. Students should read at home for 15–20 minutes every evening. If your students don't have access to books at home, you could allow them to cart some classroom library selections back and forth in their backpacks.

Independent reading is a critical part of the literacy diet you provide for your students every day. Try your best not to skip this invaluable opportunity to engage, motivate, and move students along in their reading.

Guidelines for Setting Up Your Independent Reading Time

Select a consistent time each day for independent reading.

It is best to provide the same time slot every day for independent reading. The amount of time will vary depending on grade level—ideal is 15–20 minutes. However, consider that, initially, your students can probably only read for the number of minutes that matches their age, so a 7-year-old may read for 7 minutes and a 9-year-old for 9 minutes (Taberski, cited in Moss & Young, 2010). If you find that students become inattentive or antsy

after this short time, change up the independent reading to involve partners, different books, or moving to new positions. Over a few weeks, students should build the endurance and stamina to read for the entire independent reading period.

Set up a reading environment and classroom library.

Select an area of your classroom for your classroom library. Many teachers use a carpet remnant or area rug as a way to separate the space. You may want to pick up some beanbag chairs, big pillows, or even a comfy couch to position in the book area. Or if you are tight on space, you can skip the furniture and simply have students read at their desks after visiting the classroom library to check out books.

Find a way to display books that works for you. Books look more inviting when positioned with the covers facing out instead of the spines, so a percentage of your books, if not all, should face

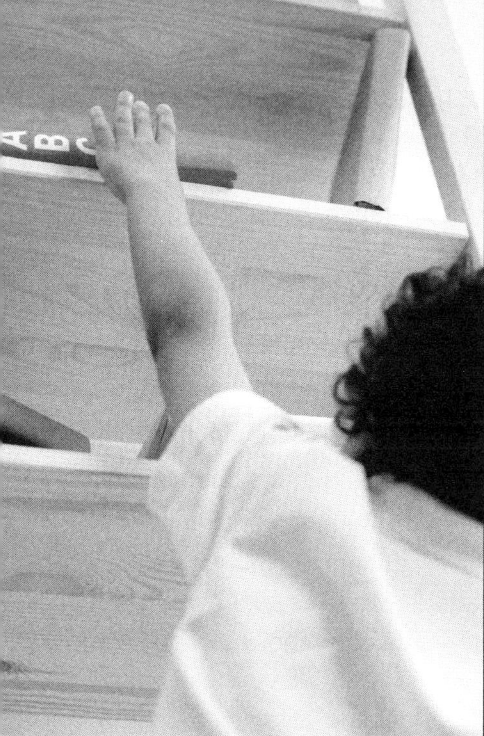

Ways to Organize Books

- Author
- Genre/type (e.g., science fiction, joke books, legends, fairy tales, poetry, picture books, chapter books, ABC books, magazines)
- Theme (e.g., courage, perseverance, friendship)
- Topic (e.g., animals, science, social studies)

out, inviting students to grab, open, and read. Many teachers hang rain gutters—available for just a few dollars at hardware stores and super easy to mount—under windows or whiteboards to display books facing out around the room. What a great way to decorate! Of course, you will want to change your displays often to entice students to read more.

Inexpensive plastic bins or baskets are one of the easiest ways to display, store, and organize books in your classroom library. Students can easily flip through books that are housed in bins. You can group books by author, illustrator, series, genre, or reading level.

Author and expert teacher Tony Stead cautions teachers against organizing the bins by reading level only. It is disheartening to visit a classroom and hear a student say, "I can't read that book. I'm only a level E and that is an F." Stead suggests organizing by student interest and topic first, then by reading level. One compromise is to have no more than 30% of the books in your collection organized by reading level alone. You might have bins of books for levels (Fountas & Pinnell, 2001), especially in grades K–2, but organize the rest of your bins by genre and topic, and perhaps place reading level on the back of books if your school requires that.

Your students need lots of practice in books that are at their independent reading level. One way to get buy-in from your students is to ask them how they would like to organize the classroom library, then to put them to work sorting and placing books in bins or on shelves (Routman, 2003).

Be sure to change your displays every few weeks. You might want to feature a certain age-appropriate author, series, or genre. Fifth-grade teacher Sandy Buscheck devotes an entire bookshelf to her collection of "Top 100 Picture Books" that she suggests students shouldn't miss during their childhoods. Her collection started as a bin and expanded to its own bookshelf, which she acquired at a garage sale. You may want to include student-generated posters that advertise books, or create as a class "Top 10" favorite booklists or a place to display student reviews of books (Routman, 2003). Have fun enticing your students to read.

Gather books for your classroom library.

The key to a successful classroom library is filling it with appropriate books. An adequate library holds around 200 books, and after a few years, many classroom libraries reach a thousand or more titles for a rich and varied collection (Routman, 2003). For new teachers, starting the library is daunting. Exactly how many books does one need to get started? Set up your classroom library corner and, for the time being, borrow books from the school library. Check out new ones every couple of weeks. In the meantime, there are creative ways to build your book collection on a budget. Soon you will find yourself on a constant book hunt at garage sales, bookstores, discount stores, and library sale racks. Once you get started, it isn't hard to find inexpensive books everywhere.

Building Your Classroom Library on a Budget

- Ask the parents' club to donate funds for books
- Invite students to donate used books, and ask parents to donate a book on their child's birthday
- Be on constant lookout at thrift and discount stores, garage sales, public library sale racks, and bargain online retailers such as www.bookcloseouts.com
- Use points from book clubs (e.g., Scholastic, Troll)
- Include magazines and student-authored materials, as well as read-aloud and shared reading materials

I know some first-grade teachers who include a bin of student-published books in their reading corner. Students race to that bin, and the covers of those popular reads become worn. What a wonderful way to honor your students' writing. You may even want to place a comments card or page at the back of these books so other students can compliment the author.

Keep track of student reading with independent reading folders.

It's helpful for students to do a bit of record keeping during independent reading time. Provide a folder for each student to house an independent reading log, interest inventory, and possibly a list of other books they wish to read. When you select the forms you want students to use during independent reading, consider how you read. After you read, do you feel like writing an

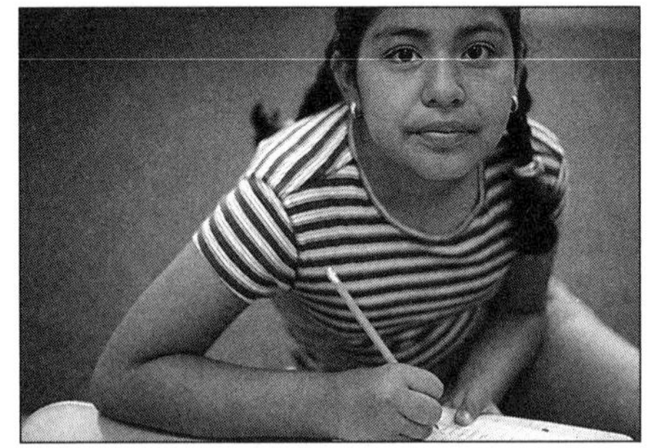

essay or long summary? Probably not. Remember, the purpose of independent reading is to encourage students to spend time reading, not filling out forms or worksheets. One option is to use a basic Reading Log Form, or simply ask students to record the information on a paper they store in their reading folders.

Some teachers allow their students to create their own forms for recording the basic book log information. Keep in mind that you are requiring a number of minutes per day in class and then again at home for reading. Emphasize stamina and minutes spent reading rather than number of pages read. (When you make recording the number of pages the goal, students tend to read quickly and carelessly rather than for comprehension, understanding, and enjoyment.)

In addition to a simple book log, it is helpful to give your students an inventory of their interests. Administer this several times per year, as interests change, so you can refer to students' interest inventories to guide book choices when they say, "I don't know what to read next."

Online, you can find many free downloadable interest inventories for a variety of grade levels. Or you might design your own quick interest inventory especially for your class. If you work with students in K–1, you could invite older students in to administer the inventory to your little ones.

Sample Reading Log Form

Title	Genre	Date started	Date finished	Rate the book (smiling face) = Great (smiling face) = OK (neutral face) = Didn't care for/ didn't like

Sample Interest Inventory

1. What is your favorite book or books?
2. What authors do you enjoy reading?
3. What do you like to do after school?
4. What are your hobbies?
5. Do you have any pets? If so, what?
6. Do you collect anything? If so, what?
7. Are you on a team or do you take lessons after school? What do you do?
8. What are your favorite television shows?
9. What is your favorite movie?
10. What would you like to learn about?
11. What do you want to be when you grow up?
12. Circle the topics you are interested in.

Animals	Social studies	Real stories	Scary stories
Dogs	Natural disasters	People from history	Funny stories
Cats	Volcanoes	Famous people	Science fiction
Horses	Hurricanes	Mysteries	How-to books
Other ____________	Earthquakes	Poetry	
Science	Rocks	Music	

Note. Adapted from *Creating Lifelong Readers Through Independent Reading* by B. Moss & T.A. Young, 2010, Newark, DE: International Reading Association, p. 57.

Establish independent reading procedures.

It helps to keep a consistent routine and to model what you want students to do during independent reading time so the students will use the time efficiently to get the most out of the allotted 20 minutes.

Teach students how to select books.

Help students select appropriate books by teaching them to use the five-finger test: Students count on one hand any hard words they encounter; if on a given page there are five or more hard words, the book may be too difficult. The Goldilocks method (Ohlhausen & Jepsen, 1992) is also helpful when students select books on their own: Is the book easy, just right, or too hard? Encourage students to select a variety of easy and just-right books to build their reading stamina. If a student is set on reading a book that is too difficult for him or her (many kids are dying to cart around one of the Harry Potter books by J.K. Rowling), then consider ways to make it more accessible, such as partner reading or listening to the book on tape.

Choosing a Book to Read Using the Goldilocks Method

Easy

- Have you read this book or one by the same author before?
- Is this an easy story for you to understand?
- Did you read it easily without stumbling on any words?

Just Right

- Do you like this book? Why or why not?
- Can you retell the story in your own words?
- Do you need to look at the story again?
- Did you read it easily without stumbling on very many words?

Too Hard

- Do you like this book?
- Do you feel like finishing it? Why?
- Are you confused about what is happening in this book?
- Is it hard to understand?
- Do you need help?

Note. Adapted from "Lessons From Goldilocks: 'Somebody's Been Choosing My Books but I Can Make My Own Choices Now!'" by M.M. Ohlhausen & M. Jepsen, 1992, *The New Advocate*, *5*(1), p. 36, and *Reading Essentials: The Specifics You Need to Teach Reading Well* by R. Routman, 2003, Portsmouth, NH: Heinemann, p. A-6.

Make time for students to share books.

A nice way to end the independent reading block is to encourage students to share their reading with others. You can invite one or two volunteers to create and present a book "commercial," without giving away the entire book, to entice others to read it. Videotape these presentations—students will love it!

Teach minilessons on procedures/quick reading strategies.

One surefire way to ensure success during the independent reading block is to model procedures and reading strategies for your students. In the beginning, you will need to show students how to select a just-right book, select a spot to read, sit still and read, discuss a book with a partner, partner read, and fill in the reading log. To make the modeling more interesting, consider inviting a student or two to do a demonstration while the rest of the class observes and comments.

From time to time, take a few minutes to model reading strategies such as how to figure out a difficult word or use a comprehension strategy (e.g., making personal connections) during reading. After you model in a text of your choice, invite students to use the strategy during their independent reading. If you want to provide students with a sticky note or two to mark their text during reading, model that in a read-aloud first, and then ask students to find a spot to mark. You don't have to require that they write on the sticky note but rather that they mark the spot and discuss with a partner afterward.

Conference with students.

While students read on their own, circulate around the room to check the text for the student to read first silently, then aloud. Ask the student to retell. Ask a few questions. If the student is 95% accurate on the questions, the book is at the reading level of the student. If the student struggles with comprehension or decoding, then it is too difficult, and you can redirect his or her choice of reading material.

Things to Mark With a Sticky Note During Reading

- A favorite part
- A descriptive paragraph
- A connection to one's own life (e.g., This reminds me of....)
- A place where you have a question

Questions to Ask During a Reading Conference

- Let's look at your reading log. What kinds of books are you reading? What do you want to read next?
- What are you reading now? Do you like your book? Why or why not? Why did you pick this book? Would you recommend it to a friend?
- Tell me about your book. What is happening? What is your favorite part?
- Who is in the story? What is the setting or problem? Does the character change?
- How does the character react to others and solve problems?
- How does the story end? Do you agree with the way the author wrote this story? Would you have done something differently?

Lori's Top 5 Surefire Strategies for Independent Reading

Try these proven strategies that will enhance your independent reading time!

Map It

ReadWriteThink.org offers a student interactive Graphic Map, which is a great way to encourage students to track events during their reading and improve their abilities to create better summaries. See www.readwritethink.org/classroom-resources/student-interactives/graphic-30039.html.

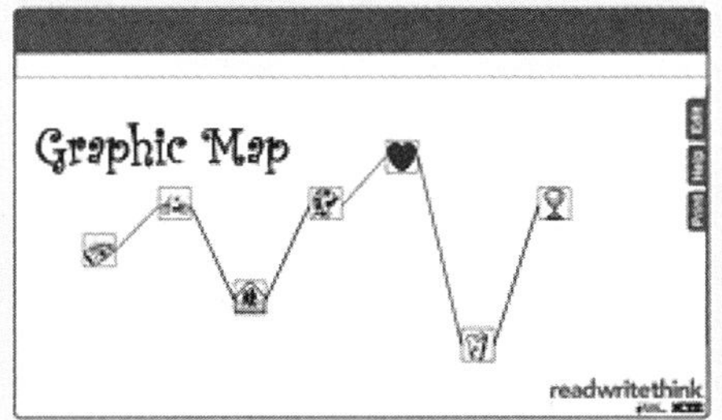

2 *Judge a Book by Its Cover*

Most likely you select reading material based on recommendations of friends, bookstores, ads, or even Oprah's Book Club. Sometimes you pick something up just because you like the cover. Using the ReadWriteThink.org Book Cover Creator (www.readwritethink.org/classroom-resources/student-interactives/book-cover-creator-30058.html), your students can create their own book jackets to display and inspire others to read, read, read!

Be a Super Model

Some years ago, I took the advice of Regie Routman (2003) and began logging my own reading. I write the title, author, and a brief summary, and I give my books a letter grade and tell why. I write in a pretty little notebook that I stash in my nightstand and that I often bring to show students. When I explain my own literature log, they are all ears. (Students love hearing about our lives outside of school—watch them perk up if you share a story about your dog, or the time your car broke down! They pay attention to your reading, too.) I share my "what I want to read next" list, as well. Sometimes this model is all the students need to inspire them to keep their own reading logs up to date.

4 *Discussion Buddies or Circles*

One of the most effective ways to increase comprehension is to allow students to discuss their reading with a partner or group (Allington, cited in Moss & Young, 2010; Applebee, Langer, Nystrand, & Gamoran, 2003). Here are some helpful discussion starters:

- What is going on in your book?
- Do you like it? Why or why not?
- Does it remind you of anything in your life, another book, or something else? What? How?
- What is your favorite part and why?
- What is a well-written passage? Great illustration?

Technology Tips

There are many exciting ways for students to engage in discussions and responses to literature using technology. Here are a few you may want to try:

- Load popular books onto MP3 players for struggling readers to listen to.
- Using an inexpensive video camera, videotape presentations of student-created commercials for their books. Students can also role-play, conducting "interviews" with the author or a character using a pretend microphone.
- Use an online platform for social networking such as Ning (www.ning.com) to create your own secure message board where students can write comments to one another about books (Moss & Young, 2010).

Before Reading: Activate Prior Knowledge

- What are some acronyms for independent reading? Discuss.
- What are some ways you have managed independent reading in your classroom?
- How do your students like independent reading time? What works for you? What are some problems you (and your students) encounter during independent reading? Why is independent reading much more than just "grabbing a book to read"?

During Reading: Respond While Reading

- While reading this chapter, mark your text with self-stick notes. Use symbols to indicate questions (?), things you want to try (T), something you connect with (+), something interesting or surprising (!) (adapted from Hatt, n.d.).

After Reading: Think About and Discuss

- Why do you think students who spend more time in independent reading do well on standardized tests? What are other benefits of independent reading?
- Which of your students read more?
- Discuss guidelines for setting up an independent reading time in your classroom.
- What are some effective ways to organize a classroom library?
- How can you help students become independent in selecting their own appropriate just-right books?
- What difficulties do students experience in selecting titles? What are some ways you can monitor students' independent reading through book logs, conferences, self-stick notes, or other writing procedures? Which questions do you prefer asking students during a reading conference?
- What procedural minilessons do you need to teach so that independent reading time will run effectively?

Putting Independent Reading Into Practice

Professional Development Breakout Groups

- Make a chart listing problems students experience with independent reading. Brainstorm solutions.
- Research ways to use technology as a form of book sharing for students. Try www.spaghettibookclub.org or www.ning.com.
- List different ways to create an effective and appealing classroom library. Check out these ideas on Scholastic's Teachers website:
  - www.scholastic.com/teachers/article/best-practices-teaching-classroom-libraries
  - www.scholastic.com/teachers/top_teaching/2009/10/classlibrary

Lesson Sharing

- Try one of Lori's Top 5 lessons with your class. Be prepared to share. On a scale of 1–5, how did the lesson go? Explain. What do you want to try next?
- Record yourself conducting an independent reading conference with one or two of your students. Share the video with colleagues. Discuss what you like and want to improve. How can you move students along in their reading by conferring with them?

Teacher as Reader

- Keep a reading log of your reading materials. Share it with students.
- Conduct a think-aloud as you reflect on your reading habits. For example: *"I read one fiction book this month, and the rest were nonfiction online articles about taking care of my new puppy. My goal is to read two more novels next month and a few kids' books."*

Before the Next Meeting

Read: Select the next chapter your group will read. Mark the text during reading.
Try: Try one of the lessons from the next chapter, or try something new from this chapter.
Observe: Visit a colleague's classroom to observe a lesson on independent reading, or record yourself teaching a lesson and share the video at a meeting.

Going Deeper With Independent Reading

- Try a book study using this practical resource loaded with everything you need to set up an independent reading program:

  Moss, B., & Young, T.A. (2010). *Creating lifelong readers through independent reading*. Newark, DE: International Reading Association.

- Or consider studying the resources listed on page 46.

My Independent Reading/My Independent Reading Evaluation Bookmarks Lesson

Objective: To provide students with two bookmarks with prompts that they can use as they "turn and talk" to one another about their independent reading behaviors.

Common Core Connections: Students provide evidence from the text when using the prompts. Students set goals to read their level of books as well as increasingly more difficult fiction and informational texts. Students evaluate their reading goals and strive to read attentively and collaborate in discussions with others.

Teacher Modeling: Model how to use each of the prompts on the My Independent Reading Bookmark by using any reading material from your grade level. During independent reading, students will be reading from different books. When you model, place your reading material on a document camera so that students can see the page you are modeling from. Conduct a think-aloud using each of the prompts on the bookmark. You can select one a day or several at a time. From time to time, return to modeling the prompts. For example, "My favorite part is...because...."

Also model prompts from the My Independent Reading Evaluation Bookmark. Discuss your reading material. For example, "This book is what I am reading now. It is easy to read, so I will finish it this weekend. Next I want to read..., and it is a bit challenging. But I am interested in it, so I will read it more slowly and reread parts to keep up."

Tip: You may want to duplicate the bookmarks back to back to use in lessons on independent reading.

Guided Practice: Ask students to turn to their partners and use the same prompt you just modeled from one of the independent reading bookmarks, but with their own independent reading books. Eventually, give students choices among several prompts. Listen to the pairs and invite students to share with the whole class. Praise their efforts. Model for students who need more support in using their texts.

Independent Practice: Students may use the same prompts as in your read-aloud lesson for their independent reading books. They can mark with self-stick notes those passages they wish to share with the group or a partner. Use the bookmarks in your reading conferences with individuals.

Wrap Up: Ask students how the discussion has helped deepen their comprehension. Ask which of the prompts on the bookmarks is their favorite or the most helpful and why.

Quick Buddy or Circle Conversation Lesson

Objective: Students write or sketch reflections about a book they are reading independently. They turn to partners or students at their table to share points.

Common Core Connections: Students collaborate in rich discussions. Students discuss themes and compare/contrast the different books they are reading.

Teacher Modeling: Tell students that when good readers share with one another the books they are reading, whether they liked the book or not, they often tell a quick summary, their favorite parts, and the connections they are making. Using a text that the class is reading or even your novel, conduct a think-aloud for each of the four boxes. Do all the boxes in one day, or cut the boxes apart and ask students to do one each day for four days.

Guided Practice: Invite students to turn to a partner or a small group and share their responses. Circulate and join in the conversations, modeling and prompting when necessary. Invite some of the students to share with the class or to model for the class their partner or group discussions.

Independent Practice: Students work on filling out their boxes as they read the next portion of their books. Give a plus, check, or minus for completed work.

Wrap Up: Invite students to tell partners and the class to share each of the four conversation boxes. Have students stand in two lines across from one another and discuss one box at a time. Play music or signal students to move to new partners and share the next box. Ask students to share which box they enjoyed the most and why.

Not Your Normal Book Report

Directions: Invite your students to share their independent reading books in creative ways! Here are just a few examples:

Shelf Talkers	***New York Times* Best Seller List of Favorites**	**Create a Book Show**
Bookstores post reviews on cards placed next to the books for sale on the shelf. Often store employees or local readers write the reviews. Create an index-card review for your classroom or school library. (Idea from Doyne & Schulten, 2011.)	Study your local paper for samples of online lists of popular fiction and nonfiction books. Survey students at your school to find out which books are most popular in your school and create a Top 5 list of "best sellers" for different grade levels. (Idea from Doyne & Schulten, 2011.)	Form a panel of three students role-playing as judges and rate and discuss a book. (For fun, copy the personalities of any television judges from music or dance competition shows.)

Assessment Tips

Observe students during independent reading time. Keep a clipboard nearby to jot down quick notes and observations. Share the rubric results with students. Model the behaviors you want them to develop.

My Independent Reading Bookmark

Name______________________________

What I am reading now:

(title) ______________________________

(author) ____________________________

I chose this book because_______________

BEFORE READING

Predict

- "I think this is about...because...."

(look at pictures, headings, skim the words)

DURING READING

Summarize/Predict

- "So far...."
- "Next I think...."

Connect

- "This reminds me of...because...."

Clarify

- I didn't get [the word, idea, page, chapter], so I...[reread, figured out the word, read on]."

Visualize

- "On this page I can see...."

Question

- "I am wondering...."

AFTER READING

Evaluate

- "My favorite part was...because...."
- "I would or would not recommend this book because...."

WHAT I WANT TO READ NEXT

1. Next I want to read ___________ because _______________________________.
2. And ____________ because___________.

Best Ever Literacy Survival Tips: 72 Lessons You Can't Teach Without by Lori D. Oczkus.

My Independent Reading Bookmark

Name______________________________

What I am reading now:

(title) ______________________________

(author) ____________________________

I chose this book because_______________

BEFORE READING

Predict

- "I think this is about...because...."

(look at pictures, headings, skim the words)

DURING READING

Summarize/Predict

- "So far...."
- "Next I think...."

Connect

- "This reminds me of...because...."

Clarify

- I didn't get [the word, idea, page, chapter], so I...[reread, figured out the word, read on]."

Visualize

- "On this page I can see...."

Question

- "I am wondering...."

AFTER READING

Evaluate

- "My favorite part was...because...."
- "I would or would not recommend this book because...."

WHAT I WANT TO READ NEXT

1. Next I want to read ___________ because _______________________________.
2. And ____________ because___________.

Best Ever Literacy Survival Tips: 72 Lessons You Can't Teach Without by Lori D. Oczkus.
© 2012 International Reading Association. May be copied for classroom use.

My Independent Reading Evaluation Bookmark

I stay in my spot and read for the entire independent reading time.

☐ Yes ☐ Sometimes ☐ No

I choose books at my level.

☐ Yes ☐ Sometimes ☐ No

I also choose books I am interested in that are at harder levels.

☐ Yes ☐ Sometimes ☐ No

I record my books in my reading log.

☐ Yes ☐ Sometimes ☐ No

I talk with others about my books.

☐ Yes ☐ Sometimes ☐ No

I set goals for reading.

☐ Yes ☐ Sometimes ☐ No

My Independent Reading Evaluation Bookmark

I stay in my spot and read for the entire independent reading time.

☐ Yes ☐ Sometimes ☐ No

I choose books at my level.

☐ Yes ☐ Sometimes ☐ No

I also choose books I am interested in that are at harder levels.

☐ Yes ☐ Sometimes ☐ No

I record my books in my reading log.

☐ Yes ☐ Sometimes ☐ No

I talk with others about my books.

☐ Yes ☐ Sometimes ☐ No

I set goals for reading.

☐ Yes ☐ Sometimes ☐ No

Best Ever Literacy Survival Tips: 72 Lessons You Can't Teach Without by Lori D. Oczkus.
© 2012 International Reading Association. May be copied for classroom use.

Quick Buddy or Circle Conversations

Directions: Fill in the boxes with ideas from the book you are reading independently. Meet with a partner or group to take turns sharing.

What I'm reading now: (title) ____________________ (author) ____________________

Summarize	**Evaluate**
This book is about ____________________ ____________________ . Draw a picture to summarize.	I like or dislike this book because ________ . I give it a (circle one) 1 = I love it! 2 = It is good. 3 = It's OK. 4 = I don't like it much. 5 = I don't like it at all! Tell why you gave that score. Draw a picture of the cover.
Connect	**Evaluate**
This book reminds me of ______________ ____________________ because ____________________ . Draw a picture.	I like the way the author (or illustrator) wrote (or drew) this part on page ________ because ____________________ . Draw a picture.

Independent Reading Evaluation Rubric

Characteristics of an Engaged Reader	1 Missing Expectations for an Engaged Reader	2 Developing Expectations as an Engaged Reader	3 Meeting Expectations as an Engaged Reader	4 Exceeding Expectations as an Engaged Reader
Uses independent time to read	• Stalls, out of seat, pretends to read, or looks around the room during independent reading time • May distract others • Always relies on teacher prompting	• Stalls or looks around for about half of independent reading time • Needs teacher prompting	• Reads for most of the independent reading period • Needs some teacher prompting	• Stays completely on task without teacher prompting for the entire independent reading time
Selects books of just-right reading level and interest	• Selects books that are consistently too hard or too easy • Spends too much time finding a book to read	• Sometimes selects books that are too hard or too easy • Sometimes spends too much time finding a book	• Most of the time quickly selects a book that is at the right level • Most of the time quickly moves into a new book	• Consistently selects books at the appropriate level • Moves from one book to the next with ease
Keeps an up-to-date reading log	• Rarely fills out reading log • Needs teacher support	• Fills out the reading log most of the time • Needs some prompting	• Most of the time fills out reading log with little prompting	• Consistently fills out reading log
Reads a variety of genres	• Reads one type of reading material	• Reads at least two different genres	• Reads three or more genres	• Reads many types of genres
Sets goals for reading (pages, genres, etc.)	• Is not motivated to set goals and needs teacher help	• Sets some goals but needs teacher help	• Sets one or two goals	• Sets detailed motivated goals

Q&A

We have so much to fit in with our core reading program. Many teachers at our school have abandoned independent reading, only requiring it at home. How can I justify my independent reading program?

This chapter provides you with research and resources to defend your program. Remember the third-grade teachers with the flat reading scores, except the one who held on to her independent reading block? Keep in mind the wonderful benefits. Just make sure you are modeling for students and conferencing with them to keep your independent reading program strong.

"Research tells us that the time students spend in independent reading is one of the best predictors of reading achievement—in comprehension, decoding, fluency, and vocabulary (Anderson, Wilson, & Fielding, 1988)."

Resources on Independent Reading

Great Professional Books

***The Book Whisperer: Awakening the Inner Reader in Every Child* by Donalyn Miller**
This popular title by a sixth-grade teacher flies off shelves in bookstores and at teacher conferences. This is a no-nonsense guide to helping students love to read.

***Comprehension Shouldn't Be Silent: From Strategy Instruction to Student Independence* by Michelle J. Kelley and Nicki Clausen-Grace**
These teachers have created their own model for the reading block that has become all the rage. They demonstrate how to move your strategy instruction into the independent reading block with ease!

***Creating Lifelong Readers Through Independent Reading* by Barbara Moss and Terrell A. Young**
This is a wonderful, detailed resource devoted to reading independently. It has everything you might want to know and more.

***Reading Essentials: The Specifics You Need to Teach Reading Well* by Regie Routman**
This book is a must-have for teachers! Not only does this expert, veteran teacher explain all you need to know about independent reading in simple steps, but she covers all reading topics well. This is a handbook/bible/guide/lifesaver for new and experienced teachers alike.

Website

Spaghetti Book Club: www.spaghettibookclub.org
A place for kids to connect, on a personal level, with the books they are reading and then share their thoughts with family members, friends, and kids around the world.

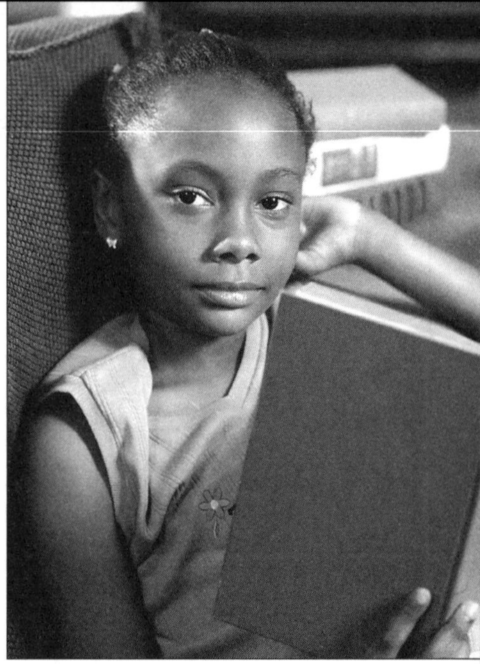

References

Anderson, R.C., Wilson, P.T., & Fielding, L.G. (1988). Growth in reading and how children spend their time outside of school. *Reading Research Quarterly, 23*(3), 285–303.

Applebee, A.N., Langer, J.A., Nystrand, M., & Gamoran, A. (2003). Discussion-based approaches to developing understanding: Classroom instruction and student performance in middle and high school English. *American Educational Research Journal, 40*(3), 685–730.

Doyne, S., & Schulten, K. (2011, November 10). Beyond the book report: Ways to respond to literature using New York Times models [Web log post]. Retrieved from learning.blogs.nytimes.com/2011/11/10/beyond-the-book-report-ways-to-respond-to-literature-using-new-york-times-models

Fawson, P.C., Reutzel, D.R., Read, S., Smith, J.A., & Moore, S.A. (2009). The influence of differing the paths to an incentive on third graders' reading achievement and attitudes. *Reading Psychology, 30*(6), 564–583.

Fountas, I.C., & Pinnell, G.S. (2001). *Guiding readers and writers: Grades 3–6*. Portsmouth, NH: Heinemann.

Hatt, C. (n.d.). *Better discussions in study groups*. Retrieved from www.choiceliteracy.com/public/796.cfm

Hiebert, E.H., & Reutzel, D.R. (Eds.). (2010). *Revisiting silent reading: New directions for teachers and researchers*. Newark, DE: International Reading Association.

Miller, D. (2009). *The book whisperer: Awakening the inner reader in every child*. San Francisco: Jossey-Bass.

Moss, B., & Young, T.A. (2010). *Creating lifelong readers through independent reading*. Newark, DE: International Reading Association.

Ohlhausen, M.M., & Jepsen, M. (1992). Lessons from Goldilocks: "Somebody's been choosing my books but I can make my own choices now!" *The New Advocate, 5*(1), 31–46.

Reutzel, D.R., & Fawson, P.C. (2002). *Your classroom library: New ways to give it more teaching power*. New York: Scholastic.

Reutzel, D.R., Jones, C.D., Fawson, P.C., & Smith, J.A. (2008). Scaffolded silent reading: A complement to guided repeated oral reading that works! *The Reading Teacher, 62*(3), 194–207. doi:10.1598/RT.62.3.2

Routman, R. (2003). *Reading essentials: The specifics you need to teach reading well*. Portsmouth, NH: Heinemann.

CHAPTER 4

Surefire Ways to Engage Students and Improve Comprehension: Guidelines and TOP 5 Comprehension Strategies

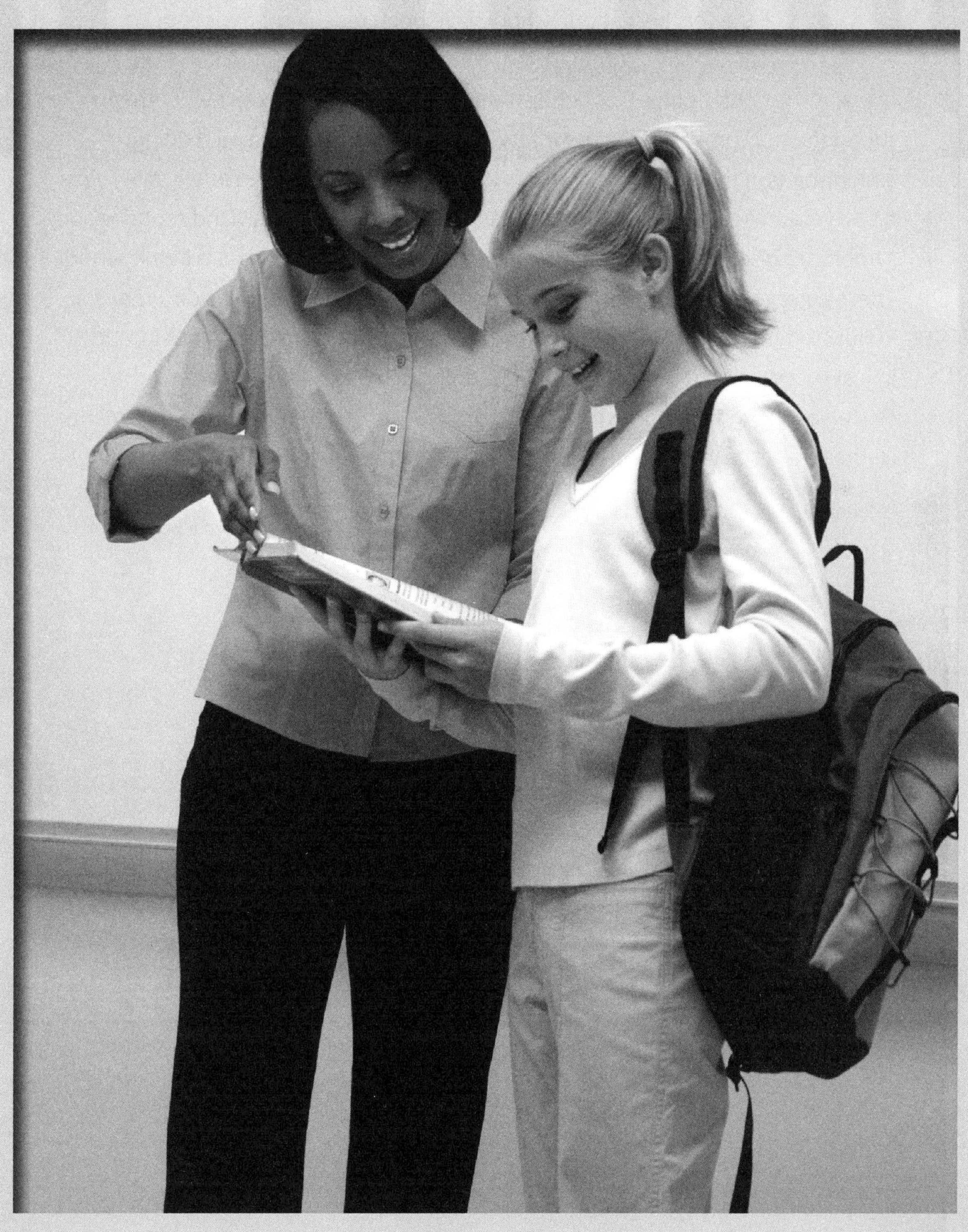

Best Ever Advice on... Comprehension

All the teachers at our school have been teaching predicting, questioning, summarizing, connecting, and inferring for years. Consistently, the Tier 2 students struggled to connect what they successfully accomplished in the intervention room to the general reading assignments in their regular classrooms. It was not until we used *Interactive Think-Aloud Lessons* (Oczkus, 2009) that all the students started using hand motions and symbols to discuss the key reading strategies they used everywhere in the school. These common props, motions, and sentence starters have made a difference in our students' overall reading and thinking skills. Our state data came in, and in just one year we raised our Hispanic reading scores 15.2%. I know that these strategies, along with our extra reading groups at the differentiated levels, made all the difference in the world. We met our growth targets in all areas of reading!

—Jennifer Reilly, Reading Consultant Specialist

Common Problems Students Have With Reading Comprehension

- Some students decode well but do not comprehend what they've read.
- Primary students may be so focused on decoding that they lose comprehension.
- Students may not be able to identify the main ideas of a text.
- Students do not make logical predictions based on the text or their background experiences.
- Students do not infer themes, character feelings, or other deeper interpretations of the text.
- Students of all ages may lack strategies for figuring out confusing or difficult words.
- Students may not make meaningful personal connections to the text including connections to their lives, other books they've read, and the world around them.
- Students may not ask questions about the text or anticipate questions the teacher may ask.

It is no wonder that reading comprehension manages to hold a prominent place on the list of "very hot" topics in literacy when the annual "What's Hot" in literacy research survey comes out (Cassidy & Cassidy, 2010). Teachers across the globe continue to report that their students experience difficulty comprehending what they read.

Do any of these scenarios sound familiar to you?

- Sixth grader Hector only selects comic books or magazines to read during SSR time. He says reading is "really boring."
- Henry accurately decodes the second-grade basal story but after reading can't recall any of the highlights or important details.
- Swanceria experiences difficulty reading the social studies text.
- Mr. Johnson's fourth graders range from first- to sixth-grade reading levels.
- Ana arrived from Mexico two years ago and reads fluently in English in third grade but experiences much difficulty comprehending what she reads.

Maybe some of these students are just like the ones in your classroom. Your students probably range greatly in their reading levels and skills. You may find that some of your students decode words but have difficulty understanding the text. Many students experience difficulty summarizing and pulling main ideas from the text. Even our very best readers may find nonfiction texts challenging. Then there are the students who simply are not engaged in their reading.

Just know that you are not alone. In recent years, an alarming 69% of fourth graders and 70% of eighth graders read below the proficient reading level on the National Assessment of Educational Progress (National Center for Education Statistics, 2009). The National Reading Panel (National Institute of Child Health and Human Development [NICHD], 2000) pointed out that comprehension is a complex process. However, the good news is that we know more now about effective ways to improve comprehension than ever before (Oczkus, 2009).

What Is Comprehension and Why Is It So Important to Teach?

The goal of reading is to comprehend or understand what we read (Lipson, 2007). Simply decoding or reading the words isn't enough if the reader cannot make sense of the text.

Recent reading research suggests that an urgent need exists for educators to teach comprehension strategies at all grade levels from primary to secondary. Reading experts agree that students need to be taught to use the "good reader" strategies (i.e., comprehension strategies) flexibly and with many different types of text (Duke, 2005).

The National Reading Panel identified comprehension, vocabulary, fluency, phonics, and phonemic awareness as the pillars or key building blocks of teaching reading (NICHD, 2000). Comprehension strategies can be taught to dramatically improve reading comprehension (Duke & Pearson, 2002). This chapter will explore practical and effective techniques for improving reading comprehension in your classroom.

What Are the Most Important Comprehension Strategies to Teach?

Although the list of comprehension strategies differs slightly depending on the study, the core list is consistent. I like to call the six essential reading comprehension strategies the "Super Six"—a kid-friendly term that will stick with your students (Oczkus, 2004, 2009):

1. Making connections
2. Predicting and inferring
3. Questioning
4. Monitoring and clarifying
5. Summarizing and synthesizing
6. Evaluating

These research-based comprehension strategies are the critical ones that good readers use before, during, and after reading. They are universally accepted, and any published reading program that you use will include them. If your district uses leveled texts and novels or a readers' workshop approach, you can also easily incorporate lessons on the comprehension strategies. I suggest teaching each of the strategies in think-aloud lessons using mentor texts and other interactive techniques (see the "Guidelines for Effectively Teaching Comprehension Strategies" section and Oczkus, 2009).

Connect

When we read, we naturally make connections to our own life experiences, other books we've read, and the world around us. When I read the popular book *Because of Winn-Dixie* by Kate DiCamillo, students are reminded of dogs or pets they've owned, books they've read about dogs, and movies they've seen. Personal connections help make reading more fun and meaningful.

Predict/Infer

Predicting is a student favorite. Students love guessing what will happen next. The trick to making good predictions is to go beyond wild guessing and make logical or more sophisticated predictions based on what is happening in the text and the reader's prior knowledge. Throughout the reading of a fiction text, you can pause and ask your students to predict what they think will happen next; with nonfiction, ask what they think they will learn next.

I like to tell students that inferring is the cousin of predicting. Both predicting and inferring require that students use text clues and clues from their own minds to figure out what is happening in the text. Students can think of themselves as reading detectives trying to decode an author's hidden message. Inferring is often called "reading between the lines" and is a strategy that the very best readers use constantly.

Question

Good readers ask questions before, during, and after reading. I bring a plastic microphone to class (all grade levels!) and tell students that asking questions is like three kinds of television shows: a game show for more literal recall, a Discovery Channel show for "wondering," and a talk show for asking open-ended discussion questions. Children come to school brimming with questions; when we harness and encourage their natural curiosity, comprehension improves dramatically (Keene & Zimmermann, 1997; NICHD, 2000).

Monitor/Clarify

Monitoring comprehension—or clarifying, as it is sometimes referred to—is much like checking the gauges on your car and then using tools to fix the problem. Some of our readers are simply not aware that they are supposed to pause frequently to try to figure out confusing words or portions of text. Monitoring comprehension involves using "fix it" strategies such as breaking words into syllables, sounding out words, and rereading for meaning. Monitoring also requires that students keep track of the big picture in the story by rereading and making "mind pictures" or visualizing while reading.

Summarize/Synthesize

Summarizing is a whopper of a strategy that involves lots of tough skills such as remembering details, sorting out important points and themes, and putting it all in a logical order. Students may moan (and you might, too) when you say it is time to summarize. Yet, researchers tell us that when students summarize, their comprehension improves (Duke & Pearson, 2002). My best advice is to make it fun. Try asking students frequently to summarize little chunks of text for practice rather than always making a summary for an entire story or chapter. Allow students to sketch drawings and create dramatizations as summaries, too.

Synthesis is related to summarizing, but when students synthesize they go beyond just recalling the text and they create new meanings. Students synthesize when they answer these questions: How has this text changed my thinking? What new ideas do I have about the topic?

Evaluate

Reality television provides us with a wonderful metaphor for evaluating during reading. Our students are familiar with the judges who spew results for music, dance, or cooking competitions. Good readers evaluate whether they liked the text, the author's craft, characters' actions, and even their own progress as readers. It is especially important to ask students to include reasons or a "because" to complete their evaluations. Evaluating moves students to higher levels of comprehension and thinking.

Helpful Strategy Starters

Strategy	Metaphor	Prop	Strategy Starters
Connect	Builder	Paper-strip connection chain	"This reminds me of... because...."
Predict/Infer	Fortune teller	Fake crystal ball or a snow globe	"I think...will happen because...."
	Detective	Magnifying glass	"I can tell that...because...."
Question	TV host, game show or talk show	Microphone	"I wonder...." "Who, what, when, where, why, how?" "Why do you think...?"
Monitor/ Clarify	Mechanic	Tool box	"I didn't get [the word, idea, page, chapter]...so I [reread, read on, chopped up the word, sounded it out]."
	Clarifier lady with eye glasses	Eye glasses	
Summarize/ Synthesize	Cowboy/cowgirl or tacky tourist	Yarn lasso or camera	"This is mainly about...."
	Chef	Chef's hat or shaker bottles	"I used to think..., now I think...."
Evaluate	Reality show judge	Gavel or score sheets	"I rate...because...."

Note. Ideas found in *Interactive Think-Aloud Lessons: 25 Surefire Ways to Engage Students and Improve Comprehension* by Lori Oczkus, 2009, New York: Scholastic; Newark, DE: International Reading Association.

Guidelines for Effectively Teaching Comprehension Strategies

Here are some practical guidelines to help you introduce and reinforce the comprehension strategies all year long.

Provide metaphors for each strategy.

The very best teachers put metaphors to good use and make their teaching come alive. Students from kindergarten to high school remember the strategies better when we attach a metaphor to each (Wormeli, 2009). For example, for questioning as we read, I bring a microphone (the fake *American Idol* one I have is always a hit) and tell students that asking questions is like being on a game show or talk show.

You can choose on the "scale of kookiness" to show a picture representing the metaphor, to hold up a prop, or to dress up like a character to share the metaphor. You do not have to dress up if that is not you, but I suggest at least holding up a prop for students. Be sure to use the Helpful Strategy Starters to provide students with the language they need for each of the strategies. This is especially helpful if you have English learners in your classroom.

Teach using think-alouds.

Think-alouds are a great way to model comprehension strategies for students and make the thinking behind them more visible. A think-aloud starts with teacher modeling and moves to guided practice with peers and eventually independent practice. This is called the gradual release of responsibility so that students become responsible for learning, as in the following example.

> *Mrs. Carpenter shows the nonfiction text* Zipping, Zapping, Zooming Bats *by Ann Earle and tells the class that when they read it is helpful to clarify, especially when reading nonfiction. She engages the students in a quick partner discussion to see what the students know about bats. Then she asks the third graders what they know about clarifying their comprehension. Some hands go up, and students share that good readers reread, read on, and sound out hard words.*
>
> *She continues by telling the students that clarifying is like wearing clarify glasses as she puts on a pair of giant yellow glasses. The students giggle, but Mrs. Carpenter has their undivided attention. As she reads aloud from the book, she pauses frequently to model for students how to clarify a difficult word or phrase using the strategy starter "I didn't get..., so I...."*
>
> *After a few pages and examples, she pauses on a word and asks the students to turn to partners to try out the strategy starter and to clarify the word* echolocation. *At the end of the lesson, she tells students they will collect five hard words to clarify in their own reading today and share ways to clarify words with their table teams.*

Steps for a Well-Crafted Think-Aloud at Any Grade Level

1. Introduce the strategy

- Say, "When good readers read they [name the strategy], and it helps them...."
- Ask students what they know about the strategy: "What do you know about...?"
- Explain the strategy: "When we [name the strategy], we first..., then we..., then finally we...."
- Optional: Use picture, prop, or character costume.

2. Model in an interactive think-aloud

- Select a passage from a text to read aloud and show the steps you use with a given strategy: "I am stopping here to [name the strategy]. Watch me as I show you how it helps me understand what I am reading."
- Optional: Add props or strategy starters to your think-aloud.

3. Guide practice

- Read on in the text, pausing to allow students to turn and talk to a partner to try out the strategy. Or have table groups try the strategy in teams and then share.

4. Provide independent practice

- Students use sticky notes to mark their texts as they read on their own and hunt for places they will use the strategy you are working on.

5. Wrap up

- The class discusses how the strategy helped them with the reading today: "The strategy helped us because...."

Mrs. Carpenter invites a student up to the front of the room to wear the big glasses and to reflect on the lesson. The student says, "I reread the sentence, and I can chop the word in parts when I clarify."

Teach comprehension strategies in different settings.

In most of my schools, we post the comprehension strategies on the wall in every room. Some teachers even hang the props on the wall for a colorful display and for reference during all sorts of reading lessons. You can easily reinforce the comprehension strategies throughout the day in a variety of settings, including the following:

- Whole-class lessons—Refer to the strategies and conduct mini think-alouds during read-alouds, novel or basal study, or content area lessons. Besides modeling, be sure to allow partners and groups to find examples in the text.
- Guided reading—Guided reading is the perfect setting for selecting just one or a few of the strategies to reinforce at a student's reading level.
- Independent reading—After a read-aloud in which you model one of the strategies and provide practice with partners, try asking students to find examples of their strategy use with independent reading books. Have students provide examples on a bookmark, self-stick notes, or a Strategy Collection Sheet (they can fold a paper into fourths and record strategy examples in each box).

Encourage higher level thinking skills.

If you focus on only lower level literal thinking skills, that is what you will get from your students. When you teach a balance of literal, inferential, and critical thinking, students grow in their comprehension (Pearson, 2010). Don't fall into the trap of providing only your best readers higher level thinking questions. Struggling readers benefit from critical thinking as well!

Try discussion starters that promote deeper thinking, such as

- "What are you wondering?"
- "Why do you think?"
- "How...?"
- "I think...because...."
- "I used to think..., now I think... because...."
- "I rate this...because...."

Require students to always give a "because" after every response.

Sample Strategy Collection Sheet

My Predictions	My Connections
Page ______ I think…will happen because…. Page ______ I think…will happen because….	Page ______ This reminds me of…because…. Page ______ This reminds me of…because….
My Questions Page ______ I wonder…. Page ______ I wonder….	**My Summaries** Page ______ This was mostly about…. Page ______ This was mostly about….

Lori's Top 5 Surefire Strategies for Comprehension

Try these proven lessons that you can use over and over to strengthen your students' reading comprehension.

1 *Connection Chains (Oczkus, 2009)*

Provide three different colors of paper cut into strips. One color is for text-to-self connections, one for text-to-text, and the other for text-to-world. Students write their connections on the papers using the frame "This reminds me of...." Then they roll and glue or tape the strips into paper chains, which we hook together and hang around the room.

2 *Roll Your Prediction (Oczkus, 2010)*

This lesson focuses on the language of predicting. Write the following strategy starters on blank foam or large, plastic cubes from the teacher store, or use regular dice and assign a strategy starter to each number. Students roll the cubes or dice every few pages and take turns using the starters to make predictions about the text.

1. "I think I will learn...."
2. "Maybe...because...."
3. "I think...will happen because...."
4. "Next, I think...because I know...."
5. "I'll bet...because...."
6. "So far...so now I think...will happen."

3 *Pop the Question (Oczkus, 2010)*

Students generate questions they might ask the main characters in the text and use toy microphones (or their fists as a pretend microphone!) to interview one another. During reading, students collect and record the questions they will use as they role play. This is a quick, impromptu activity that you can engage students in any time to improve questioning and deepen comprehension, because students are forced to make inferences as they role play and answer one another's questions. As you listen to the pairs, encourage open-ended questions rather than yes/no questions.
You may even want to audiotape students and make a quick, fun, class DVD to show during parent nights or to show other classes.

4 *Pause to Clarify (Oczkus, 2009)*

Every student in your classroom has experience with remote controls. Ask students to show you with their hands what a pause button looks like. (Have them put their arms parallel like ||.) Tell them that when good readers read, they pause when they do not understand something. Good readers either rewind (reread) or fast forward (read ahead) or even chop up the word or part to fully understand it. Use motions to demonstrate:

- Pause—Bend arms at elbows and hold parallel to form two lines like a pause button.
- Rewind—Point to indicate rewinding.
- Fast forward—Point to indicate fast forwarding.

Read aloud from a text and ask students to put their arms up in a pause when they hear something they do not understand. Stop reading and ask for examples and model/discuss how to clarify the points the students selected. Using hand motions this way improves comprehension, because the kinesthetic motions help students create mental representations for abstract concepts (Collins, 2005).

5 *So Far/Next (Oczkus, 2009)*

This is one of my favorite lessons because it engages students on many levels. After reading a portion of text, students stop to sketch what has happened so far in the story and then sketch what they think will happen next. I model and conduct this as a read-aloud for the first few times, but this activity makes wonderful independent work as well. You can assign reading and indicate stopping points (pages or ends of chapters) when students will sketch their two drawings: a "so far" and a "next." I like providing strips of cut paper for the students to fold into boxes, or you can have them sketch in a reader's notebook. Allow students to share their summaries and predictions with partners and their tablemates.

Before Reading: Activate Prior Knowledge

- How do you define reading comprehension?
- What are some problems your students experience when comprehending texts?
- Which comprehension strategies do your students struggle with the most?

During Reading: Respond While Reading

- While reading this chapter, mark your text with self-stick notes. Use symbols to indicate questions (?), things you want to try (T), something you connect with (+), something interesting or surprising (!) (adapted from Hatt, n.d.).

After Reading: Think About and Discuss

- Discuss each of the comprehension strategies and the problems your students encounter with each.
- How do metaphors for each strategy and strategy starters help students understand and apply the strategies in their reading?
- What are the steps of a well-crafted think-aloud?
- How is the interactive think-aloud model the same as or different from other think-alouds you have used in your lessons?
- How can you promote higher level thinking skills in your comprehension lessons?
- Discuss the idea of bringing in your own reading habits and materials to show students how to use the strategies.

Putting Comprehension Into Practice

Professional Development Breakout Groups

- Make a chart of problems your students have with comprehension. Which lessons or ideas in this chapter will help build understanding for each problem listed?
- At a meeting, break into grade-level groups. Using reading material from your grade level, practice on one another a think-aloud using the protocol listed on page 52. Share with the entire staff. What will you have students do to demonstrate their comprehension?
- View and discuss Lori Oczkus's online clips and articles and review Interactive Think-Aloud Lessons at www.scholastic.com/teachers/collection/interactive-think-aloud-lessons.

Lesson Sharing

- Try one of Lori's Top 5 lessons with your class. Be prepared to share. On a scale of 1–5, how did the lesson go? Explain. What do you want to try next?
- Bring student samples or a video from one of the lessons you try.
- Try the same lesson in a whole-group setting as well as with small groups. Discuss and reflect upon the differences.

Teacher as Reader

- When you read, pay attention to how you use each of the comprehension strategies. Share with your students how you used a particular strategy with a book, newspaper, or other reading material. Read aloud from your reading material and say how you used the strategy. For example, "I read this newspaper article this weekend about this dog that warned his master about a fire in the home. I reread and clarified this part of the text to figure out just how the dog did that. Now I can see a picture in my head!"

Before the Next Meeting

Read: Select the next chapter your group will read. Mark the text during reading.
Try: Try one of the lessons from the next chapter, or try something new from this chapter.
Observe: Visit a colleague's classroom to observe a lesson on comprehension, or record yourself teaching a lesson and share the video at a meeting.

Going Deeper With Comprehension

- Try a book study using this practical resource loaded with comprehension lessons:

  Oczkus, L.D. (2009). *Interactive think-aloud lessons: 25 surefire ways to engage students and improve comprehension.* New York: Scholastic; Newark, DE: International Reading Association.

- Or consider studying the resources listed on page 58.

Comprehension Strategy Bookmark Lesson

Objective: To provide students with a bookmark with prompts that they can use to discuss the comprehension strategy used during lessons with peers and when reading on their own.

Common Core Connections: Students ask and answer questions, provide evidence, compare/contrast, infer, determine the meanings of words/phrases, identify main ideas/details, summarize, and participate in collaborative discussions.

Teacher Modeling: Model how to use each of the prompts on the independent reading bookmark with reading material from your grade level. Conduct a think-aloud using each of the prompts. You can model one a day or several at a time. From time to time, return to modeling the prompts.

Guided Practice: Ask students to turn to their partners and use the same prompt you just modeled. They can mark the point in the text where the strategy helped them by putting a symbol for the strategy on a self-stick note or writing out and completing the strategy starter. (An example for making connections: The students may sketch a chain on a self-stick note and place it on the page or write, "This reminds me of....") Eventually, give students choices among several prompts. Listen to the pairs and invite students to share with the class. Praise their efforts. Model for students who need more support in using their texts.

Independent Practice: Students may use the same prompts as in your lesson for either their independent reading books or the whole group basal or content-area reading assignment. They can mark with self-stick notes the passages they wish to share with the group or a partner.

Wrap Up: Ask students how the discussion and use of the comprehension strategies have helped deepen their comprehension. Ask which of the strategies on the bookmark is their favorite or most helpful and why.

Assessment Tips

Using the reproducible Assessment Checklist on page 57, use symbols to indicate quick observations of skills that are evident (+), developing (✓), and not evident yet (–). Keep track of student progress through observations and samples of student work. Form and meet with strategy groups containing students who need to work on developing the same strategies.

Comprehension Strategy Bookmark

BEFORE READING

Make Connections
"This reminds me of...because...."

Predict
"I think this is about to [or will] happen... because...."

Question
"I wonder...because...."

DURING READING

Make Connections
"This reminds me of...because...."

Predict
"I think this is about to [or will] happen... because...."

Question
"I wonder...because...."

Clarify/Monitor
"I didn't get...so I...."

Synthesize
"Now I think...."

Summarize
"So far this is about...."

AFTER READING

Summarize
"This was about...."

Evaluate
"I liked...because...."

Synthesize
"I agree (disagree) with...because...."

Comprehension Strategy Bookmark

BEFORE READING

Make Connections
"This reminds me of...because...."

Predict
"I think this is about to [or will] happen... because...."

Question
"I wonder...because...."

DURING READING

Make Connections
"This reminds me of...because...."

Predict
"I think this is about to [or will] happen... because...."

Question
"I wonder...because...."

Clarify/Monitor
"I didn't get...so I...."

Synthesize
"Now I think...."

Summarize
"So far this is about...."

AFTER READING

Summarize
"This was about...."

Evaluate
"I liked...because...."

Synthesize
"I agree (disagree) with...because...."

Best Ever Literacy Survival Tips: 72 Lessons You Can't Teach Without by Lori D. Oczkus.
© 2012 International Reading Association. May be copied for classroom use.

Assessment Checklist

Directions: Use symbols to indicate quick observations of skills that are evident (+), developing (✓), and not evident yet (–).

Connect

The student
- Makes logical and relevant connections to self, other texts, the world
- Explains connections

Predict

The student
- Uses text clues plus other clues to form logical predictions, including text structure, previous events, actions
- Changes predictions during reading based on clues

Question

The student
- Asks questions that go with the text
- Asks questions that are literal only
- Asks questions that are inferential
- Ask questions of the author

Infer

The student
- Uses text clues plus background knowledge to infer
- Uses the language of inferring ("I can tell... because....")

Monitor/Clarify

The student
- Identifies words and ideas to clarify
- Uses a variety of strategies to clarify, including word level (sounding out, syllables) and context clues (rereads, reads on)
- Identifies and clarifies sensory images

Summarize

The student
- Retells in his or her own words

- Includes main ideas
- Includes important details
- Summarizes in order
- May use text structure to summarize

Synthesize

The student
- Identifies "ah-ha" thoughts about the book with rationale
- Completes the frame "I used to think...but now I think...."

Evaluate

The student
- Rates the book
- Gives reasons for rating
- Gives opinions about character actions, the author's style
- Rates performance as a reader

Web Resources

LoriOczkus.com: www.lorioczkus.com
See the Think-Aloud and Reciprocal Teaching video clips available here, in particular.

***Reciprocal Teaching at Work* Classroom Video Clips: www.reading.org/General/Publications/Books/SupplementalContent/BK507_SUPPLEMENT.aspx**

ReadWriteThink: www.readwritethink.org
ReadWriteThink is a great resource for hundreds of free downloadable lessons in reading comprehension and all aspects of reading. Here are some to try:

- "Building Reading Comprehension Through Think-Alouds" (Grades 6–8) by Laurie A. Henry
- "Family Ties: Making Connections to Improve Reading Comprehension" (Grades K–2) by Violeta L. Katsikis
- "Guided Comprehension: Making Connections Using a Double-Entry Journal" (Grades 4–6) by Maureen McLaughlin and Mary Beth Allen
- "Questioning: A Comprehension Strategy for Small-Group Guided Reading" (Grades 3–5) by John Young

"If you focus on only lower level literal thinking skills, that is what you will get from your students. When you teach a balance of literal, inferential, and critical thinking, students grow in their comprehension (Pearson, 2010)."

References

Cassidy, J., & Cassidy, D. (2010). What's hot for 2010. *Reading Today, 27*(3), 1, 8–9.

Collins, M.F. (2005). ESL preschoolers' English vocabulary acquisition from storybook reading. *Reading Research Quarterly, 40*(4), 406–408.

Duke, N.K. (2005). Comprehension of what for what: Comprehension as a non-unitary construct. In S.G. Paris & S.A. Stahl (Eds.), *Current issues in reading comprehension and assessment* (pp. 93–104). Mahwah, NJ: Erlbaum.

Duke, N.K., & Pearson, P.D. (2002). Effective practices for developing reading comprehension. In A.E. Farstrup & S.J. Samuels (Eds.), *What research has to say about reading instruction* (3rd ed., pp. 205–242). Newark, DE: International Reading Association.

Hatt, C. (n.d.). *Better discussions in study groups*. Retrieved from www.choiceliteracy.com/public/796.cfm

Keene, E.O., & Zimmermann, S. (1997). *Mosaic of thought: Teaching comprehension in a reader's workshop*. Portsmouth, NH: Heinemann.

Lipson, M.Y. (2007). *Teaching reading beyond the primary grades: A blueprint for helping intermediate students develop the skills they need to comprehend the texts they read*. New York: Scholastic.

National Center for Education Statistics. (2009). *The nation's report card: Reading 2009 National Assessment of Educational Progress at grades 4 and 8* (NCES 2010–458). Washington, DC: Institute of Education Sciences, U.S. Department of Education.

National Institute of Child Health and Human Development. (2000). *Report of the National Reading Panel. Teaching children to read: An evidence-based assessment of the scientific research literature on reading and its implications for reading instruction* (NIH Publication No. 00–4769). Washington, DC: U.S. Government Printing Office.

Oczkus, L.D. (2004). *Super six comprehension strategies: 35 lessons and more for reading success*. Norwood, MA: Christopher-Gordon.

Oczkus, L.D. (2009). *Interactive think-aloud lessons: 25 surefire ways to engage students and improve comprehension*. New York: Scholastic; Newark, DE: International Reading Association.

Oczkus, L.D. (2010). *Reciprocal teaching at work: Powerful strategies and lessons for improving reading comprehension* (2nd ed.). Newark, DE: International Reading Association.

Pearson, P.D. (2010, October 5). *Facilitating comprehension: The role of text, talk, and task* [Webinar]. Retrieved October 27, 2010, from www.reading.org/General/Publications/webinars-archive/webinars-free-text-talk-task.aspx

Wormeli, R. (2009). *Metaphors & analogies: Power tools for teaching any subject*. Portland, ME: Stenhouse.

CHAPTER 5

Reciprocal Teaching—The Reading Super Vitamin: Guidelines and TOP 5 Strategies for Dramatically Boosting Comprehension

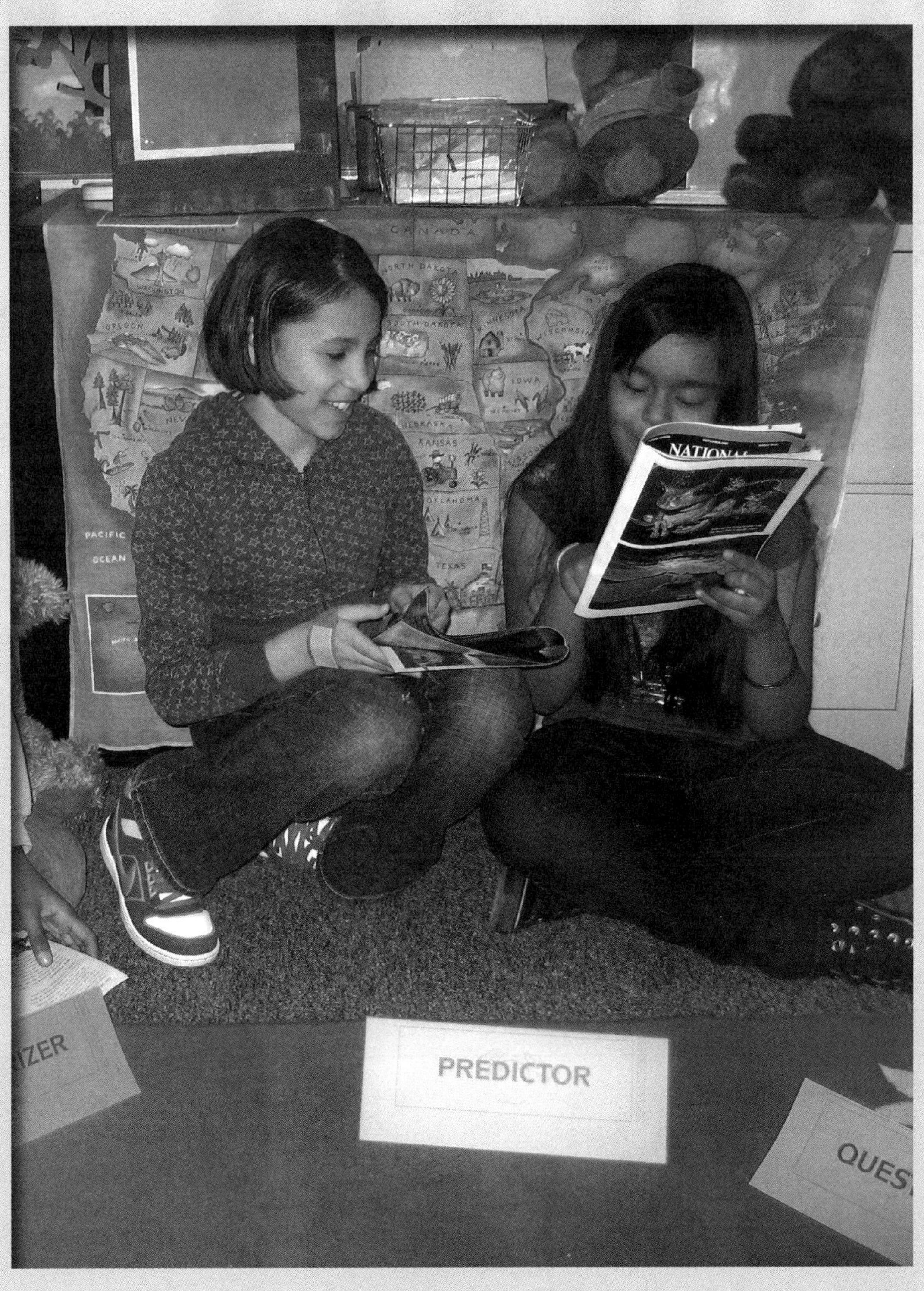

Best Ever Advice on... Reciprocal Teaching

Reciprocal teaching (RT) is that magic bullet we've all been wanting. After 10 years of use, I am still amazed at its power for improving reading comprehension. My favorite lesson (and my students' favorite as well) with RT uses the "placemat" with groups of four children. The placemat is a large paper (at least 18" x 24") divided into four rectangular sections, with a small square at the intersection of the four lines. Each section is labeled with a different RT strategy: predict, question, clarify, and summarize. Then, four children sit down at the placemat, with one child at each strategy. Each child signs his or her name and writes with a different color of pen/marker for accountability and possible evaluation of completed work. The children are assigned to read a certain amount of text and should use the assigned strategy. Material is read (silently or aloud, depending on the choice of the group or teacher), and the strategy is used and written on the placement and then shared with the group. A line is drawn under the information in each section. Everyone moves to the right and has to use a new strategy for the next chunk of text. The process is repeated until the story is finished. The last person sitting at the summary section reads to the group each of the summaries, and a final summary of the story is written by the group and put in the square at the intersection of the four lines.

—Mary Jo Barker, Reading Specialist

The best advice I can give is to rotate the roles you assign to your students during reciprocal teaching literature circles. Every student is capable of being the discussion director and enjoys taking on that role.

—Rob Malling, Principal

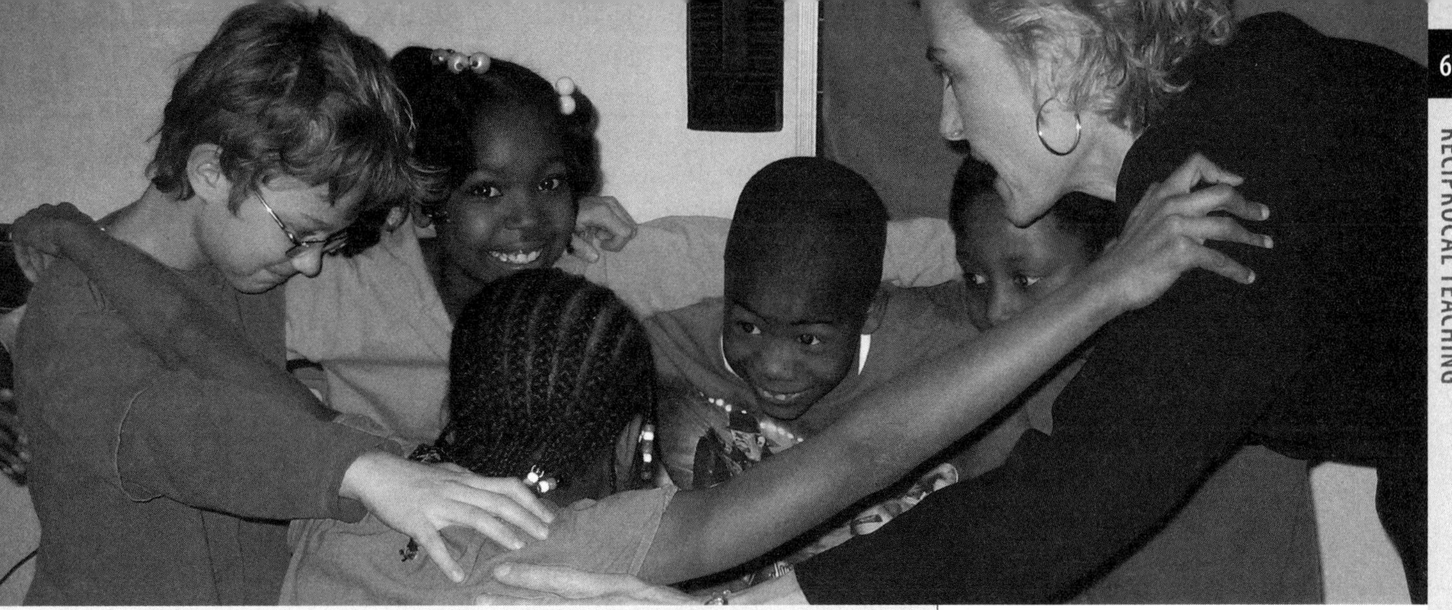

Do your students read and decode but often not deeply understand what they are reading? If so, you are not alone! Teachers across grades K–12 worry that even though they are teaching comprehension strategies more than ever before, students aren't actually *applying* the strategies when they read on their own.

Do you ever feel that your students could use a "reading vitamin" to boost their reading motivation, comprehension, and scores? Reciprocal teaching (Palincsar & Brown, 1986), or the Fab Four (Oczkus, 2008), is an effective research-based technique that dramatically boosts reading comprehension. Reciprocal teaching is engaging and student centered so that your students learn to apply the strategies when they read independently. This chapter presents new ideas for improving the comprehension of all students using this powerful reading supplement. In just a couple of doses per week, your students may improve as much as six months to two years in a six-month time period. In just 15 days you will see students reading with more confidence. With 25 years of solid proof behind it, reciprocal teaching continues to wow teachers everywhere with results that work to improve reading comprehension. Our students need the Fab Four more than ever, not only to demonstrate improved test scores but also to survive in the information age (Lubliner, 2001).

What Is Reciprocal Teaching?

Reciprocal teaching is a scaffolded discussion technique (Oczkus, 2010) that invites students to work cooperatively using four strategies: predict, question, clarify, and summarize. The strategies are used in any order and are modeled, practiced, and discussed with a teacher and peers. The trick is that in order for a lesson to be labeled reciprocal teaching it MUST include *all four strategies* in *one* lesson or reading session, rather than spreading them across several days.

Use the Fab Four every time you read!

Every time we read, we naturally use all of the Fab Four strategies in concert with one another to make meaning. For example, as you look over a magazine article on how to walk your dog properly, you first predict by skimming over the title and headings. Then throughout the reading process you ask questions and wonder thoughts such as, "I wonder if this works with little dogs." Or "How does the author deal with a dog that continually pulls on the leash and tries to run ahead?" As you read further, you may wish to clarify words or concepts that

Common Problems Students Experience With Reading Comprehension

Perhaps these are familiar problems your students experience with comprehension:

- Sixth graders race to finish a chapter in the social studies text or novel but then experience difficulty recalling what they read.
- Budding new first-grade readers plod through their leveled and decodable readers, sounding out words without paying attention to the meaning of the stories.
- Fourth graders, many of them ELL students, struggle with vocabulary and comprehension as they attempt to read the history text.
- When tenth-grade students are asked to discuss their most recent novel, most only summarize. They experience difficulty coming up with higher level thinking questions for the group to discuss.

Do any of these examples sound familiar? The National Center for Education Statistics (2009) reports that 69% of fourth graders and 70% of eighth graders read below the proficient reading level on the National Assessment of Educational Progress. Fortunately, reciprocal teaching is a research-based technique that we can use to help boost the comprehension of all students.

are difficult. "I don't get what they mean by choke collar." Lastly, you probably summarize the steps in your head that will help you utilize the information when you walk your dog. "Walk over the threshold first so your dog knows you are in control. Have the dog walk on your left. Don't allow him to pull on the leash."

Observe renewed confidence in 15 days.

In just 15 days you will see struggling students raise their hands with confidence and participate in class discussions. Anne Palincsar and Anne Brown (1986), the original researchers and creators of reciprocal teaching, found that when reciprocal teaching was used with a group of students for just 15–20 days, the students' reading on a comprehension assessment increased from a mere 30% to 80%!

Witness dramatic growth in just a few months.

Teach using reciprocal teaching at least two to three times per week, and in just a few months you may witness growth of three to six months, documented with running records, informal reading inventories, and district basal reading tests.

Document six months' to two years' growth in reading in three months.

When I work with grades 3–12 and we implement reciprocal teaching as an intervention, students' reading abilities grow as much as two years in just three months. Low-performing students in urban settings (Carter, 1997) do especially well with reciprocal teaching. Struggling readers also show positive growth in a short time—three to six months (Cooper, Boschken, McWilliams, & Pistochini, 2000). In a Berkeley, California, after-school intervention program, fourth graders moved from a level 20 on a DRA to 40 and above in a three-month period! In other settings, it has taken six months for the gains to show, but the results are consistent, strong, and astounding (Oczkus, 2010).

Experience consistent results with staying power.

Rosenshine and Meister (1994) reviewed 16 studies and concluded that reciprocal teaching is a technique that consistently improves comprehension. Palincsar and Klenk (1991) found that the gains students made due to reciprocal teaching were maintained one year later.

Note improved comprehension in content areas.

Students who engage in reciprocal teaching—a multiple-strategy approach—not only improve in their overall reading level but also retain more of the material (Reutzel, Smith, & Fawson, 2005).

What Effective Comprehension Instruction Looks Like

Primary example

Wiggly, toothless first graders gather around Mrs. Lopez on the reading rug ready to enjoy *Mr. Gumpy's Outing* by John Burningham (Holt, 1990), a lively tale about too many barnyard animals crowding onto a boat. She holds up her Reciprocal Teaching Dial, displaying the four strategies—predict, question, clarify, summarize—in a circle, as she asks the students to turn the dial in their heads first to predict. Every few pages, Mrs. Lopez pauses, selects one of the Fab Four to model, and invites the students to observe her example of a summary, quick question to ask Mr. Gumpy or one of the animals, a new prediction, or a word to clarify. After each of Mrs. Lopez's examples, student pairs immediately try out the strategies using the same strategy starters: "I think...will happen because...so far...." (summary), "I didn't get the word...so I [reread, read on, looked for parts, etc.]" (clarify), or "I think...will happen next because...." (predict). Arms wave wildly when Mrs. Lopez asks for volunteers to act out the story and then to interview the characters using a plastic microphone. Later in the day when fifth-grade buddies come to visit, the cross-age pairs will read together, pausing throughout to practice using the Fab Four (Oczkus, 2010).

Intermediate example

The small group of struggling fifth graders meet with their teacher, Mr. Ling, to read the next chapter in *Because of Winn Dixie* by Kate DiCamillo (Candlewick, 2001). After summarizing yesterday's chapter and discussing Opal's choice to give Winn-Dixie a bath, the students predict that Opal will convince her father to keep the dog. Stacks of colorful self-stick notes are available in the center of the group so the members can grab them to mark their texts with either a C for clarify or a Q for a question. Mr. Ling quickly models a question: "Why does Opal want to keep the dog?" Responses flow as the group debates the reasons, including her need for friends and a desire for a pet. Mr. Ling circulates around the group to ask each student to whisper read for him. As each student reads, he asks, "Would you like to clarify or question?" Arem clarifies, "I didn't get what the author meant by Opal and the dog being orphans." Mr. Ling coaches him by suggesting that he read on to find out why. Arem places a self-stick note with a C on it next to the paragraph and reads on. The other students are lost in the story but pause occasionally to grab a self-stick note to mark a question or word to clarify. The group summarizes what happened in the chapter today. Tomas adds, "I like the picture I am making in my head better than the movie!" Later in the day the entire class of fifth graders will participate in Fab Four nonfiction discussion circles as they work their way through the social studies text. Students take on roles as predictor, questioner, clarifier, and summarizer.

Middle school/secondary example

The eighth graders scoot desks together to work in their literature circle teams to read *The Invisible Man* by H.G. Wells (Aerie, 1992). Miss O'Leary asks the students to create a four-door organizer to keep track of their ideas for each of the Fab Four. She circulates around the room to observe and coach the groups as students participate as either a discussion director, predictor, clarifier, questioner, or summarizer. Individuals record their thoughts on their four-door organizer. For questions, Miss O'Leary encourages the students to discuss "I wonders..." with their teams. She also asks the students to write and discuss at least one question they might ask the author about his craft and use of flashbacks. For a summary, the teams work together to write a 20-word summary to share with the entire class. Students keep track of difficult passages and make predictions for the next chapter.

Practical Guidelines for Boosting Comprehension With the Fab Four

Here are some guidelines to help you teach students to use reciprocal teaching.

Keep the band together!

You do not have to wait until your students are proficient at all the strategies before presenting them as a package so your students can benefit from the power of multiple-strategy instruction. However, some teachers do like to first introduce one strategy at a time for just a few days before moving on to the next. Keep in mind that even after you put all four together you can always back up and teach a focused minilesson on one of the strategies to strengthen

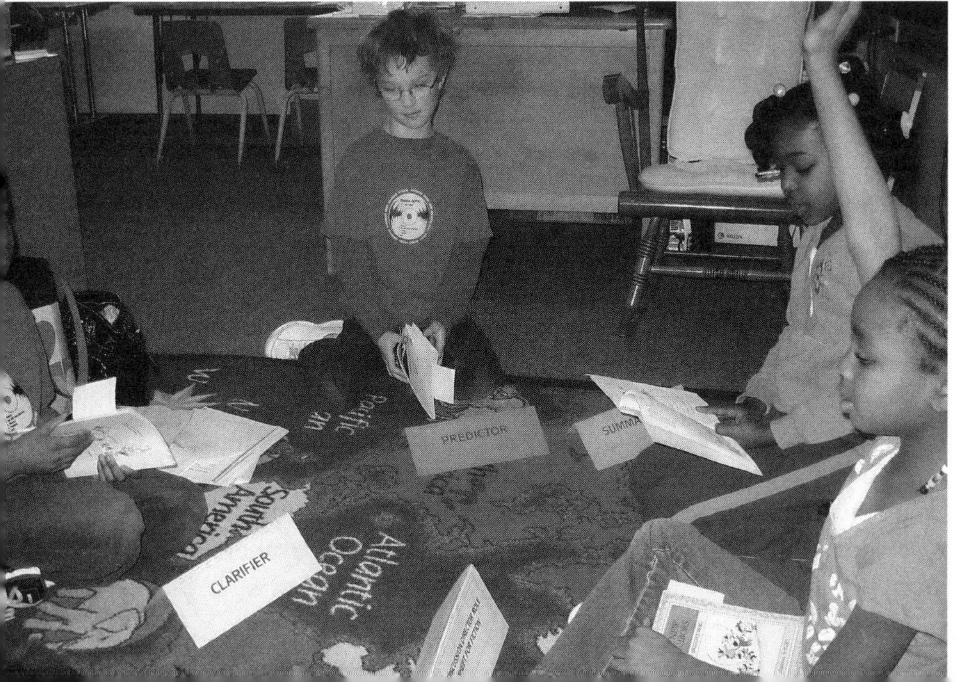

Comprehension Strategies

- Connect
- Predict
- Infer
- Question
- Summarize
- Synthesize
- Evaluate

Predict

Summarize

The Fab Four

Question

Clarify

its use. There are many creative ways to introduce the strategies.

Teach all of the comprehension strategies.

Although reciprocal teaching is extremely effective, it does not stand alone as the only comprehension instruction you need to teach! Keep in mind that reciprocal teaching is like a reading supplement. Our students also need a balanced diet that includes other comprehension strategies, including making connections to one's life, other texts, and the world (Keene & Zimmermann, 2007); creating a synthesis of ideas based on the reading; and evaluating the reading material and one's progress in reading. Try displaying a list of all of the comprehension strategies in your classroom next to a dial with the four reciprocal teaching strategies. You may teach the strategies one at a time in your reading program or you can use all four. Students should note that the Fab Four make both the comprehensive list of comprehension strategies as well as the Fab Four circle!

Teach the Fab Four two to three times per week.

If you are on a diet or exercise program, you know that following your regimen only once a week will not yield results. Students need to participate in reciprocal teaching at least two to three times per week in order to make progress in their reading. Your struggling readers benefit greatly from small-group guided reading using reciprocal teaching two to four days per week (Cooper et al., 2000).

Incorporate the four foundations of effective lessons.

In addition to the four strategies, four foundations must also be present for the optimal growth in reading to take place (Oczkus, 2010). These foundations are teacher think-alouds, cooperative learning with pairs or small groups, scaffolding or support such as bookmarks or language prompts for the strategies, and metacognition, or reflecting on the use of the strategies and their steps.

Use read-alouds to start.

You can introduce reciprocal teaching to your students at any grade level using read-alouds. You can read a chunk of text (a page or a few paragraphs), pause, and model all four strategies, or you can read a bit, pause, and model just one strategy at a time. The key is to pause between each strategy to invite students to try the strategy with partners.

Scaffold using characters and props for each strategy.

Try using metaphors and simple props for each of the strategies to help explain the strategies and make them "visible" for students (Oczkus, 2010).

- **Predicting** is like a fortune teller using clues. Students think about text and picture clues, along with background knowledge to think what the text is about or what they will learn. Try bringing in a snow globe to represent a fortune tellers crystal ball to hold up during your lesson.
- **Questioning** is like a television program with a game-show host leading the way through a text. Invite students to use a pretend microphone (their fist or a pencil) and ask each other questions about the text.

- **Clarifying** is like using a remote control to "pause" on the text to reread, read on, or to figure out words and ideas. When clarifying, you might put on glasses to "see" what you are reading or visualize and make pictures in your head.
- **Summarizing** is like a cowboy roping up ideas. You can also use the metaphor of a tourist taking a zillion pictures and then having to select just a few of the important ones to show.

Try reciprocal teaching in a variety of settings.

Your students will make reading growth using reciprocal teaching using any materials in any setting. It is up to you to decide how you will incorporate it into what you already do!

- **Whole class:** Use the basal or trade books, novels, read-alouds, and content area reading, and allow students to turn to partners to discuss each strategy.
- **Guided reading:** Using leveled texts or grade-level text, read chunks of text and rotate through the strategies. Coach students individually to try one of the strategies with you as you circulate.
- **Readers' workshop:** Teach the strategies during minilessons. Ask students to mark strategy use with self-stick notes, and allow them to select which strategy they want to work on as you confer with them.
- **Literature circles:** First teach lessons to the whole class and in guided reading so students are familiar with the strategies. Assign roles of discussion director, predictor, questioner, clarifier, and summarizer. If you already have set literature circles, use the Fab Four during content area reading!

Lori's Top 5 Surefire Strategies for Improving Comprehension With Reciprocal Teaching

1 *Fast Fab Four (Oczkus, 2010)*

Any time you want to verbally "whip" through the strategies with your students you can run through a Fast Fab Four. Simply ask students to join you as you predict, question, clarify, and summarize for each page you are reading together. No writing allowed! Try a Fast Fab Four with read-alouds, during guided reading, or with students working in teams. Ask students to "check off" each strategy in their heads as you use it. Be sure to cover all four. You may wish to create a simple dial of the Fab Four as a visual aid. Turn the dial to each strategy as you model and invite students to use the strategy. Literature circles may also run through a Fast Fab Four using a dial. The discussion director may call on students who are the respective roles—predictor, clarifier, questioner, and summarizer—to share their thoughts about the text.

2 *Which One Do We Need? (Oczkus, 2010)*

This lesson promotes megacognition to the maximum—or independent use of the strategies! Another name for this lesson is "Name That Strategy!" The goal is to describe how you are using a particular strategy and have students guess which strategy you are employing. This is a lesson that can be taught over and over many times; just choose different examples.

- Explain to students that you are going to play a guessing game using all four reciprocal teaching strategies—predict, question, clarify, and summarize. The objective is for them to know which strategy is needed during reading and how to use that strategy to better understand the text.
- Read a portion of the text aloud and pause to ask students which strategy you need. Don't tell the students which strategy you have selected; rather, allow them to guess! Give examples:

  For predicting: " I want to see what will happen next. Which strategy do I need? How do I use it?"

  For questioning: "If I could talk to the author about this I would ask...Which one do I need?"

  For clarifying: "I don't get how to say this word. Which one do I need? How can I do this?"

  For summarizing: "I need to identify the main ideas in this text. Which strategy do I need to help me? What are the steps?"

3 *Mark Your C's and Q's (Oczkus, 2010)*

This is a child-centered favorite that you can use to promote independent strategy use during guided reading. After discussing their predictions, students read silently and watch out for either C's—points to clarify—or Q's—questions they have about the text. They mark their points with self-stick notes.

- Model asking a question and clarifying: Read aloud a portion of text as students follow along. Model one type of questioning with question words (*who, what, when, where,* or *why*), with "I wonder..." statements, or with questions that begin with "Why do you think...?" Place a self-stick note with a Q on it directly on the portion of text where you asked a question. Read aloud another portion of text and pause on a confusing word or sentence or even paragraph. Begin your clarification with "I didn't get..." and then tell how you figured it out (syllables, sounded it out, read on, reread, and so on) or ask the group to help you do so. Put your self-stick note with a C on it directly on the portion of text where you experienced difficulty reading.

- Students find examples: During reading, give each student two different-colored stacks of self-stick notes. Students label one C for clarify and the other Q for question. Students mark paragraphs, words, or sentences where they want to clarify and question. After reading, discuss with students their findings. Place self-stick notes on a two-column chart labeled Clarify and Question. Chart ways to figure out points to clarify and to answer questions.

(See the lesson for C's and Q's in action with Lori Oczkus teaching a guided reading lesson at vimeo .com/13517419.)

4 *Table Runners and the Fab Four (Oczkus, 2010)*

This lesson makes a wonderful introductory lesson to reciprocal teaching, or you can use it several times per week to ensure that students are comprehending core reading or content area reading material. Students work in teams of four to six. One student is selected to be the "table runner" to record the group's responses on a self-stick note and then "runs" the note up to a class chart to post and share.

- Read aloud from the text, pausing after one or two pages to conduct a think-aloud with each of the reciprocal teaching strategies. Alternate modeling and inviting students to read more and try the strategy at their tables. The table runner shares the group's response on a self-stick note with the class.
- During literature circles, you may also wish to assign "jobs" to students at each table—predictor, clarifier, questioner, summarizer, and discussion director/table runner. Each student takes a turn leading the discussion on their assigned strategy. The group discusses and the table runner posts the strategies on the class chart.

Directions for Making a Four Door

1. Place an 8.5 by 11 sheet of paper horizontally on a flat surface.
2. Fold both sides of the paper toward the middle to form two doors.
3. Using scissors, cut the doors in half horizontally, making four doors.
4. Have students write the words *predict, question, clarify,* and *summarize* on the outside of the doors and their names on the back of the four door.

5 *Four Door (Oczkus, 2010)*

Teachers appreciate the four door (a simple paper folded into four sections with flaps for recording responses) because it provides an individual assessment for each student during the group discussions. Students love the four door because they only have to write brief responses and it is fun! As a note of caution: Don't overuse the four door because writing slows down the reciprocal teaching discussions! Use the four door only occasionally as an assessment tool and scaffolding support for discussions.

- During whole-class lessons, alternate modeling and allowing students to respond in their four doors. Also, invite students to share their responses with a partner. Use the four door during literature circles or to prepare for literature circles as students share their responses with team members.

Before Reading: Activate Prior Knowledge

- What do you already know about reciprocal teaching? Have you ever used it with students?
- Do you have students who decode but do not understand what they read? Explain.

During Reading: Respond While Reading

- While reading this chapter, mark your text with self-stick notes. Use symbols to indicate questions (?), things you want to try (T), something you connect with (+), something interesting or surprising (!) (adapted from Hatt, n.d.).

After Reading: Think About and Discuss

- Define reciprocal teaching and explain why it is considered a "reading vitamin." What must be in place for a lesson to be considered reciprocal teaching?
- Why do you think multiple-strategy instruction is effective?
- What results can you expect with reciprocal teaching in 15 days? In 3–6 months?
- Reciprocal teaching works K–12! Study the examples in the chapter under the heading "What Effective Comprehension Instruction Looks Like." What appeals to you? What do you have questions about? Why is keeping the four strategies in one lesson effective?
- What are the four foundations of effective lessons, and how can you ensure that you are using them? Why is it important to teach all the comprehension strategies, not just the Fab Four?
- How might metaphors, via characters and props, be useful in explaining the strategies?
- How can you fit reciprocal teaching into an already packed schedule? How does one start? What appeals most to you about reciprocal teaching? What is the one lesson you saw in the chapter that you can see yourself repeating over and over in your classroom?

Putting Reciprocal Teaching Into Practice

Professional Development Breakout Groups

- Reciprocal teaching works K–12. Study the lessons in this chapter and, with a team, create a lesson for your materials.
- Discuss the four foundations: think-alouds, metacognition, scaffolding, and cooperative learning. How are these in place during your lessons?
- Plan lessons to get started using either poetry or a read-aloud.
- Discuss how using the four strategies (predict, question, clarify, summarize) is different with fiction vs. nonfiction. It works with both!

Lesson Sharing

- Try one of Lori's Top 5 lessons with your class. Be prepared to share. On a scale of 1–5, how did the lesson go? Explain. What do you want to try next?
- Observe Lori Oczkus teaching lessons at www.reading.org/General/Publications/Books/SupplementalContent/BK507_SUPPLEMENT.aspx.

Teacher as Reader

- When reading on your own, notice how you put into action the Fab Four (predict, question, clarify, summarize). Discuss.
- Bring an example from your own reading to share with your class so that they can see how you naturally use the Fab Four.
- Bring in a short article or chapter from a book to read with other teachers using the Fab Four. Discuss.

Before the Next Meeting

Read: Select the next chapter your group will read. Mark the text during reading.
Try: Try one of the lessons from the next chapter, or try something new from this chapter.
Observe: Visit a colleague's classroom to observe a lesson on reciprocal teaching, or record yourself teaching a lesson and share the video at a meeting.

Going Deeper With Reciprocal Teaching

- Try a book study using this practical resource loaded with everything you need to know about reciprocal teaching:

  Oczkus, L.D. (2010). *Reciprocal teaching at work: Powerful strategies and lessons for improving reading comprehension* (2nd ed.). Newark, DE: International Reading Association. Note: Visit www.reading.org/General/Publications/Books/bk507.aspx to download the free PD study guide.

- Or consider studying the resources listed on page 72.

Fab Four Bookmark Lesson

Objective: To introduce and use the Fab Four Bookmark as a personal reference tool during reading lessons throughout the school year.

Common Core Connections: Students collaborate to discuss the reading following specified roles. Students predict/infer using evidence from the text, answer and ask questions, determine meanings of words/phrases using a variety of strategies, and determine main ideas, details, and themes while summarizing.

Teacher Modeling: Read a text aloud, pausing every few pages to model one of the four reciprocal teaching strategies. Rotate through them. As you think aloud, use the language from the bookmark and examples from the text. Have students follow along with their own copies of the bookmark as you think aloud. Alternate the teacher read-alouds and strategy modeling, with students trying the strategy with a partner using language prompts from the bookmark. For example, say,

- "I think this is about...because...." (Predict)
- "I wonder...." (Question)
- "I didn't get...so I...." (Clarify)
- "This part is about...." (Summarize)

Guided Practice: Immediately after you model one of the strategies, ask students to turn and talk with one another as they try out the strategy with either the next portion of text or the same text you just modeled. For example, say, "I think this next part is about how ants use their antennae because I see the headings and picture clues are about antennae. Turn to a partner and tell one thing you think you will learn about the antennae." Continue modeling and asking students to practice the same strategy you just modeled.

Independent Practice: Students work in pairs or teams to read more text, stopping on various pages to run through the strategies together. Circulate to listen and coach oral responses.

Wrap Up: At the end of the lesson, ask students to reflect upon which strategy helped them the most and why.

Assessment Tips

To assess student progress during whole-class or small-group discussions, try to

- Observe conversations and record student responses on self-stick notes.
- Occasionally use the Four Door strategy (see page 66) for brief written responses as a means of formative assessment.
  Warning! Don't overrely on written responses or burn out students by assigning too much writing with the strategies. The research on results of reciprocal teaching is based on *oral*, not written, responses. Student comprehension will improve using the strategies orally.
- Use the information gained as a way of planning minilessons focused on a particular strategy that students need to work on. For example, when using reciprocal teaching with nonfiction texts, students might need extra, specific lessons on how to summarize with that type of text.

Fab Four Bookmark

Predict

Use clues from the text or illustrations to predict what will happen next.

I think...because...

I'll bet...because...

I suppose...because...

I think I will learn...because...

Question

Ask questions as you read. Some are answered in the book, and others are inferred.

I wonder....

Who? What? When? Where? Why? How?

Why do you think?

Clarify

How can you figure out tricky or hard words and ideas?

I didn't get the [word, part, idea] so I:

- Reread
- Ask if it makes sense
- Read on
- Talk to a friend
- Sound words out

Summarize

Using your *own* words, tell the main ideas from the text in order.

This text is about.... Next,....

This part is about.... Then,....

First,.... Finally,....

Fab Four Bookmark

Predict

Use clues from the text or illustrations to predict what will happen next.

I think...because...

I'll bet...because...

I suppose...because...

I think I will learn...because...

Question

Ask questions as you read. Some are answered in the book, and others are inferred.

I wonder....

Who? What? When? Where? Why? How?

Why do you think?

Clarify

How can you figure out tricky or hard words and ideas?

I didn't get the [word, part, idea] so I:

- Reread
- Ask if it makes sense
- Read on
- Talk to a friend
- Sound words out

Summarize

Using your *own* words, tell the main ideas from the text in order.

This text is about.... Next,....

This part is about.... Then,....

First,.... Finally,....

Best Ever Literacy Survival Tips: 72 Lessons You Can't Teach Without by Lori D. Oczkus. © 2012 International Reading Association. Bookmark reprinted from *Reciprocal Teaching at Work: Powerful Strategies and Lessons for Improving Reading Comprehension* (2nd ed., p. 74) by L.D. Oczkus, 2010, Newark, DE: International Reading Association. May be copied for classroom use.

Fab Four Checklist

Predict

The student

- Previews illustrations
- Previews headings
- Uses background information, experiences
- Gives reasons for predictions
- Changes predictions when necessary
- Makes logical predictions based on text clues and background information

Question

The student

- Consistently asks a mix of appropriate recall questions as well as higher level questions that require inferring
- Asks questions of the author
- Wonders based on the text
- Answers a mix of questions

Clarify

The student

- Identifies words as well as ideas that are unclear or difficult
- Uses a variety of strategies to clarify words and ideas, including figuring out words by sounding out; breaking into beginning sounds, ending sounds, familiar parts, syllables; rereading, reading on; using context
- Identifies and seeks to clarify high-level ideas such as metaphors and idioms

Summarize

The student

- Retells in own words using new key vocabulary
- Gives most important ideas and details
- Tells in order
- Uses text structure or graphic organizer to summarize

"Students who engage in reciprocal teaching—a multiple-strategy approach—not only improve in their overall reading level but also retain more of the material (Reutzel, Smith, & Fawson, 2005)."

Q&A

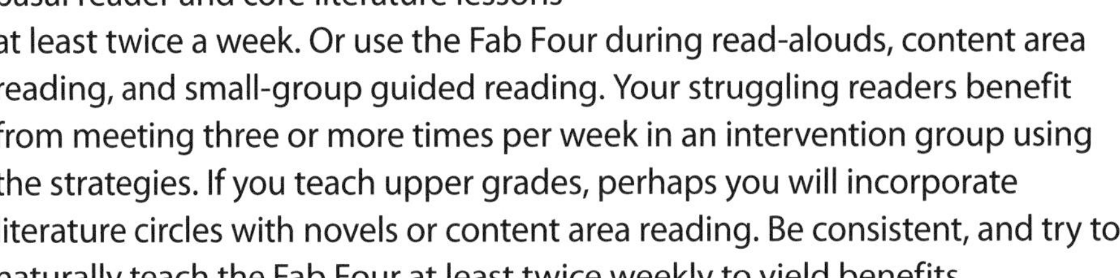

How can I fit reciprocal teaching into my already-packed schedule?

You do not need to overhaul your program to slip in reciprocal teaching. Simply incorporate the Fab Four into your basal reader and core literature lessons at least twice a week. Or use the Fab Four during read-alouds, content area reading, and small-group guided reading. Your struggling readers benefit from meeting three or more times per week in an intervention group using the strategies. If you teach upper grades, perhaps you will incorporate literature circles with novels or content area reading. Be consistent, and try to naturally teach the Fab Four at least twice weekly to yield benefits.

How do I get started with reciprocal teaching?

The easiest way to begin is during read-alouds. Decide if you will introduce the strategies all at once or one at a time over a couple of weeks. Read a portion of text aloud, pause, and model one of the strategies—predict, question, clarify, or summarize—then invite students to turn and try the same strategy with a partner or small group. Continue alternating modeling with partner discussions as you work through all four strategies.

Online Resources

Reciprocal Teaching Video Preview
www.reading.org/General/Publications/Books/SupplementalContent/BK507_SUPPLEMENT.aspx
View quick previews of reciprocal teaching in action from *Reciprocal Teaching at Work* DVD (2005), available from the International Reading Association. See examples of reciprocal teaching in action, including using the Fab Four puppets, reading aloud, and using C's and Q's during guided reading.

Reading Rockets: Reading Comprehension
www.readingrockets.org/atoz/reading_comprehension
Find additional articles, videos, and other resources to build comprehension in your classroom.

Comprehension Puppets
www.primaryconcepts.com/rdgcomp/Comprehension-Puppets.asp
Engage your students with puppets that represent each of the four comprehension strategies. Download free activities.

ReadWriteThink
www.readwritethink.org
ReadWriteThink is a great resource for hundreds of free downloadable lessons in all aspects of reading. Here are some lessons to boost your students' comprehension:

- "Get the Gist: A Summarizing Strategy for Any Content Area" (Grades 6–8) by Che-Mai Gray
- "Questioning: A Comprehension Strategy for Small-Group Guided Reading" (Grades 3–5) by John Young
- "Using Prediction as a Prereading Strategy" (Grades 3–5) by Geraldine Haggard

References

Carter, C.J. (1997). Why reciprocal teaching? *Educational Leadership, 54*(6), 64–68.

Cooper, J.D., Boschken, I., McWilliams, J., & Pistochini, L. (2000). A study of the effectiveness of an intervention program designed to accelerate reading for struggling readers in the upper grades. In T. Shanahan & F.V. Rodriguez-Brown (Eds.), *49th yearbook of the National Reading Conference* (pp. 477–486). Chicago: National Reading Conference.

Hatt, C. (n.d.). *Better discussions in study groups*. Retrieved from www.choiceliteracy.com/public/796.cfm

Keene, E.O., & Zimmermann, S. (2007). *Mosaic of thought: The power of comprehension strategy instruction* (2nd ed.). Portsmouth, NH: Heinemann.

Lubliner, S. (2001). *A practical guide to reciprocal teaching.* Bothell, WA: Wright Group.

National Center for Education Statistics. (2009). *The nation's report card: Reading 2009* (NCES 2010-458). Washington, DC: Institute of Education Sciences, U.S. Department of Education.

Oczkus, L.D. (2008). The fabulous four: Reading comprehension puppets. Berkeley, CA: Primary Concepts.

Oczkus, L.D. (2009). *Interactive think-aloud lessons: 25 surefire ways to engage students and improve comprehension*. New York: Scholastic; Newark, DE: International Reading Association.

Oczkus, L.D. (2010). *Reciprocal teaching at work: Powerful strategies and lessons for improving reading comprehension* (2nd ed.). Newark, DE: International Reading Association.

Palincsar, A.S., & Brown, A.L. (1986). Interactive teaching to promote independent learning from text. *The Reading Teacher, 39*(8), 771–777.

Palincsar, A.S., & Klenk, L.J. (1991). *Learning dialogues to promote text comprehension* (PHS Grant 05951). Washington, DC: U.S. Department of Education; Bethesda, MD: National Institute of Child Health and Human Development.

Reutzel, D.R., Smith, J.A., & Fawson, P.C. (2005). An evaluation of two approaches for teaching reading comprehension strategies in the primary years using science information texts. *Early Childhood Research Quarterly, 20*(3), 276–305. doi:10.1016/j.ecresq.2005.07.002

Rosenshine, B., & Meister, C. (1994). Reciprocal teaching: A review of the research. *Review of Educational Research, 64*(4), 479–530.

CHAPTER 6

Navigating Nonfiction: Guidelines and TOP 5 Strategies for Helping Kids Comprehend Informational Text

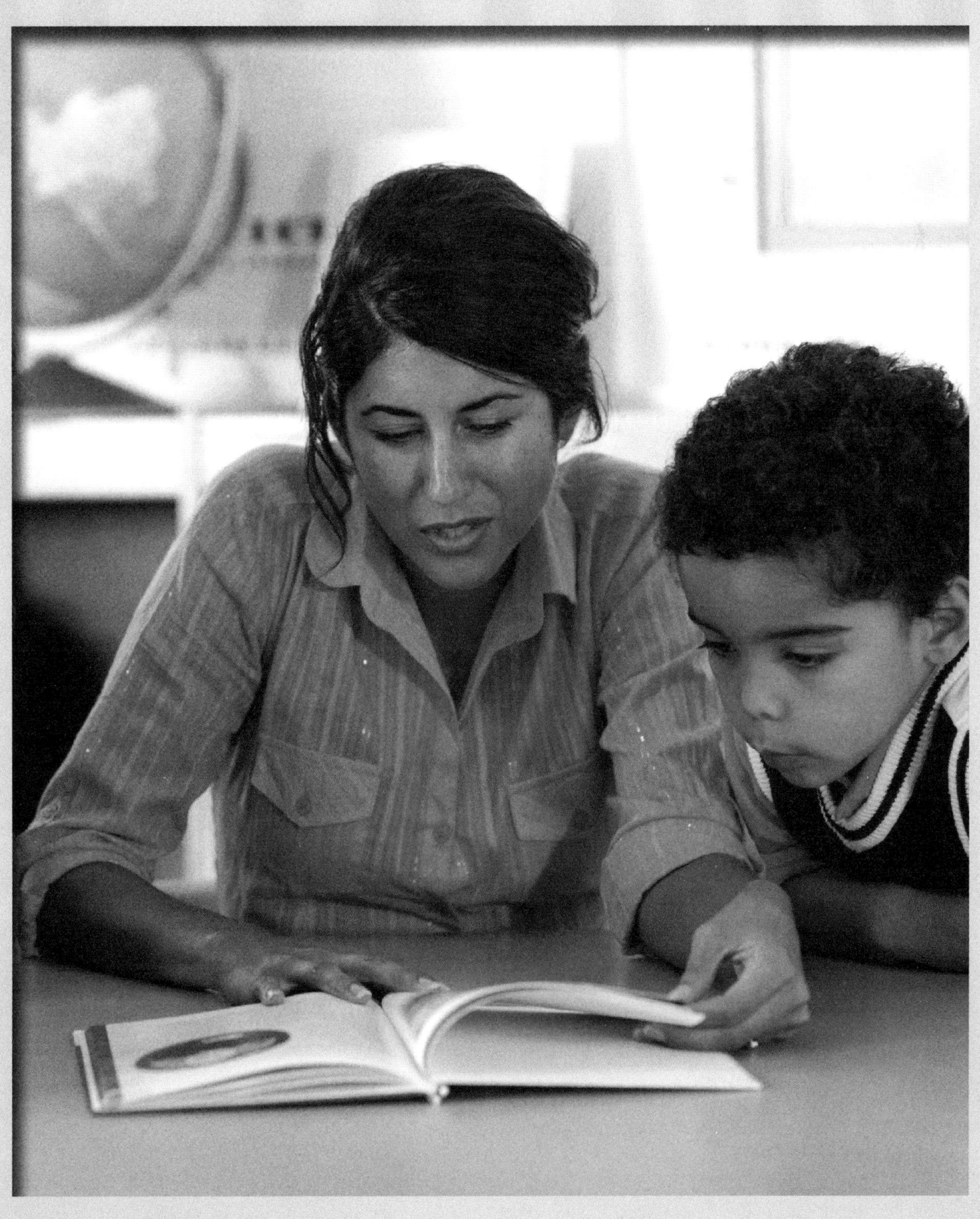

Best Ever Advice on... Informational Text

We want to make sure that we have students reading informational text because they want or need information. And we want to have students writing informational text because they actually want to convey information to someone who wants or needs it. Research suggests that students will develop as informational readers and writers more quickly in those situations (Purcell-Gates, Duke, & Martineau, 2007). I have seen teachers create very compelling reasons for students to read and write informational text—to research and write guides for their city zoo, to fact-check and send corrections to a website, to research and write science texts to send to a partner school in Uganda (Duke, Caughlan, Juzwik, & Martin, 2012). Let's get more purposeful about getting kids reading and writing purposefully!

—Nell K. Duke, Coauthor of *Reading and Writing Genre With Purpose in K–8 Classrooms* (Heinemann, 2012)

In Students' Shoes

What are your earliest memories reading nonfiction or informational text? Do you remember devouring nonfiction books and articles to satisfy your desire to learn about the planets, stinkbugs, or lands far away?

In the days before the Internet, I fondly recall paging through *National Geographic* and poring over volumes of encyclopedias for glimpses of the interesting and varied topics the letter *N* had to offer, including the North Pole, nomads, and famous nurses. However, I also remember dreading reading nonfiction, especially the school variety. Maybe you, too, recall struggling to concentrate while plodding through a dull social studies chapter or struggling with difficult vocabulary in a challenging science text.

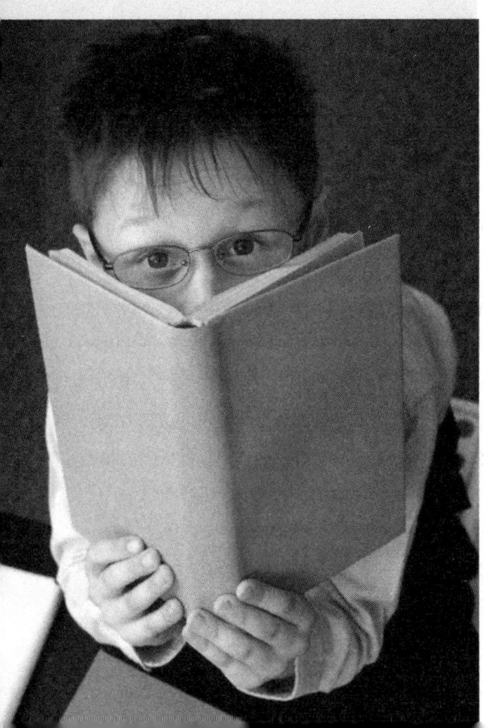

Clad in their winter coats, wet boots, and damp gloves from an outdoor recess, fifth graders file into their classroom and eagerly take their seats, anxious to see what nonfiction titles I've brought today. As I open my book bag, the students watch with wide-eyed enthusiasm. They practically gasp when I reach in my bag and reveal the contents. You'd think I'd just awarded the class with ice cream, candy, or bubble gum; instead, I pull out copies of the inviting nonfiction text *Sharks* by Seymour Simon.

Have you noticed that many of your students really enjoy nonfiction topics and texts? Many of our boy readers especially love nonfiction texts. Some students—boys and girls—may even *prefer* reading about "real" or "true" topics (Jobe & Dayton-Sakari, 2002). This chapter will explore practical ways to build on the natural curiosity of students and specific strategies to help kids better comprehend nonfiction texts.

Problems Students Encounter Reading Nonfiction Texts

In today's fast-paced, digital world, our students need to develop savvy for reading informational texts. The new U.S. Common Core Standards (Common Core State Standards Initiative, 2010) include more content area reading and writing throughout the grades and are forcing districts, publishers, and tests to require that students be exposed to more informational text.

Although many of the nonfiction texts in schools today have improved dramatically in their appeal and accessibility, content area reading poses challenges for our students. Common problems students of all ages experience when reading nonfiction include

- Lack of background knowledge for the topic
- Difficulty figuring out content area vocabulary
- Unfamiliarity with nonfiction text structures and text features

Students need plenty of exposure to effective comprehension strategies that help unlock meaning in informational texts, such as skimming and scanning and determining what is important.

Real-World Reading

It is estimated that nonfiction reading constitutes 85–95% of adults' daily reading material (Smith, 2000; Venezky, 1982). In addition, around 95% of the sites on the Internet contain nonfiction text (Kamil & Lane, 1998).

Think about what you might read in a given day and make a quick mental list of the informational texts. Your list probably includes a rich variety: web-based materials, news stories, brochures, maps, business letters, editorials, health documents, reports, directions, shopping, articles about your hobbies. The average elementary child, however, spends only 50% of his or her reading time (and often much less) with nonfiction texts. Researcher Nell Duke (2000) reports that primary students spend just 3.6 minutes per day reading nonfiction texts. The demands of our information-saturated world require that we increase students' exposure to informational text—and teach strategies to comprehend it.

Why Teach Nonfiction?

Some solid reasons to teach kids to read nonfiction include the following (see Duke, 2000):

1. Nonfiction is the key to success in school. Beginning in primary grades, students need exposure to nonfiction texts to help them succeed in both reading and writing.
2. As adults they will read mostly nonfiction (Smith, 2000; Venezky, 1982).
3. Kids like nonfiction. You can greatly affect the attitudes of your students toward reading by including exciting nonfiction in your classroom library and by teaching specific lessons on nonfiction.
4. Nonfiction appeals to students' interests. Allow students to read about nonfiction topics they are interested in to increase their motivation and reasons for reading!
5. Informational text builds background and vocabulary. When students read about a wide variety of topics, they build their background knowledge about the world around them (Duke & Kays, 1998). Nonfiction reading also strengthens vocabulary knowledge (Duke, Bennett-Armistead, & Roberts, 2002, 2003).

What Effective Nonfiction Instruction Looks Like

Primary example

The first graders are busy recording the titles of their independent reading books on their reading logs. Mr. Paige encourages the budding young readers to read a balance of fiction and nonfiction. He invites them to think about reading more nonfiction: "Turn to your partner and tell him or her one topic you hope to read a nonfiction book about next."

After lunch, the students gather around the rug area and eagerly listen as Mr. Paige reads aloud from *Meet the Octopus* by Sylvia M. James. He begins the lesson by asking students to watch as he models how to make connections to the text. He previews the text and uses the illustrations to jog his ideas: "I think I already know that the octopus uses some sort of ink to protect itself from predators. Now turn to your partners and tell one thing you think you already know." The room is buzzing with comments: "I know they swim." "I think that they have lots of arms." "I think they eat fish."

Mr. Paige asks the students to make predictions after modeling the strategy frame "I think I will learn... because...." Students talk over one another with excitement and their teacher reminds them to take turns. He continues the lesson by reading aloud from the text and pausing every few pages to ask the students to discuss what they think they will learn on that page.

Intermediate example

The fifth graders prepare to read the science text by reading each heading and then skimming that section to come up with a logical "I wonder" question. The students work in table teams to write their wonders after each section. Mrs. Baumgartner fields the wonders and the class discusses.

Later that day, Mrs. Baumgartner meets with a group of five struggling readers for a guided reading lesson using a text on volcanoes. The students gather on the floor and discuss the illustrations as they make their predictions about what they will learn. During reading, Mrs. Baumgartner stops the readers periodically and encourages them to turn to a partner and wonder something about the paragraph they are on.

During little buddy time on Friday, the students will read aloud a nonfiction text on a topic they've selected based on the buddies' interests. Later during social studies, the students work in teams on their hand motion summaries (Oczkus, 2009) for a chapter on the colonies. Each team selects five vocabulary words or phrases from the reading and creates hand gestures to represent that concept. Giggles abound as teams perform for the class, but everyone remembers the content better this way!

Practical Guidelines for Teaching Nonfiction

Here are some guidelines to help you teach students to use effective strategies as they navigate their way through nonfiction.

Recognize that reading nonfiction is different from reading fiction.

When reading nonfiction, the reader may skip around instead of reading from beginning to end, read some parts more deeply, reread often to summarize the information, or spend time studying the illustrations and other visuals. Readers have varied purposes for reading nonfiction, and those purposes affect how carefully they read. For example, if you are interested in vacationing in Florida, you might skim several websites before reading a text deeply. However, if you are house training your puppy or making pizza, you may read directions and methods very carefully. The reader needs to understand how the nonfiction book is organized (text structure) and its special text features, such as headings and captions.

Teaching idea for distinguishing nonfiction from fiction. Ask your students, "How is reading fiction different from reading nonfiction?" Record their findings on a chart. Have your students ask adults in their home why they read nonfiction and to bring in examples (e.g., maps, newspapers, magazines, how-to books, recipes).

Teach text structures.

Once when I asked second graders, "What is nonfiction?" Carlyn replied, "Nonfiction books don't start with 'once upon a time.'" Fiction books are organized around a story with a problem and solution or maybe by events or a timeline. Nonfiction texts are written to inform, describe, or report and are usually organized around basic structures: cause/effect, compare/contrast, description, problem/solution, question/answer, sequence. Cue words and phrases are often used in these structures.

Teaching idea for text structures. Try using picture books to teach the structures to your students. During the predicting phase of your book, preview the reading material and help students predict the text structure. Sketch the organizer on the board or chart and ask students to help fill it in after reading.

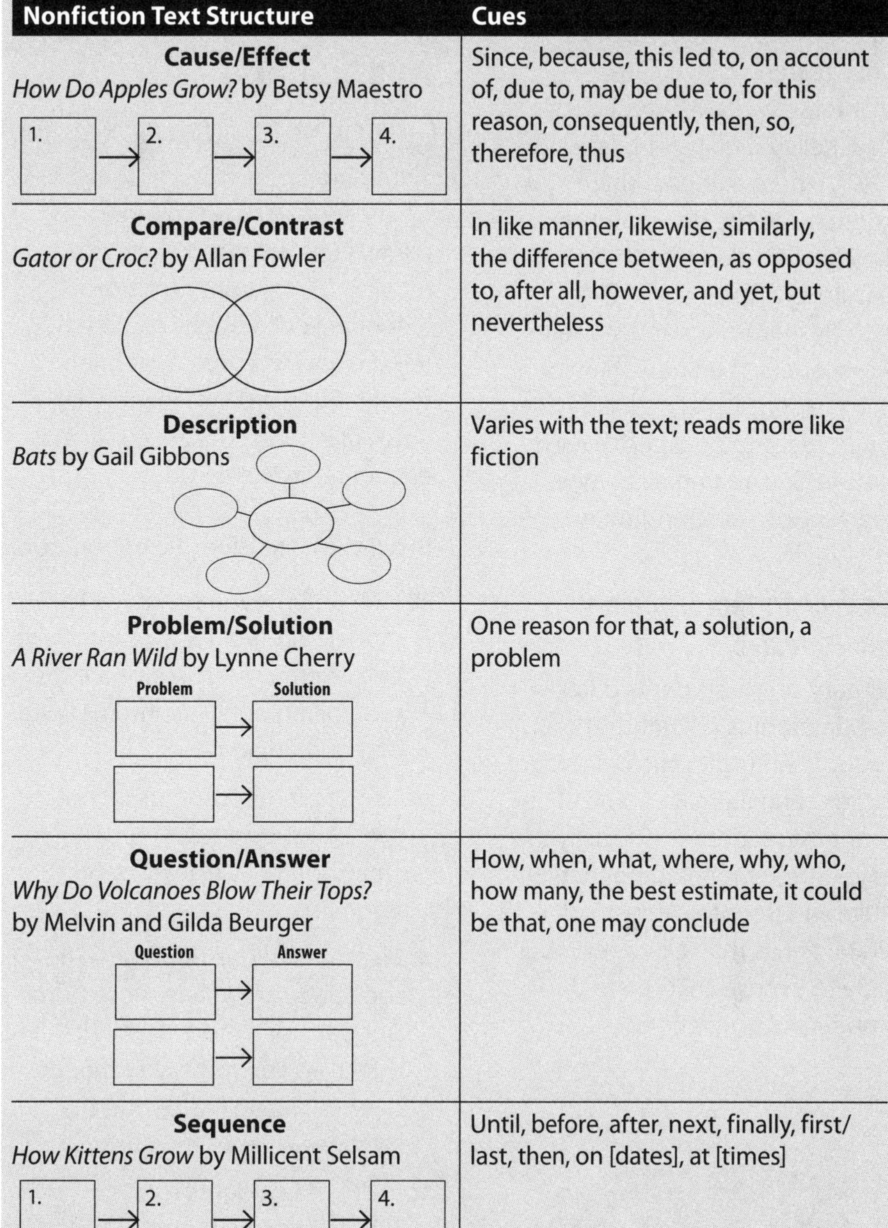

Cue Words and Phrases for Nonfiction Text Structures

Nonfiction Text Structure	Cues
Cause/Effect *How Do Apples Grow?* by Betsy Maestro 1. → 2. → 3. → 4.	Since, because, this led to, on account of, due to, may be due to, for this reason, consequently, then, so, therefore, thus
Compare/Contrast *Gator or Croc?* by Allan Fowler	In like manner, likewise, similarly, the difference between, as opposed to, after all, however, and yet, but nevertheless
Description *Bats* by Gail Gibbons	Varies with the text; reads more like fiction
Problem/Solution *A River Ran Wild* by Lynne Cherry Problem → Solution	One reason for that, a solution, a problem
Question/Answer *Why Do Volcanoes Blow Their Tops?* by Melvin and Gilda Beurger Question → Answer	How, when, what, where, why, who, how many, the best estimate, it could be that, one may conclude
Sequence *How Kittens Grow* by Millicent Selsam 1. → 2. → 3. → 4.	Until, before, after, next, finally, first/last, then, on [dates], at [times]

Introduce nonfiction text features.

Nonfiction texts are loaded with reader supports that we can teach our students. Text features include the following:

- table of contents
- headings
- captions
- maps
- diagrams
- illustrations
- photographs
- labels
- glossary
- index

As you introduce each of these to students, ask, "How does this text feature help you understand the reading?"

Teaching idea for text features. A fun way to get students to pay attention to text features while reading is to create an Interactive Text Feature Wall (Kelley & Clausen-Grace, 2007), where students share examples of the text features they find. Students cut text-feature examples out of kid-friendly magazines and student newspapers, then glue them on chart paper. Students decide how much space to dedicate to each feature. See a sample at www.teachingcomprehension.org.

Teach nonfiction in primary grades, too!

Primary-grade students enter our classrooms full of questions about "real" topics such as spiders, rockets, and animals. Some of our youngest readers—especially the boys—prefer reading nonfiction. Duke and Bennett-Armistead (2004) tell us that it is never too early to expose children to the wonders of nonfiction.

Lori's Top 5 Surefire Strategies for Teaching Nonfiction

1 *Word Pop Prediction (Oczkus, 2010)*

Skimming and scanning is a useful prediction strategy that good readers use constantly before reading. This quick prediction technique encourages students to skim and scan over text prior to reading in order to identify key vocabulary and concepts they may encounter in the text.

Procedure for Word Pop Prediction

- Tell students you are going to model skimming and scanning to help them predict. Compare this to scrolling down an Internet page before reading.
- Use a text the students can all see while you model—use a smartboard, overhead, or Big Book.
- Place your index fingers on the top edges of the text—use finger puppets for a more dramatic effect! As you move your fingers down the text, read aloud the words that "pop" for you.
- Invite the students to try skimming and scanning, and make predictions together based on the words that popped.

2 *"I think I will learn...because..." Predictions (Oczkus, 2010)*

Predicting with nonfiction can be awkward for some students. Try using the frame "I think I will learn... because..." to guide students as they predict (see www.lorioczkus.com/teachers-tips-lori-oczkus.php).

Procedure for "I think I will learn... because..." Predictions

- First select a portion of text and model for students as you predict using the "I think I will learn... because...." frame. Show how text features help you predict.
- Invite pairs of students to take turns predicting with the next portion of text.
- Discuss predictions and return to them after reading to see if students learned what they thought they would.

3 *Flip It (Oczkus, 2009)*

This fun technique teaches students how to sharpen their ability to ask and anticipate great questions as they read. Instead of asking students to make up questions about large chunks of text, try flipping sentences into questions first.

Procedure for Flip It

- Select a nonfiction text to model from. Tell students that good readers ask questions as they read, and they also think about what questions might be on a test of the material. Compare this to thinking while reading about what question the host might ask on the television program *Are You Smarter Than a 5th Grader?*
- Read one sentence aloud. Pause and think aloud as you decide what kind of question goes with the sentence and pose the question. Discuss the answer.
- Guide students to work in pairs as they find sentences to flip into questions that they then answer.
- Reflect on questioning and how it helps readers understand the text better.

4 *Hand Motion Summaries (Oczkus, 2009)*

This is a student favorite! Students brainstorm keywords and phrases from the text and create hand motions or gestures to illustrate the points.

Procedure for Hand Motion Summaries

- Select a portion of text to model. Read aloud.
- Choose five key points or words, and list them on a chart.
- For each point, make up an accompanying hand motion. Invite students to do the motions with you.
- Have pairs of students repeat the motions as they verbalize their summaries.
- Invite students to work in pairs or teams to create their own hand motion summaries.

5 *Pop-Up Thoughts (Oczkus, 2009)*

When good readers read, they constantly think about the text and thoughts pop up: "This reminds me of...." or "I already knew that...." or "Oh, I realize now that...." This lesson encourages students to think deeply and interact with nonfiction text as they read.

Procedure for Pop-Up Thoughts

- Select a portion of nonfiction text to model from, and tell students that good readers think lots of little pop-up thoughts as they read.
- As you read aloud from the text, demonstrate for students as you pause and mark on sticky notes symbols for thoughts you may have. For younger students, model only two symbols in a given lesson.
- Encourage students to work in pairs or teams to mark their texts with sticky notes for pop-up thoughts. You may even assign different pop-up thoughts per table or allow students to use them all.
- Discuss as a class. Reflect on how coding thoughts during reading helps students understand nonfiction better.

Sample Pop-Up Thoughts Symbols

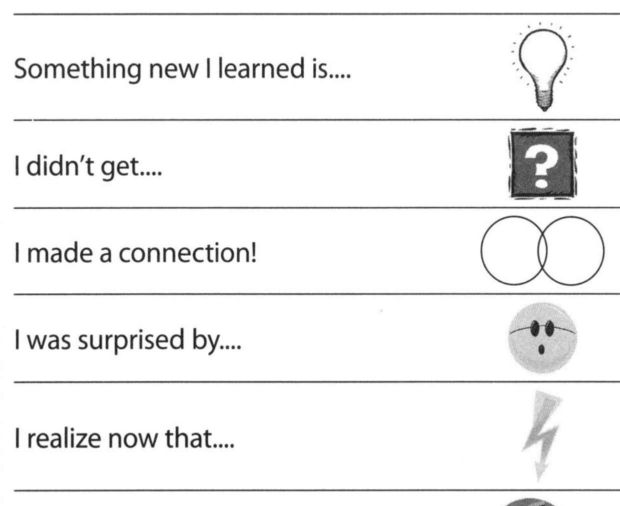

Something new I learned is....	
I didn't get....	?
I made a connection!	
I was surprised by....	
I realize now that....	
This is A+ writing!	 A+

Before Reading: Activate Prior Knowledge

- What problems do your students encounter when reading nonfiction?
- Do some of your students choose nonfiction texts for enjoyment? What nonfiction text strategies do you already teach?

During Reading: Respond While Reading

- While reading this chapter, mark your text with self-stick notes. Use symbols to indicate questions (?), things you want to try (T), something you connect with (+), something interesting or surprising (!) (adapted from Hatt, n.d.).

After Reading: Think About and Discuss

- How much nonfiction do your students read during a week? In a day?
- What are some benefits and reasons to teach nonfiction?
- Read through the nonfiction primary and intermediate examples on page 76. What do you like, notice, or wonder about the scenarios?
- How is reading nonfiction different from reading fiction?
- Discuss the various nonfiction text structures on page 77. Which ones are hardest for your students to identify?
- Which text features are difficult for your students to understand and use? How can you help them better use text features? Bring in a nonfiction text you are reading and discuss with peers which text structures and features are used.
- Look over the Top 5 Lessons and the Web Resources and select one of each to try. Discuss whether or not your students read nonfiction during independent reading time. How can you encourage students to read more nonfiction?

Putting Informational Text Into Practice

Professional Development Breakout Groups

- Make a chart listing problems students experience when reading nonfiction.
- Discuss ways fiction and nonfiction reading are different. Create a list or chart.
- Bring in a pile of nonfiction that adults read (magazines, newspapers, menus, directions, how-to manuals) and discuss the types of nonfiction we read every day and the strategies we use. Discuss ways to share this information with students.
- Bring in various nonfiction texts to use as mentor texts or examples of different text structures. (See chart on page 77.) Brainstorm ways to share with students. How do the cue words help students read nonfiction text?

Lesson Sharing

- Try one of Lori's Top 5 lessons with your class. Be prepared to share. On a scale of 1–5, how did the lesson go? Explain. What do you want to try next?
- Record yourself conducting a nonfiction lesson with a small group or the whole class. Share the video with a colleague. Discuss difficulties and successes your students have with nonfiction reading.
- Try making a Text Feature Wall (Kelley & Clausen-Grace, 2007) with your class. Walk through one another's classrooms to share your ideas. (See page 78.)
- In a staff meeting, try Lori's Top 5 Lessons using a nonfiction article from the newspaper or Internet. Or try designing lessons together for each of the Top 5 that you can use with content reading material at your grade level.

Teacher as Reader

- Make a list of all the nonfiction you read in a day. What is the percentage of time you spend reading nonfiction vs. fiction? What reading strategies do you find yourself using as you read?
- Gather nonfiction texts from around your house, including maps, recipes, newspapers, magazines, and bring them to school. Discuss with your students how you use each type. Encourage students to bring real-world reading to share. Discuss reasons people read nonfiction.

Before the Next Meeting

Read: Select the next chapter your group will read. Mark the text during reading.
Try: Try one of the lessons from the next chapter, or try something new from this chapter.
Observe: Visit a colleague's classroom to observe a lesson using informational text, or record yourself teaching a lesson and share the video at a meeting.

Going Deeper With Informational Text

- Try a book study using these practical resources loaded with everything you need to know about reading nonfiction:

  Harvey, S. (1998). *Nonfiction matters: Reading, writing, and research in grades 3–8*. Portland, ME: Stenhouse.

  Hoyt, L. (2002). *Make it real: Strategies for success with informational texts*. Portsmouth, NH: Heinemann.

- Or consider studying the resources listed on page 86.

Reading Informational Text Bookmark Lesson

Objective: To provide students with a bookmark with prompts that they can use as they "turn and talk" to one another.

Common Core Connections: Students will identify the text structure, ask and answer questions, use and evaluate text features, identify main ideas, determine meanings of words and phrases, and compare/contrast texts. Determine academic words relevant to the subject area. Discuss author's purpose.

Teacher Modeling: Read aloud from an informational text and periodically pause to model how to use one of the bookmark prompts. Conduct a think-aloud and start with something like, "In this part here, I am thinking...."

Guided Practice: Ask students to turn to partners and use the same prompt you just modeled. Eventually, give students choices among several prompts. Listen to the pairs and invite students to share with the class. Praise their efforts.

Independent Practice: Students may use the same prompts as in your read-aloud lesson for their independent reading books. They can mark with self-stick notes the passages they wish to share with the group or a partner.

Wrap Up: Ask students how the discussion has helped them deepen their comprehension. Ask which of the prompts on the bookmark is their favorite or the most helpful and why.

Nonfiction Wonders Lesson

Objective: To focus students' attention on questions while reading a nonfiction text.

Common Core Connections: Students will ask and answer questions to determine their understanding of important details in a text and use evidence from the text when making inferences.

Teacher Modeling: Pause periodically during and after a read-aloud from an informational text and think aloud as you demonstrate how good readers use "wondering" to help them comprehend a text. Select specific portions of text to use as examples. Say, "During this part I am wondering...."

Guided Practice: Invite students to turn to a partner or tablemates and share their wonders. Try assigning different types of wonders (i.e., "I wonder why....") to groups of students. Students may use self-stick notes or markers and chart paper. Students create "wonder" posters and share.

Independent Practice: Every few pages, ask students to pause to write a few "wonders." They may sketch as well.

Wrap Up: Invite students to tell partners and the class how sensory images help them comprehend as they read. Share favorite examples from the text.

Assessment Tips

During informational text lessons, observe students and listen to their responses in class and partner discussions, and analyze independent work. Encourage students to use physical, verbal, and sometimes written responses to your lessons (e.g., thumbs-up, slates, make a face, dramatize, and partner talk). Keep a clipboard or student role sheet nearby to jot down quick notes and observations during or after the lesson.

Reading Informational Text Bookmark

BEFORE READING

Connect

Look at the cover and flip through the book. What do you think you already know about the topic?

Predict

- Look at the table of contents and flip through the book. How is the book organized? What is the text structure of the reading material?
- Skim the headings, captions, and other features. What do you think you will learn? Why did the author write this text?

Question

- What are you wondering?
- What do you want to know?

DURING READING

Clarify/Monitor

- Pause to clarify confusing words/parts. Are there any confusing words or parts? How can you figure them out?

Question

- Now what are you wondering?

Summarize

- What have you learned so far?
- What is important and interesting?

AFTER READING

Summarize

- What did you learn?
- Tell what this text is about.

Synthesize

- At first, what did you think? Now what do you think?
- Compare this text to others on the topic. How is it alike, different?

Infer

- Fill in this statement with your inference. "I can tell that ________ because ________."

Evaluate

- Are there any issues to discuss?
- How do you rate this reading?

Question

- What are you still wondering?

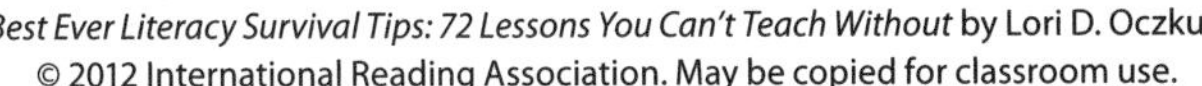

Reading Informational Text Bookmark

BEFORE READING

Connect

Look at the cover and flip through the book. What do you think you already know about the topic?

Predict

- Look at the table of contents and flip through the book. How is the book organized? What is the text structure of the reading material?
- Skim the headings, captions, and other features. What do you think you will learn? Why did the author write this text?

Question

- What are you wondering?
- What do you want to know?

DURING READING

Clarify/Monitor

- Pause to clarify confusing words/parts. Are there any confusing words or parts? How can you figure them out?

Question

- Now what are you wondering?

Summarize

- What have you learned so far?
- What is important and interesting?

AFTER READING

Summarize

- What did you learn?
- Tell what this text is about.

Synthesize

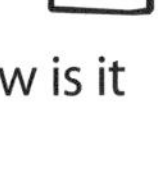

- At first, what did you think? Now what do you think?
- Compare this text to others on the topic. How is it alike, different?

Infer

- Fill in this statement with your inference. "I can tell that ________ because ________."

Evaluate

- Are there any issues to discuss?
- How do you rate this reading?

Question

- What are you still wondering?

Best Ever Literacy Survival Tips: 72 Lessons You Can't Teach Without by Lori D. Oczkus.
© 2012 International Reading Association. May be copied for classroom use.

Nonfiction Wonders

Directions: During reading today, keep track of what you are wondering about as you read. Share with your partner or group.

I wonder what
I wonder when
I wonder where
I wonder why
I wonder how

Using Comprehension Strategies With Informational Text Assessment Checklist

Connect

The student

- Tells about prior knowledge that relates to the topic after a text walk
- Knows how to access additional information to find out background knowledge (e.g., Web, glossary, reference materials)
- Participates during background-building lessons and then uses gained background to understand the reading

Predict

The student

- Identifies text structures and uses them to help make predictions
- Identifies and uses text features to predict (e.g., headings, illustrations, glossary, maps, diagrams)
- Makes logical predictions about what will be learned for a given portion of text

Question

The student

- Asks logical "wonder" questions that go along with the text
- Asks "wonder" questions that are inferential
- Asks a variety of questions that are "right there" questions
- Asks deeper, inferential questions
- Answers literal questions
- Answers higher level questions

Clarify/Monitor

The student

- Identifies words to clarify
- Uses a variety of strategies to clarify (e.g., word-level and contextual rereading, reading on)
- Identifies confusing ideas, concepts in the text
- Uses a variety of strategies to clarify confusing concepts, ideas
- Uses sensory images to clarify

Infer

The student

- Uses questions to infer from the text
- Uses background knowledge and text information to infer

Summarize

The student

- Summarizes in own words
- Uses important vocabulary from the text
- Includes important points and relevant details
- Summarizes in order
- May use text structure to summarize

Synthesize

The student

- Identifies "ah-ha" thoughts about the content
- Reads more than one text on the subject to gain answers to questions

Evaluate

The student

- Gives opinions about the text and reasons for those opinions
- Rates performance as a reader

Q&A

How can I encourage my students to read more nonfiction during independent reading time?

Encourage your students to read nonfiction on their own by having them keep a reading log that lists the titles and genres of the texts they are reading. Also, ask them to fill out an interest inventory. (See the Reading Log Form on page 34 and the Interest Inventory on page 35). When you confer with students, encourage them to read books, magazine articles, and online pieces about their topics of interest.

Web Resources for Nonfiction

ReadWriteThink: www.readwritethink.org

ReadWriteThink is a great resource for hundreds of free downloadable lessons in all aspects of reading. Here are some lessons to help your students navigate nonfiction:

- "Investigating Animals: Using Nonfiction for Inquiry-based Research" (Grades K–2) by Devon Hamner
- "Predicting and Gathering Information With Nonfiction Texts" (Grades K–2) by Bethany L.W. Hankinson
- "Traveling Terrain: Comprehending Nonfiction Text on the Web" (Grades 3–5) by Sheila K. Seitz
- "Using THIEVES to Preview Nonfiction Texts" (Grades 6–8) by Cynthia A. Lassonde

Scholastic 5-Day Unit Plan for Introducing Nonfiction: content.scholastic.com/browse/unitplan.jsp?id=109

Prepare your students to use expository texts that readers of all ages encounter daily, including newspapers, brochures, magazines, instruction manuals, recipes, and maps.

Stenhouse Publishers Author Conversations: Nonfiction Mentor Texts (Podcast): www.youtube.com/watch?v=0RdxCHu5QXA

An interview with Lynne Dorfman and Rose Cappelli, authors of *Nonfiction Mentor Texts*, recorded in 2009 at the IRA Convention in Minneapolis.

"The demands of our information-saturated world require that we increase students' exposure to informational text—and teach stategies to comprehend it."

References

Common Core State Standards Initiative. (2010). *Common Core State Standards for English language arts & literacy in history/social studies, science, and technical subjects*. Washington, DC: National Governors Association Center for Best Practices and the Council of Chief State School Officers.

Duke, N.K. (2000). 3.6 minutes per day: The scarcity of informational texts in first grade. *Reading Research Quarterly, 35*(2), 202–224.

Duke, N.K., & Bennett-Armistead, V.S. (2004, May/June). Nonfiction reading in the primary grades: How and why it's good for young learners. *Scholastic News Teachers' Edition*, pp. 3–4. Available at teacher.scholastic.com/products/classmags/files/Nell_duke_May04.pdf

Duke, N.K., Bennett-Armistead, V.S., & Roberts, E.M. (2002). Incorporating informational text in the primary grades. In C.M. Roller (Ed.), *Comprehensive reading instruction across the grade levels* (pp. 40–54). Newark, DE: International Reading Association.

Duke, N.K., Bennett-Armistead, V.S., & Roberts, E.M. (2003). Bridging the gap between learning to read and reading to learn. In D.M. Barone & L.M. Morrow (Eds.), *Literacy and young children: Research-based practices* (pp. 226–242). New York: Guilford.

Duke, N.K., Caughlan, S., Juzwik, M.M., & Martin, N.M. (2012). *Reading and writing genre with purpose in K–8 classrooms*. Portsmouth, NH: Heinemann.

Duke, N.K., & Kays, J. (1998). "Can I say 'Once upon a time'?": Kindergarten children developing knowledge of information book language. *Early Childhood Research Quarterly, 13*(2), 295–318.

Harvey, S. (1998). *Nonfiction matters: Reading, writing, and research in grades 3–8*. Portland, ME: Stenhouse.

Hatt, C. (n.d.). *Better discussions in study groups*. Retrieved from www.choiceliteracy.com/public/796.cfm

Hoyt, L. (2002). *Make it real: Strategies for success with informational texts*. Portsmouth, NH: Heinemann.

Jobe, R., & Dayton-Sakari, M. (2002). *Info-kids: How to use nonfiction to turn reluctant readers into enthusiastic learners*. Markham, ON, Canada: Pembroke.

Kamil, M.L., & Lane, D.M. (1998). Researching the relation between technology and literacy: An agenda for the 21st century. In D. Reinking, M.C. McKenna, L.D. Labbo, & R.D. Kieffer (Eds.), *Handbook of literacy and technology: Transformations in a post-typographic world* (pp. 355–376). Mahwah, NJ: Erlbaum.

Kelley, M.J., & Clausen-Grace, N. (2007). *Comprehension shouldn't be silent: From strategy instruction to student independence*. Newark, DE: International Reading Association.

Oczkus, L.D. (2009). *Interactive think-aloud lessons: 25 surefire ways to engage students and improve comprehension*. New York: Scholastic; Newark, DE: International Reading Association.

Oczkus, L.D. (2010). *Reciprocal teaching at work: Powerful strategies and lessons for improving reading comprehension* (2nd ed.). Newark, DE: International Reading Association.

Purcell-Gates, V., Duke, N.K., & Martineau, J.A. (2007). Learning to read and write genre-specific text: Roles of authentic experience and explicit teaching. *Reading Research Quarterly, 42*(1), 8–45.

Smith, M.C. (2000). The real-world reading practices of adults. *Journal of Literacy Research, 32*(1), 25–52. doi:10.1080/10862960009548063

Venezky, R.L. (1982). The origins of the present-day chasm between adult literacy needs and school literacy instruction. *Visible Language, 16*(2), 112–127.

CHAPTER 7

Assessment Survival Tips: Guidelines and TOP 5 Quick, Informal Assessments Every Teacher Should Know

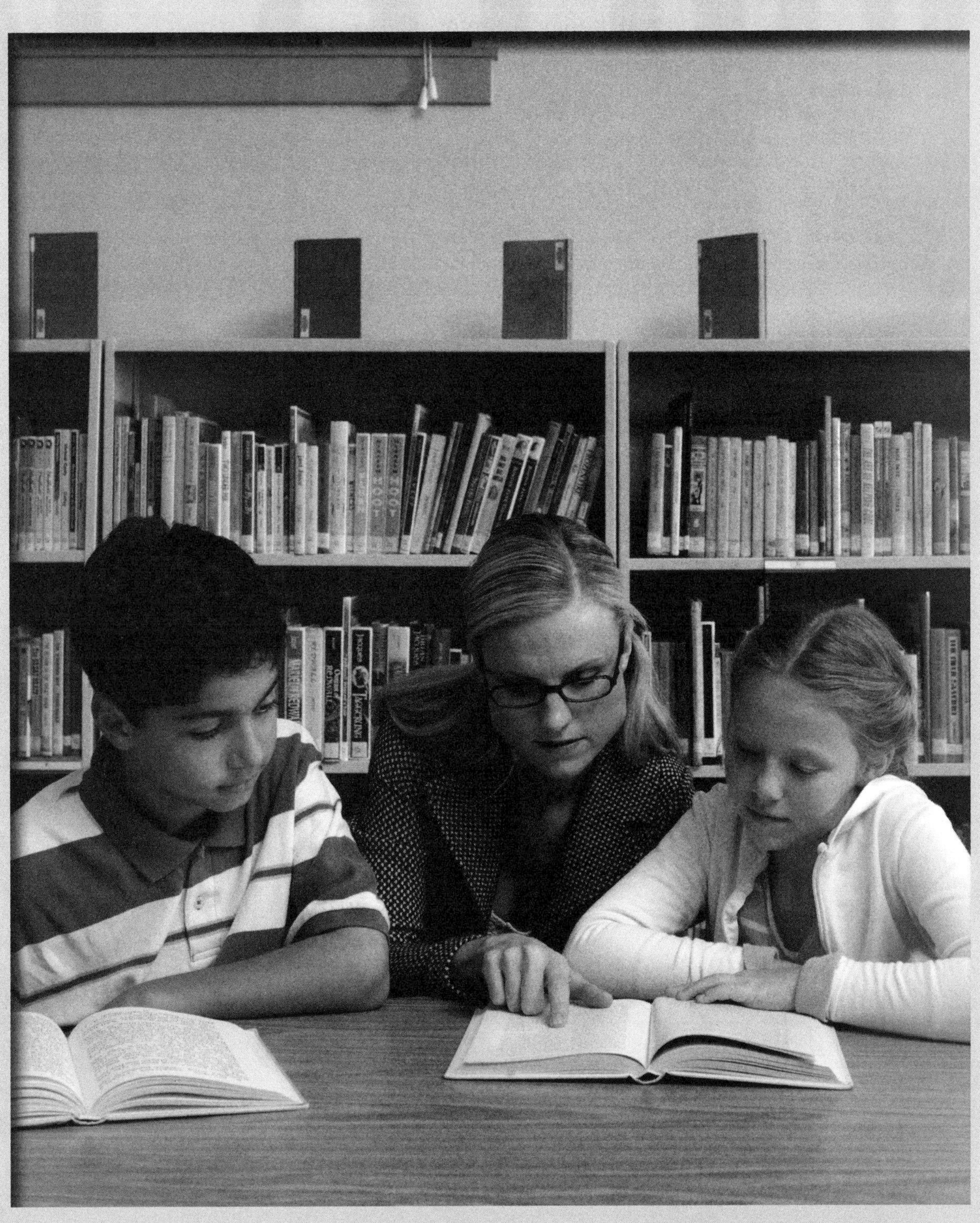

Best Ever Advice on... Assessment

Use the Informal Reading Inventory (IRI) to assess and monitor students' progress. It is the only research-based tool that teachers really have to use. Use it often and use it carefully. It will help you with classroom instruction, assessment, diagnosis, and ongoing monitoring.

—J. David Cooper, Coauthor of *Success With RTI: Research-Based Strategies for Managing RTI and Core Reading Instruction in Your Classroom* (Scholastic, 2010)

Assessment Overload

These days, we teach in an assessment-crazed environment. Politicians, the general public, and the media focus constant attention on schools and test scores. The pressure to improve student performance is everywhere.

Most likely, your district embraces a variety of required tools for you to bombard students with throughout the year: beginning-of-the-year assessments, ongoing assessments, and a parade of formal and informal district, state, and national tests. Many teachers express frustration with the constant testing and feel that they barely have time to teach the necessary information to do well on the exams or to cover the curriculum.

Questions to Consider When Assessing Students' Reading

- How do I find time to assess my students' abilities and determine their individual needs?
- What level text can each student read, and what is the independent, instructional, and frustration reading level of each student?
- Which skills and strategies do my students need to learn?
- How do my students feel about reading?
- How can I assess the pillars of reading instruction (word work, phonics, phonemic awareness, fluency, and comprehension)?
- How can I use informal assessments to inform and improve my daily instruction?

Assessment Is a GOOD Thing

There is some good news! With carefully planned assessment and consistent use of the results to inform instruction, assessment use can lead to increases in student learning. Additionally, our instruction becomes more informed and focused as we strive to vary our lessons to meet student needs and to improve performance.

This chapter covers some informal, super simple assessments that elementary and middle school teachers employ to improve reading instruction in their classrooms. Brief summaries of each tool make this the perfect quick reference for your own classroom.

When you use these easy, classroom-tested assessments, you gain rich, on-the-spot information that helps

- Back your more formal testing with additional data to inform selection of instructional materials
- Inform your instruction and provide feedback for future lessons to meet student needs
- Group students together who share the same problems or strengths

Reading Assessment 101

The main categories of all assessments we administer in classrooms today are *diagnostic*, *formative*, and *summative*. Serravallo (2010) suggests that when we understand these basic terms, we can categorize the types and purposes of assessments for ourselves, parents, and administrators. The different types of assessment measures work together to give us an accurate picture of students' progress so we can adjust our instruction to meet their needs.

Diagnostic assessments

This type of assessment gives a baseline reading level of the student. We also gain information regarding the student's strengths and needs.

How to use this information: The data gathered help us determine how to group our students for instruction. We can also analyze the strengths and weaknesses of our students and see where we need to improve our instruction. Remember: If you administer an assessment, plan time for analyzing and interpreting the information you collect, then use it!

Examples: Developmental Reading Assessment (DRA), Informal Reading Inventory (IRI)

Formative assessments

These are on-the-spot assessments given while our students are reading. This type of assessment should be given frequently to provide feedback on our lessons and student progress.

How to use this information: The data gathered give us feedback on student progress and advise us which students didn't "get it" and how to reteach or provide differentiated instruction.

Examples: Running records, observations, written responses, verbal responses, student–teacher and student–student conversations, workbook pages

Summative assessments

These are end-of-unit assessments to evaluate how well students have learned the information taught. The information provided is different from that of diagnostic or formative assessments, in that you are assessing how well students have learned what you intended to teach during a specific period of instruction.

How to use this information: The data gathered are analyzed and can be used to form groups for intervention or extension. We can also decide if we need to reteach any of the material or differentiate our instruction.

Examples: End-of-book test or a test on writing summaries after a unit on the strategies and skills for summarizing reading material, end-of-unit tests with formal reading programs, standardized tests, district assessments

Essential Guidelines for Making Assessment Meaningful

The key to making assessment work for you and your students is to involve the students in the process (DiRanna et al., 2008; Heritage, 2010; E. Osmundson, personal communication, November 2010)! Following are some basics for engaging students in assessment so they will be motivated to use strategies to improve their own reading.

Feedback: How am I doing?

Give students immediate feedback as often as possible during lessons so they know if they need to work on a given skill or strategy. Feedback includes compliments, corrections, and suggestions.

When teaching the whole class, you might have students write responses on a slate. You may then add an example to your teaching if you see that half the class didn't get the concept.

When you meet with individual students, provide feedback that they can incorporate immediately. You might say, "You are starting to make some strong inferences about character feelings. You said you think the main character feels sad right now. I see that you are having trouble finding clues from the text to justify your inferences. Let's find some clues together, and you can practice finding more character-feeling clues on the next page."

Feedback in fluency might sound like this: "You are reading more words per minute and so your speed has improved. Great! I did notice that you are reading so fast that you are speeding past the punctuation signals! Let's try reading this together, and we will try using the punctuation signals to sound more natural when you read."

Immediate feedback sets students on the correct path for learning and improving their reading. Try to build constant feedback for the class and individuals into your lessons.

Modeling: Show me!

It makes sense that if you expect students to do something, they need to know what a "good" one looks like. If you are teaching summarizing or inferring, you need to provide lots of strong examples from text, share your own think-alouds, and allow students to offer examples.

The assessment cycle includes repeated modeling from texts so that students will know what they need to do to improve. For example, if you are teaching how to make strong predictions using text clues and background knowledge, you might model with a text, ask students to practice with partners, observe their attempts, and return to modeling based on their predictions.

Be sure to praise students for their approximations. You may even want to create simple rubrics or criteria to help students know what good strategy or skill use looks like. For example, you can review with the class the steps for giving a verbal text summary and together list those steps in order for student reference when they practice summarizing.

Peer evaluation: Two heads are better than one!

Another important piece of the assessment puzzle is peer and self-evaluation. During a lesson, students might turn to partners and try a strategy such as summarizing. One student takes a turn providing a

Sample Student Goals in Reading

- I want to increase the number of books I read this month to [*number*].
- I will improve my reading fluency to [*words per minute*].
- I will read with expression.
- I will improve my fluency by reading phrases instead of word by word.
- I will read more difficult chapter books with good comprehension. I want to read the book [*title*].
- I will read for 30 minutes every night at home.
- I will explore new genres by reading books such as [*titles*].
- I will improve my use of the strategy [*rereading, using beginning sounds, visualizing, etc.*]. (Note: Have students be specific here. Say something like, "I will improve my use of predicting by looking at headings in nonfiction and thinking about what I might learn," "I will improve my use of visualizing by stopping every two pages to think about the picture I am forming in my head and rereading when necessary," or "I will improve my use of figuring out words by looking at the beginning sounds and thinking about what makes sense.")

summary while the peer observes. The observer uses a class-created rubric or checklist that includes the criteria for a good summary. (This might include filling in a frame, such as "In the beginning…, then…, next…, finally....") The peer tutor shares what the partner did well and what was missed in the summary, then the partners switch roles.

Wiliam and Thompson (2007) note that the partner who is observing and providing feedback benefits as much as the partner who is reading, because he or she internalizes the learning by evaluating another's work. When you engage students in peer evaluation, they learn with and from each other. Be sure to provide strong modeling along the way.

Goal setting: Encourage independence!

Many popular self-help books promote the idea of goal setting for success in everything from weight loss to time management to gaining financial wealth. The success gurus all seem to agree that goal setting is important if you want to reach new heights, and writing down goals is even better. So why not borrow from the experts and bring goal setting into our classrooms to improve student reading?

A powerful way of engaging students in the assessment cycle is to help them create their own specific goals for reading. Individual student conferences present a perfect opportunity to help students set goals. You can also teach quick, whole-class minilessons on goal setting and model some examples.

Encourage students to write goals and refer to them often. They can keep a record of goals in their reading logs or folders, or on an index card taped to their desks.

Lori's Top 5 Formative Assessments to Use DURING Lessons

1 *Thumbs Up/Thumbs Down*

It is easy to build quick checks for understanding during every lesson to keep track of student learning. By doing so, you provide active engagement while assessing student learning (Oczkus, 2009).

During a think-aloud during reading instruction, read from the text and model how to give a summary. Discuss with students what a good summary looks like, and

either model one or ask students to tell what they think a good summary should include. Then, model a poor short summary lacking information, and ask students to show with a thumbs up or down whether they think your summary was good.

Immediately model in a think-aloud a better summary that includes main ideas in order, and ask for a thumbs up or down. Note which students are able to demonstrate their understanding.

Give another set of examples and see how many students can identify the better summary. You may then decide what your next lesson will cover and how you will ask students to practice their own summaries based on their responses to your lesson.

In addition to asking students for a thumbs up or down, you might have students indicate responses using the following methods:

- Hold up fingers to indicate which number is correct in a multiple response.
- Hold up fingers to rate a story/ author and turn to a partner to justify response.
- Record responses to problems or questions on slates and hold up for you to see.
- Underline portions of text or put a sticky note next to text with a symbol on it.
- Use new technologies such as interactive whiteboards and clickers.

Many school districts across the United States are updating their technology and providing interactive whiteboards and clickers. Each student uses a remote to click an answer to a carefully planned question, revealing immediately which students understood the question and which need additional instruction. A written record is available for reference and lesson planning. Students love to click away and respond to the immediate feedback. The new generation of clickers enables students to type in longer written responses.

Be cautious and judicious with your use of these automated systems. Effective teachers collect evidence on student learning from a variety of sources that reflect the complex processes of reading.

2 *Pile Sorting*

Pile sorting is one of my favorite ways to flexibly group students for further instruction. After scaffolded instruction, I ask students to complete a brief assignment, such as a quick-write in their reading notebooks or a quick-write on a paper folded into fourths, requiring four examples. I read and sort their responses in three groups: those who got it, those who sort of got it, and those who didn't get it. This takes just a few minutes and identifies three groups of students with whom I can meet and do the following:

- Provide deeper examples for the group who got it.
- Give opportunities to review and move into deeper examples for the group who sort of got it.
- Reteach and provide intervention for the group who didn't get it.

Another option would be to mix students from all three groups and work through more examples after I model, of course. This way they help one another deepen their understanding. For example, I may teach a lesson on asking questions before reading. The questions begin with the words "I see...and I wonder...." (Oczkus, 2004). Students flip through the illustrations prior to reading to record what they see on each page and something they wonder. When I collect their papers, I skim them looking for wonders that match the text illustrations and follow a logical path of thinking.

In a lesson using the book *Digging Up Dinosaurs* by Aliki, I ask students to write "I see and I wonder" statements for the first 10 pages in the book. The first pages demonstrate how a fish became a fossil. One student writes, "I see a fish buried under layers of soil and I wonder how long it took to become a fossil." Another student writes in response to the same picture, "I see a fish under the dirt and wonder how long the Tyrannosaurus Rex was here." The second student has some good ideas but is not wondering specifically about the illustration at hand. A third student misses the point entirely and writes, "I see a bone and wonder if I can get a fish." So my quick piles begin: the first student in the got it pile, second in the sort of got it pile, and third in the didn't get it pile.

I plan a lesson to build more background on the topic and model examples of "I see and I wonder" for the students. I provide individual coaching and small-group work to practice wondering. As students turn in their examples, I look for evidence of growth and teach increasingly sophisticated lessons.

3 Clipboard Cruising

Another great addition to your assessment techniques is to be a super kidwatcher (see Goodman, 1985) or observer. As students are engaged in meaningful reading tasks, circulate the room and collect specific evidence of student learning. If you are teaching a lesson on inferences, for example, listen in on conversations about how students arrived at their conclusions. Make notes on your clipboard about who understands what and the evidence. Examine these notes after instruction for patterns and trends.

Clipboard cruising (Kaufeldt, 2005) is a formative assessment technique that can be done in a variety of ways.

- To get started, keep a clipboard with a piece of yarn and pen attached that you can grab at any moment to record your observations of students.

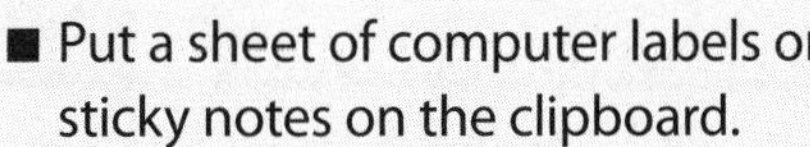

- Put a sheet of computer labels or sticky notes on the clipboard.
- Circulate around the classroom and date each note as you record information about one student at a time. You may not get to everyone in one day.
- Once you've recorded an observation for each student, use the information to form flexible groups of students who have similar needs or strengths.
- The sticky notes or labels with student names are easily removed from the clipboard and placed in a folder for each student.
- You may look for the same skill or strategy at a later date to see how each student has progressed.

For example, after teaching lessons on predicting while reading, clipboard cruise and ask each student for a prediction and reason for that prediction. Do so three times during a grading period and use the information to create more lessons and flexible groups to target the predicting strategy.

4 Individual Reading Conferences

One of the most powerful ways to instruct students is to conduct individual reading conferences (Routman, 2003). If you are already providing time for independent reading through sustained silent reading or readers' workshop, meet with individual students to discuss their reading. You may wish to use the clipboard cruising method for recording

information; however, you may need an entire sheet of paper rather than sticky notes or labels for recording in-depth interviews.

Routman (2003) points out that by second grade, children do not require oral reading as part of the conference. Use your judgment for how much oral reading you want to observe.

Here are some questions you might ask students in a one-on-one conference (Routman, 2003):

- What are you reading?
- Why did you pick this book?
- Do you like it? Why or why not?

For fiction, ask,

- Who are the main characters?
- What is the problem?
- What are your favorite parts?

For nonfiction, ask,

- What is interesting?
- What do you want to learn/what are you learning?
- How is this book organized?
- What are your reading goals? (e.g., harder books, topics, fluency)
- What do you want to read next?

As you confer with each student, you may also want to make a note of the following:

- Was the book too easy, hard, or just right for the student?
- How fluently did the student read it aloud to you?
- What strategies does the student use to figure out words?

5 Running Records

A useful reading assessment to easily implement with any text, on the spot, is a running record, where an individual student reads aloud from a 100-word passage while the teacher records and then analyzes decoding, comprehension, and fluency (Clay, 1993). A running record reveals how a student is functioning in a certain level of text and which decoding strategies the student is using, provides a quick fluency check for you to watch for intonation and prosody, and helps you plan specific coaching and lessons around student needs (Cooper, Robinson, & Kiger, 2010).

How often you give a running record depends on your purpose for giving the assessment. You may give more frequent running records, even once a week, to younger children and struggling readers to monitor their progress and to adjust your instruction to fit their needs. When using running records to monitor reading level, you may give running records in grades K–2 every three weeks and in grades 3–6 every four to six weeks.

Analyze the results: You can informally analyze the results and see what patterns the errors form. Ask, Did the student use meaning, phonics, visual clues? How fluently or word-by-word did the student read? How was his or her overall comprehension? Acceptable scores depend on the reading material (Serravallo, 2010). For independent reading material, the student should score 97% or higher in oral reading with natural-sounding fluency and good comprehension. For instructional-level text, the student may score 95% or a bit below, and comprehension and fluency may be lacking. If the score comes in below 90%, the student may be frustrated with the text and unable to maintain meaning.

Use running records to inform instruction: Taking running records is not enough. You can use this valuable information to plan lessons, coach individual students, and form groups.

- Plan lessons—The results from your running records reveal patterns across your class, and you can build lessons around student needs.
- Coach individual students—If a student needs to use more phonics, decoding, or maybe meaning clues while reading, you can model using a variety of texts. You might say, "I noticed you are substituting words that make sense but do not begin with the letter of the word in the book." Then model how to sound out the words and think about what makes sense.
- Form groups—You can group students who need to work on the same strategies, such as reading more fluently or using meaning to figure out words.

Taking Running Records Is Easy

Get started

Choose or have the student select a passage of 100 words out of any text. Make a photocopy of the page or simply take notes on another paper as the student reads to you. Sit next to and a bit behind the student so that he or she will not be as conscious of your note-taking during the reading. Date your notes for later reference and comparison.

Record student errors and self-corrections

Choose either a modified, super simple running record or a more detailed one. Both are easy to take once you've had some practice.

Take a modified, super simple running record! When taking notes without a copy of the text, you can conduct a modified, super simple running record (Routman, 2003). Listen to the student read aloud and then measure overall comprehension by asking the student to retell or to answer a couple basic questions. Record only the substitutions the student makes or the self-corrections. The easiest way to do that is to write what the student says on top and what the text says below it. For example, if the student says "dog" and the text says "pet," you write the following:

page 3 child reads: dog
text says: pet

Or take a more detailed running record: To take a more detailed running record, follow a copy of the text as the student reads. Circle omissions and record self-corrections, substitutions, and insertions. Count the number of words the student read correctly, including self-corrections, and calculate results using this formula:

$$\frac{\text{Number of words read correctly}}{\text{Number of words in the text}} \times 100 = \text{\% of words read correctly}$$

Example: Julian read 97 out of 100 words correctly.

$$\frac{97}{100} \times 100 = 97\%$$

Assess comprehension

After a read-aloud, ask the student to retell the reading in his or her own words or to answer a few questions regarding main events and ideas from the text. The student should be able to recall 90–95% of the material.

Before Reading: Activate Prior Knowledge

- Discuss briefly all the assessments you are required to administer, both formal and informal. What is the good news about all this assessment?
- What problems do you have taking what you learn from assessments and incorporating that information into useful data for planning differentiated lessons?

During Reading: Respond While Reading

- While reading this chapter, mark your text with self-stick notes. Use symbols to indicate questions (?), things you want to try (T), something you connect with (+), something interesting or surprising (!) (adapted from Hatt, n.d.).

After Reading: Think About and Discuss

- What is the difference between diagnostic, formative, and summative assessments? Name the ones you are using and explain how each is useful. What difficulties do you face with each?
- Why is immediate feedback so important?
- What is the purpose of teacher modeling? Do you enjoy modeling? What is hard about it?
- Explain peer evaluation.
- How might you incorporate more opportunities for students to set goals? What might the reading goals at your grade level look like?

Putting Assessment Into Practice

Professional Development Breakout Groups

- Prepare a quick and practical "Assessment 101" explanation that shares the definitions, differences, and tools for diagnostic, formative, and summative assessments. Use the talk with parents to help them understand the various assessments and their uses.
- Work on a team and make a list of practical and specific feedback to use during reading conferences and lessons; include compliments, corrections, and suggestions for your students

Lesson Sharing

- Select one of Lori's Top 5 lessons to deepen your understanding of formative assessments; use it during lessons. Be sure to explain how the information gained from the assessment helped you plan more targeted lessons and differentiate for students. Bring student samples to discuss.
- Form interest groups based on the Top 5 assessments you wish to try. Bring student samples to share. Try the same assessment for a month and share. What worked? What would you change?

Teacher as Reader

- Set reading goals for yourself. Include the genres and types of texts you want to read as well as the number of books you wish to enjoy. Share your goals with your students.

Before the Next Meeting

Read: Select the next chapter your group will read. Mark the text during reading.
Try: Try one of the lessons from the next chapter, or try something new from this chapter.
Observe: Visit a colleague's classroom to observe a lesson or an assessment you are using with your class, or record yourself teaching a lesson and share the video at a meeting.

Going Deeper With Assessment

- Try a book study on assessment using either of these wonderful professional books:

  Cooper, J.D., Robinson, M.D., & Kiger, N.D. (2010). *Success with RTI: Research-based strategies for managing RTI and core reading instruction in your classroom*. New York: Scholastic.

  Opitz, M.F., Ford, M.P., & Erekson, J.A. (2011). *Accessible assessment: How 9 sensible techniques can power data-driven reading instruction*. Portsmouth, NH: Heinemann.

- Or consider studying the resources listed on page 100.

Ready, Set, Goal!/More Ready, Set, Goal! Bookmarks Lesson

Objective: To provide students with bookmarks with prompts that they can use to evaluate their reading habits, fluency, and comprehension.

Common Core Connections: Students will set goals to comprehend on-level and more complex texts, both fiction and informational. Students evaluate their own progress using evidence, theme, inferences, decoding, figuring out words using multiple strategies, and compare/contrast of characters in the text and other books.

Teacher Modeling: Run the Ready, Set, Goal! and More Ready, Set, Goal! bookmarks back to back. Model how to use each of the prompts on the bookmark using any reading material from your grade level. Tell students that goal setting is an effective, proven way to improve in a sport or any endeavor, including reading. Invite students to discuss the kinds of goals athletes set. How are those goals like the goals they are setting in reading? Conduct a think-aloud using each of the prompts on the bookmark. You can model one a day or several at a time. From time to time, return to modeling the prompts. Bring a student forward to help set his or her reading goals in front of the class. Return continually to the Ready, Set, Goal! Bookmark to model throughout the school year.

Guided Practice: Ask students to turn to their partners and use the same prompt you just modeled. Eventually, give students choices among several prompts. Listen to the pairs and invite students to share with the class. Praise their efforts. Model for students who need more support in setting goals. Periodically, you may wish to duplicate new bookmarks for students to write on. Invite pairs to work together taking turns, with one student reading while the other uses one aspect of the bookmark to "assess" the partner's fluency or comprehension.

Independent Practice: Students may use the same prompts as in your modeling for either their independent reading books or the book the class is reading. Use the Ready, Set, Goal! bookmark as a guide for individual or group conferences with students.

Wrap Up: Ask students to share which goals they are reaching and which are difficult to achieve. Brainstorm ways to meet reading goals. Plan a class Ready, Set, Go! party to celebrate goals met.

Handy Assessment Teacher Bookmarks

Use the Handy Assessment teacher bookmarks as guides when you confer with students one-on-one. Use the information gained to help you form small groups to read and work on strategies.

Running Records: Take regular running records. Compare how your students grow in their reading over time. After a running record, compliment the student on what he or she is doing well, for example, "You reread that word and figured it out. That is a great strategy to use." Help the student set goals for areas to work on to improve reading, for example, "Maybe you can try looking for smaller parts within words to figure them out."

Retelling Scoring: Ask students to retell for the running record after reading aloud. Share compliments, such as, "You organized the main ideas in a compare/contrast summary, just like the text. Good work!" Help the student set goals for the next areas to work on. Say, for example, "How about trying to use a few of the key vocabulary words in your summary next time?"

Ready, Set, Goal! Bookmark

Fill in the blanks and check off your goals.

MY BOOK GOALS

☐ I want to read ______ books in the next _______.

☐ I will read harder books that I am interested in, such as ______________________________.

☐ I will read more

☐ *magazines* ☐ *picture books*

☐ *chapter books* ☐ *harder or longer chapter books*

☐ *online materials, such as* _______________

☐ I will read a variety of genres.

☐ I will read more

☐ *nonfiction* ☐ *fiction*

☐ *realistic fiction* ☐ *historical fiction*

☐ *memoir, biography* ☐ *adventure*

☐ *mystery* ☐ *science fiction*

☐ *other* ______________________________

☐ I want to read nonfiction books about __________.

Here is the list of books I want to read next:

1. ______________________________________

2. ______________________________________

3. ______________________________________

MY TIME SPENT READING GOALS

☐ I will read for _______ minutes at home every night.

☐ In class I will read for _______ minutes and/or _______ pages each day.

☐ I will pay attention during reading by staying in my seat, reading, and thinking about what I am reading.

Ready, Set, Goal! Bookmark

Fill in the blanks and check off your goals.

MY BOOK GOALS

☐ I want to read ______ books in the next _______.

☐ I will read harder books that I am interested in, such as ______________________________.

☐ I will read more

☐ *magazines* ☐ *picture books*

☐ *chapter books* ☐ *harder or longer chapter books*

☐ *online materials, such as* _______________

☐ I will read a variety of genres.

☐ I will read more

☐ *nonfiction* ☐ *fiction*

☐ *realistic fiction* ☐ *historical fiction*

☐ *memoir, biography* ☐ *adventure*

☐ *mystery* ☐ *science fiction*

☐ *other* ______________________________

☐ I want to read nonfiction books about __________.

Here is the list of books I want to read next:

1. ______________________________________

2. ______________________________________

3. ______________________________________

MY TIME SPENT READING GOALS

☐ I will read for _______ minutes at home every night.

☐ In class I will read for _______ minutes and/or _______ pages each day.

☐ I will pay attention during reading by staying in my seat, reading, and thinking about what I am reading.

Best Ever Literacy Survival Tips: 72 Lessons You Can't Teach Without by Lori D. Oczkus.
© 2012 International Reading Association. May be copied for classroom use.

More Ready, Set, Goal! Bookmark

MY FLUENCY GOALS

Rate
☐ I will increase my reading rate to ______ words/minute.
☐ I will slow down, pause, or speed up to make the reading more exciting.

Accuracy
☐ I will practice rereading to sound more fluent and to read all the words correctly.

Prosody
☐ I will read phrases/groups of words, not word by word.
☐ I will read with expression and feeling.
☐ I will improve the way I read dialogue.
☐ I will emphasize meaningful words.

MY COMPREHENSION STRATEGY GOALS

Make Connections
☐ I will watch for connections:
- ☐ *text to self*
- ☐ *text to text*
- ☐ *text to world*

Predict
☐ I will make predictions by
- ☐ *looking at the title, cover, and illustrations*
- ☐ *studying the headings, table of contents, and illustrations when I predict with nonfiction*
- ☐ *thinking about how the book is organized*
- ☐ *thinking about my background knowledge*

Question/Infer
☐ I will ask "I wonder" questions.
☐ I will ask "quiz" questions (right there and infer or me plus the book)
☐ I will ask discussion questions like "Why do you think...?" and "What if...?"
☐ I will infer using the starter "I can tell that...because...." to make inferences.

Monitor/Clarify
☐ I will make pictures in my head when I read.
☐ I will pause to clarify words and ideas.
☐ To clarify words, I will look at
- ☐ *beginning/ending sounds*
- ☐ *base words*
- ☐ *syllables*

☐ I will reread.
☐ I will read on.

Summarize/Synthesize
☐ I will summarize by including
- ☐ *main ideas*
- ☐ *important details*
- ☐ *ideas in order*

☐ I synthesize by thinking about
- ☐ *the theme or lesson*
- ☐ *how my thinking changed*

Evaluate
☐ I will rate
- ☐ *the text*
- ☐ *the author*
- ☐ *the characters*

☐ I will compare this book to other books I've read.

More Ready, Set, Goal! Bookmark

MY FLUENCY GOALS

Rate
☐ I will increase my reading rate to ______ words/minute.
☐ I will slow down, pause, or speed up to make the reading more exciting.

Accuracy
☐ I will practice rereading to sound more fluent and to read all the words correctly.

Prosody
☐ I will read phrases/groups of words, not word by word.
☐ I will read with expression and feeling.
☐ I will improve the way I read dialogue.
☐ I will emphasize meaningful words.

MY COMPREHENSION STRATEGY GOALS

Make Connections
☐ I will watch for connections:
- ☐ *text to self*
- ☐ *text to text*
- ☐ *text to world*

Predict
☐ I will make predictions by
- ☐ *looking at the title, cover, and illustrations*
- ☐ *studying the headings, table of contents, and illustrations when I predict with nonfiction*
- ☐ *thinking about how the book is organized*
- ☐ *thinking about my background knowledge*

Question/Infer
☐ I will ask "I wonder" questions.
☐ I will ask "quiz" questions (right there and infer or me plus the book)
☐ I will ask discussion questions like "Why do you think...?" and "What if...?"
☐ I will infer using the starter "I can tell that...because...." to make inferences.

Monitor/Clarify
☐ I will make pictures in my head when I read.
☐ I will pause to clarify words and ideas.
☐ To clarify words, I will look at
- ☐ *beginning/ending sounds*
- ☐ *base words*
- ☐ *syllables*

☐ I will reread.
☐ I will read on.

Summarize/Synthesize
☐ I will summarize by including
- ☐ *main ideas*
- ☐ *important details*
- ☐ *ideas in order*

☐ I synthesize by thinking about
- ☐ *the theme or lesson*
- ☐ *how my thinking changed*

Evaluate
☐ I will rate
- ☐ *the text*
- ☐ *the author*
- ☐ *the characters*

☐ I will compare this book to other books I've read.

Best Ever Literacy Survival Tips: 72 Lessons You Can't Teach Without by Lori D. Oczkus.
© 2012 International Reading Association. May be copied for classroom use.

Handy Assessment Teacher Bookmark

RUNNING RECORD HOW-TO'S

Getting Started

- Select a passage of 100 words.
- Take notes as the student reads, or record the student reading.

Modified Super Simple Running Record (Routman, 2003)

- Student reads aloud the passage. You do not need a copy of the text to record on; use another paper.
- Record only substitutions or self-corrections and the page number.

Recording a substitution

page 3	child reads: dog text says: pet

Recording a self-correction

page 3	child says dog for pet and self-corrects record: dog SC

More Detailed Running Record

- Make a copy of the passage.
- Circle omissions, self-corrections (these are not counted as errors), substitutions, and insertions.
- Count the number of words read correctly (include self-corrections).

$$\frac{\text{Number of words read correctly}}{\text{Number of words in the text}} \times 100 = \text{\% of words read correctly}$$

Example: Julian read 97 out of 100 words correctly.

$$\frac{97}{100} \times 100 = 97\%$$

Interpreting Running Record Scores

95%–100% = suitable for independent reading

90%–94% = instructional-level reading to be guided by teacher

89% and below = difficult, frustration level

Handy Assessment Teacher Bookmark

RETELLING SCORING HOW-TO'S

Quick Retell

- Student retells the running record passage. Look for the following.

The student

☐ Tells the main ideas or events in order
☐ Provides relevant important details

Student includes for fiction:

☐ setting
☐ characters
☐ problem
☐ key events
☐ ending
☐ theme or lesson
☐ new vocabulary from the selection

Student includes for nonfiction:

☐ an understanding of text structure
☐ main ideas
☐ relevant details
☐ new vocabulary from the selection

Did you prompt the student?

☐ The student retold without any prompting.
☐ The student needed some prompting.
☐ The student needed lots of prompting.
☐ Even with prompting/questioning, the student *did not* satisfactorily recall the material.

Interpreting a Retelling Score

Take notes or tally marks for points. Scoring depends on the difficulty of the reading material.

- Independent reading material recall should be at 97% or higher.
- Instructional-level text recall should be at 95% or higher.
- A score below 90% is too many errors for such a short passage! Student may be frustrated.

Q&A

Should I share assessment results with students? How can I use the results to get buy-in from my students?

You should absolutely share assessment results with students and provide feedback so they can grow and learn from the information collected. When students reflect on their results, they become metacognitive and use the information in new reading situations. The key is to be positive in the process. Here are some simple points to consider to get the most out of sharing assessments with your students:

- Ask students how they think they did on the assessment. What was hard or easy for them?
- Build on the known. Give compliments on what students do well. For example, "I noticed you check the illustrations to figure out new words or confusing parts in the text. Now you might want to try rereading difficult or confusing words or parts to also help you clarify."
- Help students set specific goals based on the assessment results and the skills and strategies you are teaching.
- Praise evidence of progress and approximations as students practice the skills, strategies, and reading behaviors they need to improve.

"With carefully planned assessment and consistent use of the results to inform instruction, assessment use can lead to increases in student learning."

Web Resources

Bright Hub: www.brighthub.com/education/special/articles/31319.aspx
"Short Cuts to Take and Use Running Records"

Busy Teacher's Cafe: www.busyteacherscafe.com/literacy/running_records.html
This page provides information on administering running records and using the information to guide your reading instruction.

Learn NC Editions: www.learnnc.org/lp/editions/readassess/1.0
"Ongoing Assessment for Reading"

ReadWriteThink: www.readwritethink.org
ReadWriteThink is a great resource for hundreds of free downloadable lessons on all aspects of reading. Here are some to try:

- "Name Talk: Exploring Letter-Sound Knowledge in the Primary Classroom" (Grades K–1) by Kathy Egawa
- "Poetry: A Feast to Form Fluent Readers" (Grades 3–5) by Sheila K. Seitz
- "Promoting Student Self-Assessment" (Grades 6–12) by Phil Wilder

Teacher2Teacherhelp: www.teacher2teacherhelp.com/uncategorized/individual-reading-conference
Educational consultant Annemarie Johnson provides information on individual reading conferences.

References

Clay, M.M. (1993). *An observation survey of early literacy achievement.* Portsmouth, NH: Heinemann.

Cooper, J.D., Robinson, M.D., & Kiger, N.D. (2010). *Success with RTI: Research-based strategies for managing RTI and core reading instruction in your classroom.* New York: Scholastic.

DiRanna, K., Osmundson, E., Topps, J., Barakos, L., Gearhart, M., Cerwin, K., et al. (2008). *Assessment-centered teaching: A reflective practice.* Thousand Oaks, CA: Corwin.

Goodman, Y.M. (1985). Kidwatching: Observing children in the classroom. In A. Jaggar & M.T. Smith-Burke (Eds.), *Observing the language learner* (pp. 9–18). Newark, DE: International Reading Association; Urbana, IL: National Council of Teachers of English.

Hatt, C. (n.d.). *Better discussions in study groups.* Retrieved from www.choiceliteracy.com/public/796.cfm

Heritage, M. (2010). *Formative assessment and next-generation assessment systems: Are we losing an opportunity?* Washington, DC: Council of Chief State School Officers. Retrieved November 29, 2010, from www.ccsso.org/Documents/2010/Formative_Assessment_Next_Generation_2010.pdf

Kaufeldt, M. (2005). *Teachers, change your bait! Brain-compatible differentiated instruction.* Norwalk, CT: Crown.

Oczkus, L.D. (2004). *Super six comprehension strategies: 35 lessons and more for reading success.* Norwood, MA: Christopher-Gordon.

Oczkus, L.D. (2009). *Interactive think-aloud lessons: 25 surefire ways to engage students and improve comprehension.* New York: Scholastic; Newark, DE: International Reading Association.

Opitz, M.F., Ford, M.P., & Erekson, J.A. (2011). *Accessible assessment: How 9 sensible techniques can power data-driven reading instruction.* Portsmouth, NH: Heinemann.

Routman, R. (2003). *Reading essentials: The specifics you need to teach reading well.* Portsmouth, NH: Heinemann.

Serravallo, J. (2010). *Teaching reading in small groups: Differentiated instruction for building strategic, independent readers.* Portsmouth, NH: Heinemann.

Wiliam, D., & Thompson, M. (2007). Integrating assessment with learning: What will it take to make it work? In C.A. Dwyer (Ed.), *The future of assessment: Shaping, teaching, and learning* (pp. 53–82). Mahwah, NJ: Erlbaum.

CHAPTER 8

Grouping Survival Tips: Guidelines and TOP 5 Grouping Strategies for Improving Reading

Best Ever Advice on... Grouping

Since small-group time is always limited, it is important to use every minute allocated to the meeting. Annette was a reading teacher I admired. Every time she would call over a small group to meet with her, she would hand a reading task card to children as they arrived at the table. The cards contained generic warm-up activities, for example, "Warm up by finding a place in the reading where the author uses interesting language, and be ready to share it with the group" or "Warm up by finding your favorite part of the reading so far, and be ready to tell us why it is your favorite part." This allowed Annette to engage each student immediately upon arrival at the table. While students worked on their warm-ups, Annette could conduct brief conferences with individual students as needed before starting the group activities.

—Michael P. Ford, Coauthor of *Do-able Differentiation: Varying Groups, Texts, and Supports to Reach Readers* (Heinemann, 2008)

When you were in elementary school, do you recall whether you read with the blue birds, red birds, or yellow birds? I distinctly remember reading in the blue or mid-level reading group. Throughout elementary school, I longed to read the interesting and "hard" books reserved for the red group! Luckily, today educators know that fixed-ability groupings do not offer a wide enough range of reading experiences to meet student needs. Instead, we employ a rich array of grouping options that are flexible and that change based on student needs and interests.

All students benefit from a variety of grouping formats. Researchers inform us that our struggling readers need frequent, quality instruction in small groups (Allington, 2006). This chapter explores the different groupings you can choose from as you build your reading program.

What Effective Grouping Looks Like

Let's peek into two classrooms to see how teachers use grouping to meet student needs while effectively engaging them in a variety of reading tasks. Notice that grouping in these classrooms includes partnerships, cooperative groups, and flexible groupings based on student needs and interests. Skilled teachers know how to use different ways of grouping students to maximize instruction.

Primary example

Mrs. Lee's first graders enthusiastically chant and sing "Itsy Bitsy Spider" from a Big Book. They then sit cross-legged and spellbound as Mrs. Lee reads aloud from a nonfiction text about spiders. Throughout the lesson, Mrs. Lee directs the students to talk to their assigned partners before she calls on a volunteer to share with the whole class.

During guided reading time, Mrs. Lee calls small groups of five or six students to meet at her reading table and read nonfiction texts about insects. She coaches them in comprehension and decoding strategies as they read books that are carefully matched to their reading levels. Students engage in literacy centers in individual and partner activities that include reading books, making words with a variety of manipulatives, and writing activities.

Three times per week, Mrs. Lee meets with her most challenged readers in small groups of three for an intervention group. Some of those students receive one-on-one, intensive instruction twice a week from the reading specialist. The rest of the class rotates around the room to centers where the students have been trained to work quietly in pairs and triads.

Later in the day, during readers' workshop, Mrs. Lee reads aloud and models how to make personal connections. Then every student reads independently while Mrs. Lee conducts individual conferences with five or six students per day. She monitors student progress using informal assessment techniques that help her to form new groups for guided reading.

Intermediate example

Lively discussion fills the room as Mr. Gallegos's fifth graders meet in literature circles twice weekly to discuss novels. Students select a novel from a list of choices and are placed in interest groups to read with the assigned roles of discussion director, predictor, questioner, clarifier, and summarizer. Mr. Gallegos circulates and coaches the groups as they talk about their books.

The class also reads from the district-adopted basal four times a week with varied groupings including partners, individuals, and sometimes literature discussion groups with assigned roles. Informal, informative assessments and observation provide valuable information that helps Mr. Gallegos group students flexibly for quick reteaching lessons.

Later in the day, the students read the social studies chapter with their tablemates and construct a summary poster to share with the class. During readers' workshop three times a week, each student reads from a self-selected text while Mr. Gallegos confers with one to three students at a time to coach comprehension, encourage critical thinking, and teach decoding strategies for unlocking words.

The five most challenged readers meet three times a week for an intervention. Once a week, the fifth graders read picture books aloud to first graders to build comprehension strategies for themselves and their little buddies.

Powerful Grouping Options

When you vary the ways you group students, the classroom becomes an engaging learning atmosphere where students become better readers, thinkers, and independent learners. Conducting regular assessments during instruction provides observations and findings that will help you group students by need and interest. (See Chapter 7, "Assessment Survival Tips.")

The Table shows some of the groupings you can choose from, and then you may select how many times per week you will implement these structures. Which grouping structures you will use over the week and how often you will implement them depend on your grade level and district requirements.

Table. Powerful Grouping Options

Grouping structure	Meeting student needs
Whole-class lessons	• Partnerships informal or assigned During whole-class lessons, ask students to talk with partners often to process the information, ask questions, and respond.
	• Table groups Students work in teams at their tables or discuss or perform a response to reading task with tablemates.
Readers' workshop	• Partnerships During teacher modeling and the guided practice portions of the lesson, individual students discuss their reading with a partner.
	• Individual conferences Students work independently or in partnerships while the teacher calls on one student at a time to confer over reading strategies and habits. Teacher takes notes and uses the information to coach the student, monitor growth, and to form flexible groups with students of like needs.
	• Teacher-led small flexible groups While the rest of the class reads independently, the teacher meets with a small group of students who are reading the same text or who have the same needs.
Flexible-needs or strategy groups	Teacher meets briefly with temporary group that has the same need. For example, after a whole-class lesson on prediction, if five students wrote predictions that didn't make sense, the teacher would gather them to model and practice making sensible predictions.
Guided reading groups	Guided reading groups are teacher-led and organized by need, interest, or reading level. The text is usually at the students' reading level. The teacher guides students as they predict, make connections, and read silently while the teacher coaches the students to decode, question, and in the end think critically and summarize.
Partnerships	Partnerships can be used during whole-class lessons or at literacy stations or centers. Partners can be assigned or can be more informal. The teacher models the partner behaviors that are expected.
Cooperative groups/ literature circles	Students work in teams of three to five students either informally at their tables or in assigned groups with roles. Literature circles are a form of cooperative/ collaborative groupings.
Interest groups	Students form groups based on their interests, which might be related to book titles or topics.
Cross-age groups	Older students are paired with younger students from another grade level to read and write together.
Intervention group	• Intervention small group The struggling readers are identified, and the teacher or reading specialist meets with these students regularly to provide instruction at their level that will boost achievement and catch them up to grade level.
	• Intervention triad for RTI In a Response to Intervention program, the goal is to help struggling readers catch up and avoid special education by providing constant monitoring through assessments and intervention with intense levels of targeted instruction. The struggling readers are taught in small groups of three.

Practical Guidelines for Grouping to Meet Student Needs

Here are some research-based guidelines that will help ensure student success as you select a variety of grouping structures to fit your classroom setting and students' needs.

Avoid the bluebird syndrome!

Unfortunately, the self-fulfilling prophecy "once a bluebird, always a bluebird" often becomes a reality through the grades, and struggling readers suffer from low self-esteem (Slavin, 1987). Studies on intervention indicate, however, that schools need to provide time for intensive interventions for struggling readers (Pikulski, 1994).

Studies on the effects of constant ability grouping are worth considering when deciding how to group your students for literacy instruction. Students needs are best met if you vary the grouping structures in your overall weekly plan and make sure to include interventions for struggling readers, flexibly organized small groups, time

to confer with individual students, student choice activities, partner work, and mixed-ability collaborative groups.

Keep groups flexible.

Try keeping your groups flexible by using constant informal, or formative, assessments. For example, if you are teaching students to summarize, then after students write or draw a summary, collect the samples and sort into piles: those who got it, those who sort of got it, and those who missed the mark. Meet with these groups, formed according to their progress in summarizing, to briefly model and practice together.

Also use random grouping techniques to keep groups flexible. Pass out playing cards—or use other color-code or number techniques—to form randomly organized groups to work on class projects.

Provide intervention in small triad groups.

Use formative assessments during instruction on a regular basis to identify exactly how your students are progressing. Try meeting with just three struggling readers at a time who share similar reading levels or needs (or at least put your three most challenged readers in a group and the rest of the class in groups of five or six). Evaluate their progress constantly to customize your instruction to their needs and to promote growth. (See Chapter 7, "Assessment Survival Tips.")

Allow students to discuss in pairs or groups.

Teachers often complain that their students are not engaged during instruction. One effective way to ensure that students process content and stay involved in your lessons is to provide time for students to work with partners or group members during lessons.

Learning is social, and students use language and discussions to construct negotiated understandings (Vygotsky, 1978). During a first-grade read-aloud, for example, you might pause several times during the book to ask students to share their predictions with a partner. You might pair English learners with more proficient English speakers. Or during a social studies lesson in sixth grade, students may work in teams of four to verbally summarize the chapter and then perform a quick dramatization of an important point they learned.

Incorporate student choice.

When you allow students to form groups based on choice, they become more engaged and motivated to learn. Students first choose a book or topic, then form groups with other students who selected that same title or topic. For example, in fourth grade, students select which type of animal habitat they are interested in and form groups that then read books on their chosen topics. In first grade, after reading aloud Clifford books by Norman Bridwell and Curious George books by Margret and H.A. Rey, I encourage students to choose their favorite character, either Clifford or Curious George. They work in groups to create murals depicting scenes from the books.

Avoid behavior problems by modeling.

Student partners and student-led groups are successful when we model the behaviors we want students to use during those groups. Make a chart with your class to help model and discuss what good partner or group behavior looks like and sounds like. Encourage volunteers to model for the class. Discuss ways to improve.

Sample Partner and Group Behavior Chart

Partner or group behavior looks like	Partner or group behavior sounds like
• Students leaning in using body language to show they are listening • Eye contact • Pleasant looks on faces • Head nodding	• Polite manners • No interrupting • Stay on topic • Piggybacking onto one another's comments: "I agree...." "I also think that...." • Praise for one another: "Nice prediction..." "I liked your summary...."

Lori's Top 5 Surefire Strategies for Grouping

1 Four Corners (Kagan, 1992)

Encourage students to form groups by interest. Four Corners is a cooperative structure that can be used in endless combinations to enhance your reading and literacy lessons. Students choose among four options and meet in a designated corner of the classroom to work with other students who've selected the same option. The teacher circulates to facilitate and direct each of the corners.

Some Ideas for Four Corners

- Four different book titles
- Four characters from a book or books—students decide which character they are most like or that they like the most and then share reasons with cornermates
- Four different response modes (e.g., one corner houses paper for sketching, another materials for creating a drama, another writing supplies, and the fourth art materials)
- Four different writing topics

Procedure for Four Corners

- The teacher presents four choices (e.g., topics, books, response modes) and designates specific corners of the classroom for each.
- Each student indicates which of the four choices he or she prefers by recording it on a paper or sticky note. The teacher may even require that students write reasons for their choices.
- Students gather in the corner of the room designated as the meeting place for their chosen topic or title.
- Encourage students to share their work with other corner groups, or students may gather in home groups made up of one member from each corner.

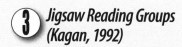

2 Partner Match-Up

Match students across ability levels to partner read. When students partner read in your classroom, you may find that some students experience frustration. For example, your most capable reader may not be patient enough or willing to read with your readers who struggle. Partner Match-Up is an easy solution to your partnering woes! This popular method involves creating a list of your students ranked by reading ability and matching students across reading levels to read together. The partnerships help both students to grow in their reading.

Procedure for Partner Match-Up

- Using your district or informal assessments, rank your students with your top reader as number 1 and your most struggling reader as last, or vice versa.
- Cut the numbered list in half.
- Position the lists side by side. Based on a list of 20 students, if number 1 is your strongest reader, you are pairing him or her with number 11, a reader who reads in the middle of the class. The student who falls in the middle of the class is paired with the one who struggles the most.
- Revise your list and change partners from time to time.
- Occasionally allow students to read with the partner of their choice or their tablemates!

Sample Partner Match-Up List

1. Jose	11. Roberto
2. Maria	12. Angel
3. Rebecca	13. Fernando
4. Vince	14. Keiko
5. Ishmael	15. Jermaine
6. Gretta	16. Otis
7. Cai	17. Vanessa
8. Olivia	18. Tatiana
9. Destiny	19. Lee
10. Ricky	20. Tito

3 Jigsaw Reading Groups (Kagan, 1992)

Engage students in cooperative reading. The students in Mrs. Lopez's fifth-grade class work in groups to read and discuss portions of the social studies chapter. After mastering a portion of the text, students are assigned to home groups, where each student shares his or her expertise on a chunk of the text. The group then collaborates on a quick response, or all members take a quiz to measure their learning.

Procedure for Jigsaw Reading

- Divide the reading material into logical portions by headings, chapters, or pages.
- Place students into home groups of four to six students. Mix ability levels so that students may help one another. Either randomly assign students to groups or

strategically select students for groups. Either name the groups (e.g., after the assigned leader) or allow students to name their groups.

- Count off so that each home group member has a number from 1 to 4. Then call each numbered group to meet either with you or on their own to work through an assigned portion of the text to master that text. You may wish for the jigsaw expert groups to meet simultaneously while you rotate to each to observe or facilitate.
- End the lesson by asking students to return to home groups and share what they've read with their team members. The home group can work on a culminating project or prepare for a quiz.

4 *Little Buddies, Big Buddies*

Provide opportunities to work with cross-age buddies. When you provide time for younger and older students to read together, something magical happens. The first graders and fifth graders pair up around the room, snuggling with books on the floor, at desks, and sprawled together on the carpet. The little ones are spellbound as they look adoringly to their "cool" buddies, and the older students puff up their chests as proud, responsible "teachers" and leaders. The room hums as the 30 pairs of students read, discuss, and laugh their way through books. The best news about this free and engaging intervention is that both cross-age buddies improve in their reading (Topping, 1989), especially the older struggling reader who is teaching a younger child.

Procedure for Cross-Age Buddies

- Select a classroom from a few grade levels above or below yours to partner with for the year. Meet with the other teacher to carefully match up students. Try keeping partners together all year long to bond.
- Set aside a 30-minute time slot for the classes to meet and work together.
- Older students select a title based on the little buddy's interests. The older student practices reading the selected book in the classroom and marks it with sticky notes in spots where he or she will stop and ask questions or promote discussion. Model read-aloud techniques for the older students.
- The older student reads the selected book to the younger student, pausing to predict, make connections, and ask questions. When finished, the pair works together to write and sketch a quick summary of the story.
- Time permitting, you can also provide time for the younger student to read a short leveled text to the older student.
- Keep the session short!

5 *Best Line Cooperative Reading Responses*

Teach students to respond to reading. Written responses help students deepen their comprehension. When coupled with cooperative group work, comprehension soars. A wonderful first-grade teacher, Jenny Dodd, came up with this fun and easy lesson that works at all grade levels. Students select one best sentence from their writing and copy it onto paper strips to combine with those of other students for Best Line Poetry or Responses.

Procedure for Best Line Writing

- Students write a poem about the reading or a character from the text, or they write a response to literature using a variety of starters (Oczkus, 2009), including
  - "I was surprised by...."
  - "Something new I learned was...."
  - "I made a connection to the part where...."
- Students underline their best line or favorite line and copy it onto a paper strip.
- Students work in groups of three or four and combine their best lines to create poems about the reading.
- They prepare to present their best line poems to the class by reading chorally, dramatizing, or acting out their poem.

Before Reading: Activate Prior Knowledge

- Preview the headings in this chapter and the table on page 104. What types of small-group formats do you use to differentiate instruction in your classroom?
- Which are the easiest for you to implement and which are the most difficult? Why?
- Are there any types of groups you'd like to begin using that you have not previously tried?

During Reading: Respond While Reading

- While reading this chapter, mark your text with self-stick notes. Use symbols to indicate questions (?), things you want to try (T), something you connect with (+), something interesting or surprising (!) (adapted from Hatt, n.d.).

After Reading: Think About and Discuss

- Why is it important to employ a rich and varied array of grouping options in classrooms today?
- Study and discuss the Powerful Grouping Options table on page 104. Which options do you implement already? Which would you like to begin using with your students, and what steps will you need to take to start?
- Why is "bluebird syndrome" dangerous?
- How can you avoid the stigma of grouping but still provide the necessary scaffolding and intervention that students need?
- Discuss ways to keep grouping flexible. What is the ideal size for the various groupings at your grade level?
- How does discussion impact reading comprehension?
- What are some effective ways to provide student choice in your groupings?
- Discuss effective ways to model appropriate group discussion behaviors at your grade level. What are the challenges with student-led discussions? How can you make time for the most important grouping models that will meet the needs of your students?

Putting Grouping Into Practice

Professional Development Breakout Groups

- Try a cooperative grouping strategy that you might use with students in a workshop with other teachers.
- Use Four Corners (Kagan, 1992; see description on page 106) with four different children's book titles or response modes to reading the same article. How can you adapt Four Corners for your grade level?
- Make a list of grouping options with a list of possible obstacles to each. How can you overcome these?

Lesson Sharing

- Try one of Lori's Top 5 lessons with your class. Be prepared to share. On a scale of 1–5, how did the lesson go? Explain. What do you want to try next?
- Decide on a simple whole-school plan for cross-age buddy reading (see page 107). At least two grade levels try it and report back to the staff. What is effective about cross-age tutoring? How can you make time for it?

Teacher as Reader

- Do you remember what reading group you were in as a child? Explain. How did that experience make you feel?
- If you are or have ever been in a book club, describe how discussing books can be helpful.
- When you discuss a book with others, how is your comprehension impacted? What are the kinds of comments you make about books? How can you use this information to help you design meaningful group discussions in your classroom?

Before the Next Meeting

Read: Select the next chapter your group will read. Mark the text during reading.

Try: Try one of the lessons from the next chapter, or try something new from this chapter.

Observe: Visit a colleague's classroom to observe a grouping lesson, or record yourself teaching a lesson and share the video at a meeting.

Going Deeper With Grouping

- Try a book study using these practical resources loaded with good ideas about grouping:

  Opitz, M.F., & Ford, M.P. (2008). *Do-able differentiation: Varying groups, texts, and support to reach readers.* Portsmouth, NH: Heinemann.

  Serravallo, J. (2010). *Teaching reading in small groups: Differentiated instruction for building strategic, independent readers*. Portsmouth, NH: Heinemann.

  Tyner, B. (2009). *Small-group reading instruction: A differentiated teaching model for beginning and struggling readers* (2nd ed.). Newark, DE: International Reading Association. Note: Visit www.reading.org/General/Publications/Videos/V9243.aspx for information on the DVD training series.

  Tyner, B., & Green, S.E. (2012). *Small-group reading instruction: Differentiated teaching models for intermediate readers, grades 3–8* (2nd ed.). Newark, DE: International Reading Association.

- Or consider studying the resources listed on page 115.

Small-Group Reading Plan/Think-Aloud Modeling and Coaching Bookmarks Lesson

Objective: There are two bookmarks for teachers. One is for an effective small-group guided-reading lesson plan to use with fiction or nonfiction. The other is a think-aloud model to use along with a coaching-prompt model during small-group lessons.

Common Core Connections: Students provide evidence from the text for all responses. They also ask and answer questions, read closely, compare/contrasts ideas, use decoding and word analysis, discuss text structure, and summarize and determine theme, main ideas, and key details.

Teacher Modeling: Use the Small-Group Reading Plan Bookmark as you guide small groups of readers. Use the Think-Aloud Modeling and Coaching Bookmark when you want to model a particular strategy for your students.

Guided Practice: Ask students to turn to partners and use the same prompt you just modeled. Listen to the pairs and invite students to share with the group. Praise their efforts. As students read silently and independently, work with individuals and coach them on the reading strategies they need.

Independent Practice: Students may use the same prompt as in your think-aloud or any other you choose. They can use self-stick notes to mark the passages they wish to share with the group or a partner.

Wrap Up: Ask students which strategy helped them the most and why. Ask students to set goals. Which strategies do they want or need to work on next?

Independent Work Choices Lesson

Objective: To provide students with a menu of independent work to reinforce key reading strategies and to help them build reading comprehension. Students engage in the work choices during guided reading groups.

Common Core Connections: Students complete each of the work choices using evidence from the text as they compare/contrast and make judgments. Students use many Common Core standards to participate in the menu choices.

Teacher Modeling: Model each of the independent work choices over a few weeks or longer, if necessary. Introduce each one by modeling and demonstrating. Use other pages from this book for further instructions for each of the following:

- Read to Yourself bookmark (page 42)
- Read to a Partner (see Paired Reading Bookmark, page 163)
- Buddy or Circle Conversation (see page 44)
- So Far...Next... (see page 113)
- Read for Real (see "I Wonder," page 84)
- Share Your Book (see page 44)
- Word Work (see Build, Fix, Mix! and other options on pages 145–146)

Guided Practice: Allow time when introducing each Independent Work Choice for students to work in pairs or to practice in teams. Circulate and offer more modeling and support.

Independent Practice: After you've modeled and students have practiced, they should try the Independent Work Choices on their own. Give feedback and return to teacher modeling.

Wrap Up: Discuss and reflect on the success of students' work choices. What problems did they have? How can they improve?

Four Corners/Character Carousel Lesson (Four Corners adapted from Kagan, 1992)

Objective: To deepen student comprehension through character study.

Common Core Connections: Students work collaboratively to discuss characters. Students describe character details, character challenges, and changes the character undergoes over time. They also compare/contrast characters.

Teacher Modeling: Model the independent portion of the lesson. Model how to select a character, explain why you picked that character, and sketch the character. Also, act out a scene with your character in it. Say why you chose that particular scene. Discuss challenges your character faces and the way your character changes throughout the story.

Guided Practice: Guide students as they work on their own to choose a character to sketch. Then designate each of the four corners of the room as meeting places for students who chose the same character. In the corner, students meet to select a scene and practice acting it out. Option: Instead of all the students in a given corner working together in a large group, they can pair up or work in threes. As each group performs a scene and reports on its character, the other students in the class sketch the group's character, reasons, and scene. Encourage students to discuss challenges their characters face and ways each character changes from the beginning of the story to the end.

Independent Practice: Students work on their character choices and reasons. They fill in what the other groups selected and performed.

Wrap Up: Ask students to compare and contrast characters they selected. Discuss. How are these characters the same or different? Discuss. Ask students to reflect on what they did well in this lesson and what they need to improve. Ask them to discuss how talking about characters helps them better understand the story.

Grouping and Assessment Tips

Whole-Class Lessons	Readers' Workshop	Flexible Strategy Groups	Small Teacher-Led Groups
• Use every pupil response, such as slates, thumbs-up, turn and talk to partners. • Observe student responses.	• Confer with individuals. • Confer with partnerships. Carefully match partnerships. • See assessment chapter, page 87. • Clip Board Cruise (page 93)	• Collect student samples. Simple is best. For example, ask students to write four questions. Collect. Make piles: *–those who get it* *–those who need lots of help or just some help* • Change strategy groups often. • See Chapter 7 on assessment.	• Use running records and retellings to place students in groups and to help monitor progress. • See Chapter 7 on assessment.
Literature Circles	**Intervention Group**	**Cross-Age Tutors**	**Independent Reading**
• Students turn in individual responses to reading. • Clip Board Cruise (page 93)	• Use informal reading inventory and other assessments outlined in Chapter 7.	• Group students so that the older student is more capable than the younger one. • Observe pairs. • Ask the older student to assess the younger child's progress.	• Use My Independent Reading Evaluation, page 43. • Confer with students.

Small-Group Reading Plan Bookmark

Grouping/Book Selection Guidelines

Choose a book for small groups based on student reading level, interest in the same titles, formative assessments (see Chapter 7).

Before Reading

- **Connect**—Invite students to briefly look over the cover and flip through the text. Ask students what they think they know about a topic or what connections they are making.
- **Predict**—Ask students to preview the illustrations, headings, text structure, key vocabulary, and text to form predictions. What do they think they will learn, or what is the selection about?

Optional: Introduce a graphic organizer for the text.

- **Question**—Invite students to discuss questions or what they wonder before reading.

During Reading

- **Silent Reading**—Students read silently and independently while you quietly coach individuals.
- **Predict/Question**—Students watch for their predictions and questions as they read.

Promote active reading by giving students a self-stick note to mark one or more strategies.

- **Clarify**—Look for words, ideas, sensory descriptions. Clarify words using beginning sounds, ending sounds, chunks, sounding out/blending, syllables, root words.
- **Question**—Ask more questions.
- **Summarize**—So far what has happened?
- **Synthesize**—What is surprising, interesting?

After Reading

- **Predict/Question**—Discuss changes in thinking.
- **Summarize/Synthesize**—Summarize.
- **Compare/Contrast**—Compare and contrast ideas within the text or with other texts students have read.

Optional: Fill in a graphic organizer for the text.

- **Clarify, Infer, Connect, Evaluate**—Choose one or more to discuss.

Think-Aloud Modeling and Coaching Bookmark

Model for a Think-Aloud (Oczkus, 2007)

Select a comprehension strategy (connect, predict, question, clarify, summarize, infer, synthesize, evaluate) to briefly model for students, using the text the small group is reading.

- **Introduce**—Tell students they will model a reading strategy. Ask, "What do you know about this strategy?" (Optional: metaphor, prop, gesture; see page 51.) Discuss purpose of the strategy. For example: "Questions help us to stay interested in the reading."
- **Model**—Read a portion of text aloud and demonstrate the strategy.
- **Guided Practice**—Ask students to turn to a partner and try the strategy using the text selected for the group.
- **Independent Practice**—Give students a self-stick note to mark where they use the strategy during silent reading in small-group time or readers' workshop.

Coaching Individuals During Small-Group Instruction or Readers' Workshop

- **Student Reads**—Ask the student to whisper or quietly read aloud a few sentences to you.
- **Choose a Strategy**—Coach the student on comprehension strategies based on one of the following:
  - *your modeling*
  - *a strategy the student needs*
  - *a strategy the student chooses*
- **Coach**—Using the questioning strategy as an example, ask the student to read a portion of text and make up a question to go with it. If the student experiences difficulty, the teacher models and asks the child to try questioning with the next portion of text. Or if a child is stuck on a word, coach and help the child figure it out (see page 150).
- **Goal Set**—Ask the student what he/she will work on during independent reading.

Independent Work Choices During Small-Group Instruction Time

Read to Yourself	Read to a Partner	Buddy or Circle Conversation
■ Read your independent reading book silently. ■ Use a self-stick note or two. Or write in your reader's notebook. Mark • *a favorite part* • *a funny part* • *confusing or cool word or part* • *a connection* • *a question* • *anything else* ■ Use your bookmark to help you read.	■ Read with a partner. Use the Paired Reading bookmark or take turns. ■ Use your bookmarks to talk about the book.	■ Fill in your Circle Conversation sheet. ■ Write or draw • *a summary* • *evaluation score for the reading* • *a connection* • *overall score for the book*
So Far...Next... (Oczkus, 2007)	**Word Work**	**Read for Real**
■ Read to page _______. ■ Stop and sketch two drawings: one for what has happened so far and one for what you think will happen next. So far... Next... ■ Read more and do it again!	■ Study spelling words. ■ Play Build, Fix, Mix! (Pinnell & Fountas, 1998) alone or with a partner. 1. Make each word using magnetic letters or cards. 2. Mix up the letters. 3. Build the word. 4. Check it. 5. Write it.	■ Pick a nonfiction book that you are interested in. ■ Fill out an "I wonder" chart in your notebook or on a paper. Write "wonders" before, during, and after reading. ■ Use your Informational Text Bookmark (see page 83). ■ Sketch something you learned in your journal.
Prep a Lesson	**Create a Cover**	**Share Your Book**
■ Prepare to read a book with your cross-age tutor. ■ Practice reading the book three times and put self-stick notes on three pages where you will stop to ask questions.	■ Make a book cover using the ReadWriteThink Book Cover Creator (www.readwritethink.org/classroom-resources/student-interactives/book-cover-creator-30058.html).	■ Make a shelf card for the library. Write or type a 15- to 20-word review. Give a score.

Four Corners/Character Carousel

Directions:

- Choose the character from the reading that you think is most interesting.
- Fill in the first Character Carousel box with your character. Leave the rest blank.
- Go to a corner of the room to join other students who also chose your character.
- Share your Character Carousel drawings and boxes. Plan your group presentation.
- Fill in the other three boxes after each group presents.

1	2
Name of character ____________ • I chose this character because ____________ ____________________. • Make a quick teeny sketch of your character. • Our group is acting out a scene from page _____ because ____________.	**Name of character** ____________ • The group chose this character because ____________________. • Make a quick teeny sketch of the character. • The group is acting out a scene from page _____ because ____________.
3	**4**
Name of character ____________ • The group chose this character because ____________________. • Make a quick teeny sketch of the character. • The group is acting out a scene from page _____ because ____________.	**Name of character** ____________ • The group chose this character because ____________________. • Make a quick teeny sketch of the character. • The group is acting out a scene from page _____ because ____________.

Web Resources

***Reciprocal Teaching at Work* Classroom Video Clips: www.reading.org/General/Publications/Books/SupplementalContent/BK507_SUPPLEMENT.aspx**
Reciprocal Teaching lessons show students in whole-class settings, guided reading groups, and literature circles.

ReadWriteThink: www.readwritethink.org
ReadWriteThink is a great resource for hundreds of free downloadable lessons in all aspects of reading. Try "Book Clubs: Reading for Fun" (Grades 3–5) by Traci Gardner.

Annenberg Learner.org Teaching Reading 3–5 Workshop: www.learner.org/resources/series204.html
Provides wonderful online videos on a variety of topics for staff development at no cost to teachers. Richard Allington and others have contributed.

"When you vary the ways you group students, the classroom becomes an engaging learning atmosphere where students become better readers, thinkers, and independent learners."

Q&A

"Time is my biggest problem. How can I meet with all my designated groups during the course of a week?"

In the course of a day, you will not be able to meet with every group, but you can rotate through your groups every few days. You may want to meet with your three to five most challenged readers daily. Literature circles meet in upper grades at least twice per week.

A readers' workshop is another effective way to meet individual needs while incorporating some guided reading groups. In a workshop, students read their self-selected books while the teacher circulates to confer with students, taking notes to keep track of student progress. During readers' workshop, the teacher may opt to gather and teach three or four students who need to work on the same skills or strategies.

Select which types of groupings best fit your grade level and situation, and create weekly routines.

References

Allington, R.L. (2006). *What really matters for struggling readers: Designing research-based programs* (2nd ed.). Boston: Allyn & Bacon.

Hatt, C. (n.d.). *Better discussions in study groups*. Retrieved from www.choiceliteracy.com/public/796.cfm

Kagan, S. (1992). *Cooperative learning*. San Juan Capistrano, CA: Resources for Teachers.

Oczkus, L.D. (2007). *Guided writing: Practical lessons, powerful results*. Portsmouth, NH: Heinemann.

Oczkus, L.D. (2009). *Interactive think-aloud lessons: 25 surefire ways to engage students and improve comprehension*. New York: Scholastic; Newark, DE: International Reading Association.

Opitz, M.F., & Ford, M.P. (2008). *Do-able differentiation: Varying groups, texts, and supports to reach readers*. Portsmouth, NH: Heinemann.

Pikulski, J.J. (1994). Preventing reading failure: A review of five effective programs. *The Reading Teacher, 48*(1), 30–39.

Pinnell, G.S., & Fountas, I.C. (1998). *Word matters: Teaching phonics and spelling in the reading/writing classroom*. Portsmouth, NH: Heinemann.

Serravallo, J. (2010). *Teaching reading in small groups: Differentiated instruction for building strategic, independent readers*. Portsmouth, NH: Heinemann.

Slavin, R.E. (1987). Ability grouping and student achievement in elementary schools: A best-evidence synthesis. *Review of Educational Research, 57*(3), 293–335.

Topping, K. (1989). Peer tutoring and paired reading: Combining two powerful techniques. *The Reading Teacher, 42*(7), 488–494.

Tyner, B. (2009). *Small-group reading instruction: A differentiated teaching model for beginning and struggling readers* (2nd ed.). Newark, DE: International Reading Association.

Tyner, B., & Green, S.E. (2012). *Small-group reading instruction: Differentiated teaching models for intermediate readers, grades 3–8* (2nd ed.). Newark, DE: International Reading Association.

Vygotsky, L.S. (1978). *Mind in society: The development of higher psychological processes* (M. Cole, V. John-Steiner, S. Scribner, & E. Souberman, Eds. & Trans.). Cambridge, MA: Harvard University Press.

CHAPTER 9

Wonderful Words: Guidelines and TOP 5 Lessons to Improve Vocabulary and Reading

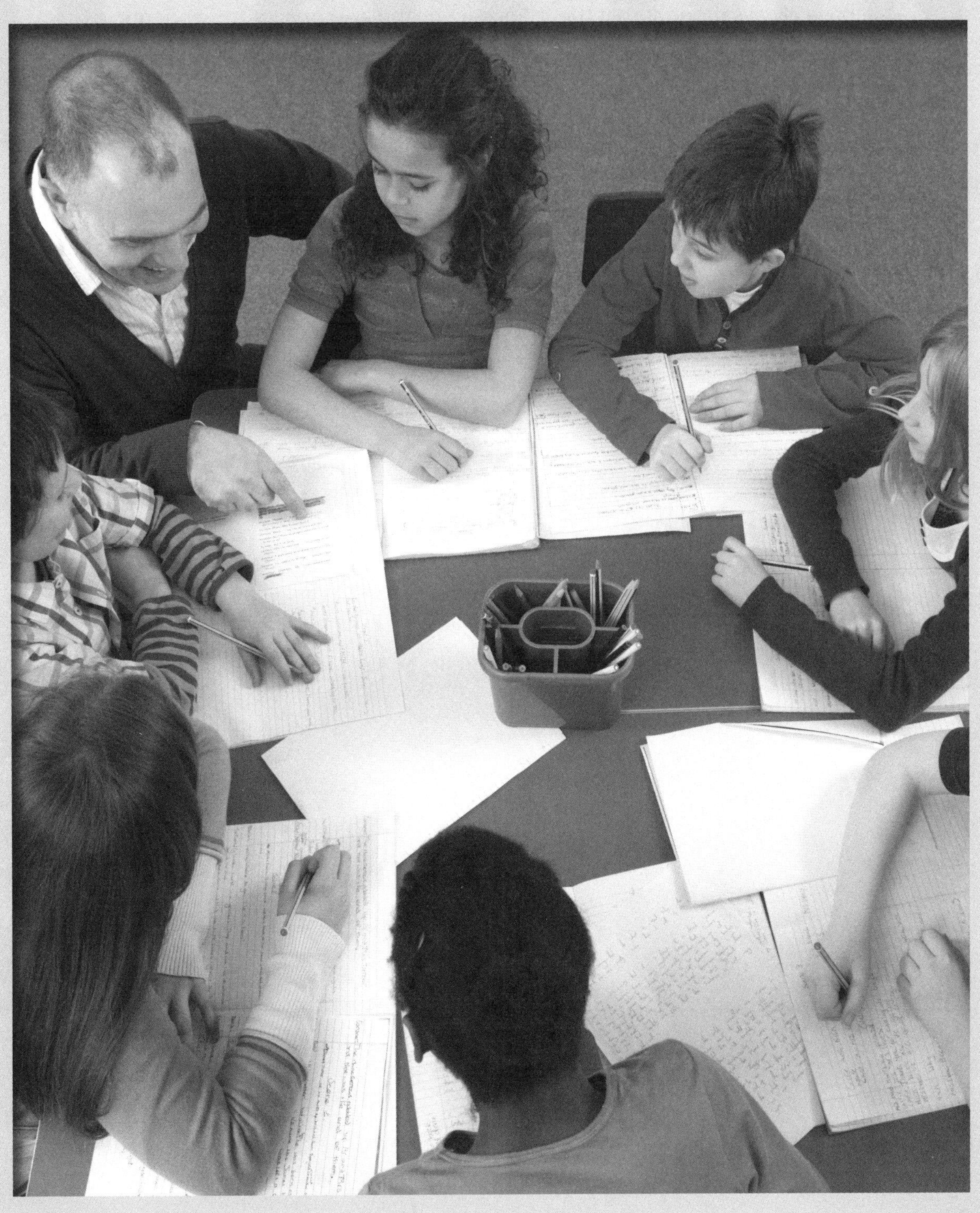

Best Ever Advice on... Vocabulary

I have always thought that the toughest vocabulary concept for students to comprehend is the idiom, because idiomatic expressions require a lot of explaining and vary greatly by culture. Think about all the idioms associated with rain: "it's raining cats and dogs," "rain check," "when it rains, it pours," "don't rain on my parade," to name just a few. Encouraging students to work with partners and in small groups to write about, illustrate, create songs, or act out skits that demonstrate idioms is a great way to engage students and differentiate instruction. Most important, teachers who encourage students to work with idioms can promote language development in a fun and meaningful way.

—Danny Brassell, Author of *Dare to Differentiate: Vocabulary Strategies for All Students* (Guilford, 2011)

Perhaps when you were a student in school you remember a teacher passing out a list of 20–30 words on Monday with the expectation that you would master and learn the words by the test on Friday.

Often not much direct teaching occurred with the words in class and you wrote sentences and copied dictionary definitions to help you "learn" the list of vocabulary. Deep learning doesn't occur when we simply ask students to memorize lists of words (Beck, McKeown, & Kucan, 2002). Unfortunately, this age-old practice still thrives in many classrooms today in spite of the fact that researchers tell us that students don't learn words this way! Each student in the classroom learns a bit differently, and fortunately today there are many interesting ways to reinforce and teach vocabulary.

Vocabulary instruction is absolutely critical to the overall literacy success of our students. When I survey audiences of teachers all over the country and ask what problems their students experience with reading comprehension, vocabulary tops the list every time. Researchers verify that vocabulary is one of the greatest predictors of reading comprehension (Baker, Simmons, & Kame'enui, 1998), and in order to learn any content area material, students need to be able to comprehend new vocabulary. Vocabulary also greatly affects writing. Students who possess richer vocabularies write better. So if vocabulary is so important, how can we best teach it?

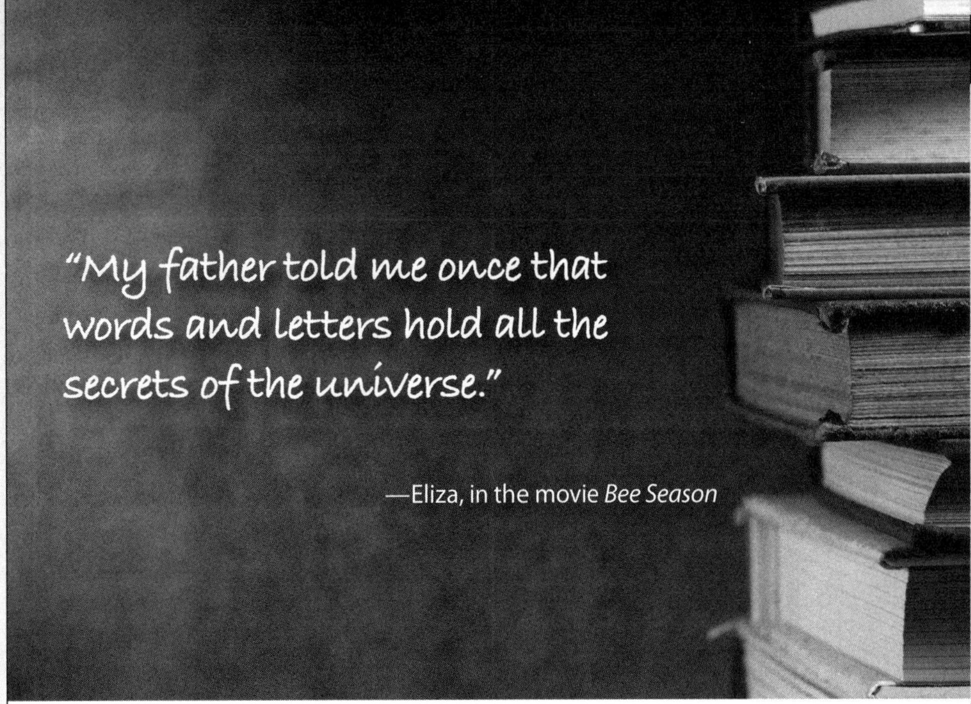

Let's take a quick peek in some classrooms to see some examples of exciting vocabulary lessons in action! These lively lessons are a far cry from the "look up the words in the dictionary, copy the definition, and write a sentence" variety that some of us experienced all through school. Vocabulary instruction today needs to be rich, interesting, multidimensional, and rigorous to prepare our students to deal with the constant barrage of words they face in school and in the world they live.

- *Sixth graders huddle around the room as they illustrate vocabulary for the social studies unit on Egypt. Some gather around computers as they create word splashes using a computer program, while others huddle on the floor and sketch with markers on large posters to create a mural of words that they will act out in skits later in the day. The class adds the history words along with illustrations to their Alpha Box word wall for the unit on Egypt (Hoyt, 1999). Later, the class plays a round of Wordo (Cunningham, 2008), a version of bingo where students select the words for their game card.*
- *Third graders, mostly English language learners (ELLs), line up in a conga line to simultaneously march around the room to music as they use movements to represent the key vocabulary words from their most recent basal story. The words flash on the interactive whiteboard, and students create gestures midmarch to demonstrate their understanding of the chosen words.*
- *First graders gather around the kidney-shaped table as their teacher leads the guided reading with a picture walk of the book* Living Dinosaurs *by Jonathan Scott and Angela Scott (HarperCollins, 2008) that includes discussions of rich vocabulary about crocodiles and lizards. Their teacher introduces words on sticky notes, and the group helps her organize the vocabulary in a word sort and Venn diagram to help the students compare crocodiles and monitor lizards. Students each select a word and sketch a drawing to accompany it on the organizer.*

The Critical Impact of Vocabulary on Literacy

Rich, interesting vocabulary usage is the hallmark of an intelligent, well-read, educated person and

is the key to unlocking reading comprehension. A handbook titled *100 Words to Make You Sound Smart* (Houghton Mifflin, 2006) rests on my desk and offers inviting word gems like *disheveled*, *capricious*, and *insidious*. The editors promise that if I use these words in my everyday, speaking vocabulary, my utterances will be memorable, thus making me sound "smarter"! (The same series also touts *100 Words Every High School Graduate Should Know* and *100 Words Every Word Lover Should Know*!)

Vocabulary directly influences not only your ability to communicate but also your ability to comprehend what you read. As you select your own summer reading for pleasure, you will likely thumb through books and choose titles based on your interest in the topic and the vocabulary load. As we skim through and sample a text, if there are too many challenging words, we, even as adult readers, might avoid selecting that book. Vocabulary load is the essential key that can make or break the reading experience for a reader.

Teachers pose many important questions regarding vocabulary instruction including:

- What are the challenges that students face while learning vocabulary?
- What vocabulary words should I teach to my students?
- How do I help my ELLs catch up in learning essential vocabulary?
- What is the best way to teach and differentiate vocabulary instruction?
- How much time should I spend teaching vocabulary to my students?

Some Important Facts You Should Know About Vocabulary

Students are bombarded every day with thousands of words from books, conversations, the media, and the Internet. Researchers tell us the following essential facts about vocabulary and our students.

- **Students need to learn a minimum of 3,000 words per year!** This incredibly staggering number (Nagy, 1988) makes it impossible to directly teach them all! Anderson (1996) estimates that we would need to teach 20 words per day every day of the school year. That is at least 100 words per week that our students need to master!
- **Children who enter kindergarten with weak vocabulary skills encounter difficulty learning to read.** Hart and Risley (1995) found huge differences in vocabulary levels of kindergarteners based on socioeconomic level. Children with parents who are professionals enter school with a vocabulary of 1,100 words, children from working-class families know around 650 words, and children whose families are on welfare know just over 400 words. This knowledge gap widens through the school years.
- **Unfortunately vocabulary used in everyday conversations and on television shows is limited.** Prime-time television shows feature less challenging vocabulary than children's books. Even most of the conversations of college graduates contain vocabulary less challenging than many preschool books (Cunningham and Stanovich, 1998).
- **Vocabulary instruction is often neglected in schools**. Schools often devote very little class time to vocabulary instruction (Scott, Jamieson-Noel, & Asselin, 2003). Practices such as writing definitions are ineffective yet often are among the most common vocabulary assignments. In addition, researchers tell us that the vocabulary instruction in basals is not enough to make up the gap that some students have in their vocabulary development.
- **Researchers agree that there are three types of vocabulary words that students need to learn:** Tier I, or general; Tier II, or specialized;

and Tier III, or technical (Beck et al., 2002; Vacca & Vacca, 2002). Tier I words are often found in our speaking vocabularies. ELL students need to be taught these words. Tier II words are considered academic and instructional and are the ones we often focus our instruction on in school. Words like *permeate*, *compare*, and *generalize* fall into this category. Tier III words are specialized and technical words that depend upon the topic in study. For example if we are discussing elections we might study the words *primary*, *campaign*, *caucus*, and *delegate*.

- **Teaching vocabulary improves reading comprehension for both native English speakers** (Beck, Perfetti, & McKeown, 1982) and English learners (Carlo et al., 2004).

Vocabulary in Action in the Classroom

Primary example

Before reading a nonfiction piece about frogs from the basal reader, Mrs. Sanchez introduces the class to a graphic organizer, a circular-shaped web to record facts about frogs. The students turn to a partner and picture walk through the text, noting what they already know before reading. The students work in pairs to write on sticky notes at least two things they know about frogs. The students take turns placing their sticky notes on the chart. Mrs. Sanchez leads the group in categorizing their words into groups, including what a frog looks like, what a frog eats, where a frog lives, and what a frog does. After reading, the students select vocabulary to dramatize.

Intermediate example

As the sixth graders meet in their literature circle to discuss the chapter from Gary Paulsen's Hatchet, *discussion of vocabulary comes up throughout their chat. Yuri, the discussion director, pauses to invite the group members to share their thoughts, which center on clarifying the actions of the main character, Brian. Vocabulary words such as* branches, weaving, *and the* whine of the mosquitoes *pop up during the lively discussion. Clayton notices the author's craft and use of rich vocabulary and his own ability to visualize when the author describes Brian's face as* bleeding, swollen, lumpy, bloody, *and* scabbed all over. *The summarizer, Elisa, finishes off the interaction with a three-sentence summary that includes many concept words like* survive, create, *and* foliage. *Students return to their desks and, in their reading journals, record interesting words along with sentences and sketches to illustrate those words.*

Guidelines for Effective Vocabulary Instruction

Set goals for vocabulary instruction.

Leading vocabulary expert Michael Graves and colleagues (Graves, 2006; Graves & Watts-Taffe, 2002) share four goals for vocabulary instruction that include the following goals:

1. Facilitate wide reading.
The importance of wide reading in the growth of students' vocabulary is critical (Nagy and Anderson, 1984). Encourage students to read both in and outside of school. Conduct read-alouds by pointing out key vocabulary before reading as well as throughout the process. Expose students to all types of genres in read-alouds and with their independent reading. Have students keep reading logs that list the titles they read independently so you can see that they are reading all kinds of texts, genres, and topics. Wide reading also includes reading aloud to younger students and less proficient students. Reading aloud to students promotes vocabulary growth. Shared reading is also a widely documented strategy for increasing vocabulary.

Teaching Idea: Discuss vocabulary before and after read-alouds. Introduce vocabulary prior to reading aloud. Create hand motions to go with each word you introduce. During the read-aloud, students listen for the key word and

demonstrate its meaning with a quick hand gesture.

2. Teach individual words.
The most helpful instruction includes working with definitions and context and then incorporating the student's prior knowledge along with comparing and contrasting meanings. Frequent exposure to words and how they are related (e.g., graphic organizers) makes instruction more "robust."

Teaching Idea: Encourage students to use words outside of class. At one elementary school, students keep a tally on a chart and also discuss when they use, see, or hear the words for the week being used outside of school. After a certain number of tally marks, the class is rewarded with a party.

3. Provide word-learning strategies.
Since it is impossible to teach all the words that students need to know, we can instead give them strategies for figuring out words on their own. Teach students to look both around words using context and in words using word parts. Use dictionaries and glossaries when necessary. Provide opportunities for students to sort words that they are studying. Put words on individual cards, pieces of paper, or sticky notes so students can sort words into categories based on meaning or word parts.

Teaching Idea: Conduct think-alouds where you select a challenging word and demonstrate how you figure it out by using both context (looking around the word) and by word parts (looking in the word). Provide practice with partners implementing the same procedure. Encourage students to share new words they encountered and figured out from their own reading. As a fun option, wear goofy glasses when conducting your think-aloud. Tell students each lens helps you to look both "around" and "in" words to figure them out! Encourage students to be word detectives as they use strategies for figuring out words.

4. Foster word consciousness.
Word consciousness means that in our classrooms we provide a word-rich environment that includes wordplay, word collecting, and games with words. Be sure to have students help you post words in the room on word walls, graphic organizers, and charts.

Teaching Idea: Create a Word-a-Day collection by asking students to collect one word every day to add to their personal dictionaries. Or make it a schoolwide initiative with Words of the Week (Frey & Fisher, 2007). Select words based on themes such as weather, animals, or government. Also try selecting words based on Latin and Greek roots e.g., Distract—attract, retract, protractor, tractor, subtract, extract (Rasinski, Padak, Newton, & Newton, 2011).

Teach from three categories of words.
Teachers may want to look at three primary sources for individual vocabulary words: (1) the new vocabulary that relates to understanding a unit's goals and objectives, (2) basic sight words and high-frequency words, and (3) words found in students' writing (Brassell, 2011).

Allow students to self-select some vocabulary to learn.
Vocabulary self-collection strategy (Haggard, 1986; Readence, Bean, & Baldwin, 2001; Ruddell, 1992) places the responsibility for learning words on the students. Students scan the reading material and select words they want to learn or that they wish to teach to the group. They can keep a word-learning journal for illustrating and saving special words. Students love generating their own vocabulary lists and are often more interested in learning words that they have selected.

Discuss vocabulary before and throughout reading.
Any time you spend teaching vocabulary that relates to the reading students are engaged in is time well spent (Beck & McKeown, 1983). Ask students what they know about a topic as they participate in

a one-minute book look (Oczkus, 2004). Students flip through a book for only one minute as they think about what they know about the topic. Then, during a second round or more detailed preview of the text, the teacher explains some core vocabulary that students will need to understand the selection as well as to encourage them to predict what the text is about. During reading, the teacher asks students to clarify and discuss words that are confusing to them. Provide sticky notes so students may note interesting or challenging words in the text. After reading, students and the teacher build a graphic organizer to fill with words.

Provide scaffolds to build the vocabulary of ELLs.

Read-alouds, shared reading, science experiments, discussions, video clips, photos, and word games all become contexts for learning more words for ELLs. It takes much exposure to words and concepts for language learning to stick. On a trip to the zoo, my first graders delighted in seeing the animals they'd read about. One ELL spotted a chipmunk and called out, "Look at the beaver!" The teachable moment prompted a rich discussion of animals with bushy tails and their specific names.

Make vocabulary learning fun!

Our students have "multiple intelligences" (Gardner, 1983) and learn in different ways. Some students may enjoy making flashcards with drawings, while others may prefer acting out words or playing games on the computer to reinforce vocabulary. Brain research supports teaching students using nonlinguistic representations for abstract concepts and vocabulary (Marzano, 2004, 2010). In order to differentiate instruction and provide a healthy, rich, and varied diet of vocabulary activities, try adding art, drama, music, and games to your repertoire of vocabulary lessons.

Here are some ideas to get you started:

Try movement or music for vocabulary.

Show a clip from the episode of the popular television program *Hannah Montana*, where Miley creates a dance and a song to help her memorize the bones in the body. Encourage students to do the same with words your class is studying.

Introduce games, drama, and art.

Games are a great way to engage students. Try charades with words. Or play a version of bingo called Wordo (Cunningham, 2008), where students use a blank card and fill it with words from the word wall in your classroom or from a list of words the class is studying. If you want to incorporate drama, have students make up skits about vocabulary and present them to the class. Try videotaping with a pocket camera and posting on the school or classroom website.

Share wordplay games and books.

Miss Alaineus: A Vocabulary Disaster by Debra Frasier

The Boy Who Loved Words by Roni Schotter

Puniddles by Bruce McMillan

Mom and Dad Are Palindromes: A Dilemma for Words...and Backwards by Mark Shulman

There's A Frog in My Throat: *440 Animal Sayings a Little Bird Told Me* by Loreen Leedy and Pat Street

Hairy, Scary, Ordinary: What Is an Adjective? by Brian P. Cleary

Lori's Top 5 Surefire Strategies for Vocabulary Instruction

1 *Colorful Words*

This activity is often called shades of meaning (Goodman, 2004) and is a teacher and student favorite that you can use with any words! The purpose of the activity is to demonstrate the differences and nuances between synonyms.

- Brainstorm as a class lists of words. Start with words for feelings (happy, sad, angry, and so on).
- Visit your local paint store and collect a variety paint chips.
- Ask students to help you select which words go with each of the colors. Display the colors and matching words on a bulletin board or word wall.

2 *One-Word Prediction and Word Sort (Oczkus, 2004, 2009)*

Students predict words that they think might be in the text based on a picture walk before reading. After predicting words, they sort, illustrate, and study them.

- Picture walk with students through a text by previewing headings, some key vocabulary, and illustrations.
- Close the book and ask students to select a word they think might be in the text.
- Students work in pairs or alone to write their word on a sticky note.
- Students all hold up their words at the count of three. Call on students who have the same words or synonyms to stand and then place their words on a chart.
- Lead students in sorting the words into logical categories. Label the categories.

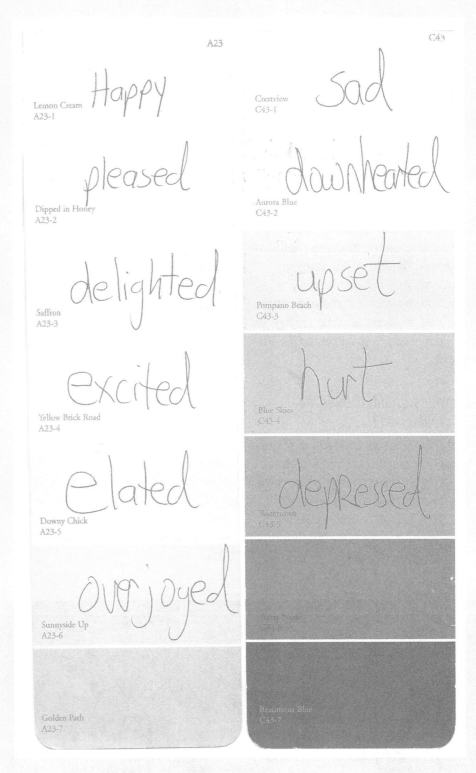

Words We Predict for ***Thunder Cake*** by Patricia Polacco

Baking a cake	Feelings	Weather
eggs	scared	rain
flour	hug	thunder
milk	scared	lightning
strawberries		

- Ask students to make predictions based on the words: "We think ________ will happen because ________."
- During reading students watch for the displayed words.
- After reading, provide students with options as they return to the words.
- Students may re-sort, illustrate, dramatize, or create drawings of the words to accompany them. You may also have students sort words by meaning or by word structure (base words, spellings, parts of speech, etc.).

 Word Jars

In the book *Donavan's Word Jar* (Monalisa Degross), Donavan is a young boy who doesn't collect snake skins, butterfly wings, or even coins. He collects words! Donavan collects big words that make him feel smart; common words, like cuddle, to warm his heart; silly words, like squabble, that tickle his ears; and strange words that make him wonder. Wouldn't it be great if we could teach all of our students to love words as much as Donavan?

- Try inspiring your students to be word collectors by reading *Donavan's Word Jar* aloud.
- Provide each student with a small container (empty milk carton, baby-food jar, or small box) and strips of paper for recording words. Students collect words and occasionally dump their collections to sort words, trade, illustrate, and act out words.

 A–Z Chart (Frey & Fisher, 2009; Hoyt, 1999)

The A–Z chart is an easy way to build a classroom word wall during a unit of study. For example create a chart when studying frogs, state history, or Egypt.

- Display a chart with 26 boxes, one for each letter of the alphabet. Or use construction paper pages for each letter or group letters (e.g., one page for A, B, C, and D).
- Invite students to brainstorm words they know about a topic, such as photosynthesis. Throughout the unit, they can help you fill in the chart.
- Periodically use the chart of words to play games, such as concentration, guessing riddles, acting out words, or charades.

 Key Word Dance or Key Word March (Oczkus, 2009)

This is a really motivating, active way to bring words to life. Students use motions to illustrate words to music. One third-grade teacher adapted my Key Word Dance idea to teach selection vocabulary with her ELLs.

- Select vocabulary from a text your class is reading.
- Together create hand motions to go with the words.
- Put the words on flashcards.
- One student holds up the word cards one at a time.
- A select group of 6–8 students from the class is chosen to move in a conga line around the room. The "marchers" look at the displayed word card and make that movement. They change their movement to match the card that the card holder chooses to show.
- Play music so students can "march" or "dance" as they review vocabulary. Try Paul Simon's "Diamonds on the Soles of Her Shoes."

Q&A

I am overwhelmed by all of this good information about vocabulary. How can I use these activities in a given week to effectively teach vocabulary?

The good news is you don't have to use all of these rich, fun activities in the same week! Just try making your classroom a word-conscious place where you teach words but also teach students to figure out words on their own.

Incorporate vocabulary ideas in some way into every lesson. One way to do that is to teach words that go with your grade-level reading selection and your content area teaching. Naturally, many words will come up in those curricular areas that you can put into a weekly list for teaching and actively reviewing. It is also important to teach high-frequency words and words the students need for their writing. These words can be included in your weekly list and can also be displayed on a word wall. Students should keep a word-learning notebook where they record words, sketches, and lists of interesting words to use in their writing. If you have centers or workstations going, students can participate in drama, art, or games with the words you are studying. Perhaps you can also select words to sort each week that can be sorted in a variety of ways by meaning, length, word part, and so on.

See the many excellent professional books suggested in this chapter for other ideas.

Before Reading: Activate Prior Knowledge

- Do you agree with the quote from the movie *Bee Season*? Why or why not?
- What vocabulary lessons, games, and techniques are successful with your students?
- Discuss problems you experience while teaching vocabulary to students.
- Which texts have more challenging vocabulary, and how do you deal with the vocabulary load?

During Reading: Respond While Reading

- While reading this chapter, mark your text with self-stick notes. Use symbols to indicate questions (?), things you want to try (T), something you connect with (+), something interesting or surprising (!) (adapted from Hatt, n.d.).

After Reading: Think About and Discuss

- Why is vocabulary so important, and what are some ways it impacts literacy development? Discuss ways to think about which words to teach.
- How does wide reading impact vocabulary acquisition? What else do students need?
- What are some ways to promote word learning and word consciousness?
- Why is it important to allow students to self-select some vocabulary?
- What kind of support do ELL students need to acquire vocabulary? How can you use nonlinguistic representations (Marzano, 2004) to help not only ELLs but all students understand and develop vocabulary?
- With so many words to teach, how can you choose which ones to teach and the best way to do so for your grade level?

Putting Vocabulary Into Practice

Professional Development Breakout Groups

- Get into groups of five. Each group studies one of the Top 5 lessons, discusses it, and creates a poster. Using a student text, write a quick lesson plan. Share with the other groups.

Lesson Sharing

- Try one of Lori's Top 5 lessons with your class. Be prepared to share. On a scale of 1–5, how did the lesson go? Explain. What do you want to try next?
- Observe your ELL students in the lessons. What extra support do they need? Which words do they self-select? Try adding a special, brief small-group time to play a vocabulary game or teach one of the lessons to your ELL students.

Teacher as Reader

- What do you remember doing to study vocabulary as a child?
- Do you enjoy word games, teasers, etc., as an adult? Explain.
- When you read, do you notice and appreciate interesting or new vocabulary? Name an author whom you enjoy reading because of the way he or she uses words.
- What special-interest topics do you read about when you need to delve deeper to understand new vocabulary?

Before the Next Meeting

Read: Select the next chapter your group will read. Mark the text during reading.
Try: Try one of the lessons from the next chapter, or try something new from this chapter.
Observe: Visit a colleague's classroom to observe a lesson on vocabulary, or record yourself teaching a lesson and share the video at a meeting.

Going Deeper With Vocabulary

- Try a book study using these practical resources loaded with everything you need to know about vocabulary:

  Bear, D.R., Invernizzi, M.R., Templeton, S., & Johnston, F. (2012). *Words their way: Word study for phonics, vocabulary, and spelling instruction* (5th ed.). Boston: Allyn & Bacon.

  Brassell, D. (2011). *Dare to differentiate: Vocabulary strategies for all students*. New York: Guilford.

- Or consider studying the resources listed on page 133.

Magic Words Bookmark Lesson

Objective: To encourage students to collect a variety of vocabulary words as they read.

__Common Core Connections:__ Determine and clarify known and unknown words while reading using an array of grade-appropriate strategies (phonics, word analysis, and context). Demonstrate understanding of word relationships.

Teacher Modeling: Read aloud from a text and think aloud as you marvel at words! Select some of the bookmark prompts to help you select words.

Guided Practice: Encourage students to work in pairs or teams and to collect words on self-stick notes. Then students can make a poster using the word categories or others they create to group their words. They may illustrate and act out words for the class.

Independent Practice: Students keep a running list of favorite words either in their journals or on the bookmark (or on paper the same size as the bookmark). Students share words with partners. Encourage and praise students for noticing interesting words as they read. Coach as necessary.

Wrap Up: Ask students to share their words and reasons for selecting them. How does awareness and appreciation of vocabulary increase one's reading? Ask students to reflect.

Wonderful Words Sorting Sheet Lesson

Objective: To encourage students to group words into different categories by cutting apart the words and sorting word cards according to varied criteria. Students participate in both closed or assigned sorts as well as open sorts in which they create the categories for the words. Words may be selected by the teacher or the students.

__Common Core Connections:__ Demonstrate understanding of word relationships and meanings. Demonstrate connections among words. Categorize words by key attributes and shades of meaning.

Teacher Modeling: Model how to sort words using word cards and the various word-sort categories listed on the Wonderful Word Sort sheet. Use either a Smart Board, pocket chart with index cards, or overhead projector so that all students may see the words you are sorting. Think aloud as you read each word and show how you decide which category to place it in.

Guided Practice: During your lesson, pause so that pairs can discuss the words you are sorting; invite them to show whether or not they agree with your group choices by giving a thumbs-up or thumbs-down. You may also give pairs some words to sort; circulate as they do so to prompt and offer support.

Independent Practice: Give students words to sort or allow them to fill the boxes with words they select from the reading. Encourage students to word sort on their own and sort the cards into at least three categories before gluing them down and labeling the categories. (Alternatively, you can make a pocket or give students an envelope in which to store the words.)

Wrap Up: Ask students to reflect on the word-sorting activity. What did they learn? What words do they enjoy the most? Which are the most difficult to categorize? Which words do they think they will use the most in their reading and writing?

Assessment Tips

Assessing vocabulary can be tricky. The depth of "knowing" a word varies for each word and student. Beck, McKeown, and Omanson (1987) refer to word knowledge as a continuum that includes

- No knowledge of a word
- General understanding of a word
- Knowing a word in one context only
- Knowing a word but not recalling it for use in a situation
- Depth of knowledge of a particular word's meanings, origins

Assessing vocabulary requires multiple measures including classroom observations, formal reading program assessments (such as multiple choice or end of unit vocabulary tests), and classroom informal measures. The wonderful vocabulary ideas shared in this section are Stahl and Bravo (2010).

Examples of Classroom Informal Vocabulary Measures

Before students read a selection, you can give a quick vocabulary pretest to use again as a posttest to gauge what they've learned. Possible informal pretests for vocabulary:

- A graphic organizer
- A vocabulary pretest (see sample)
- Cloze procedure: Use a paragraph or two from the book and leave out key words for students to fill in. Or write a paragraph and ask students to select words from a list to fill in.

Students self-assess and check off which words they know and to what extent. Even young students can do this activity successfully. The teacher fills the column with the vocabulary words, or students can skim the chapter and self-select some. After reading, use the same list of words and see if students can fill out the chart.

Vocabulary Pretest

Vocabulary Word List	I have never heard this word before.	I have heard this word and I know a little bit about it.	I think it means… (give another word).	I can write a sentence or sketch it.

Note. Adapted from "Contemporary Classroom Vocabulary Assessment for Content Areas" by K.A.D. Stahl & M.A. Bravo, 2010, *The Reading Teacher*, *63*(7), p. 572.

Vocabulary Recognition Task

The Vocabulary Recognition Task (Stahl, 2008) is a wonderful and easy way to assess student knowledge of vocabulary before and after reading. Here is how to create one:

1. Create a list of words from a unit or book.
2. Students read the list of words and circle the words they think they know.
3. Students categorize the circled words into a graphic organizer (a web or other shape) that contains headings from the text.

See the sample on page 130. For a scoring guide and additional examples, see Stahl and Bravo (2010).

Vocabulary Recognition Task: Flies

1. Picture Walk/Text Walk
Look through the book at the illustrations and headings. Take one minute to flip through.

2. Circle Words
Before reading the book *Fly Facts* by Janice Marriott (Pacific Learning, 2008), circle the words you know that have to do with flies.

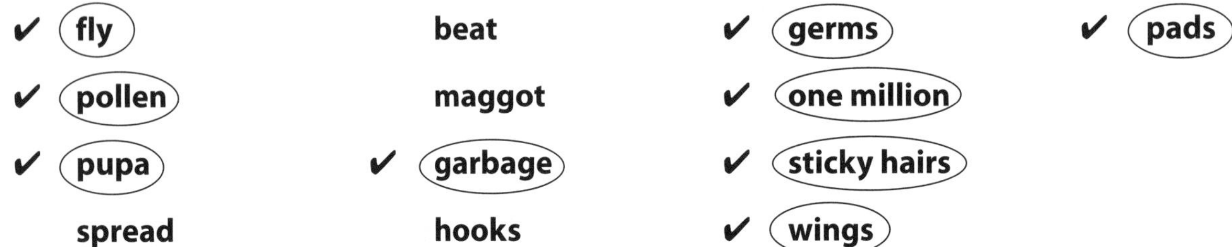

✔ fly
✔ pollen
✔ pupa
spread
beat
maggot
✔ garbage
hooks
✔ germs
✔ one million
✔ sticky hairs
✔ wings
✔ pads

3. Group Words
Write your circled words in the categories. Check them off as you write each one. Predict where you think they go.

Facts About Flies	What Use Are Flies?	Life Cycle of a Fly	Favorite Foods	Parts of a Fly
fly	pollen	pupa	garbage	wings
one million				pads
germs				sticky hairs

Note. Adapted from "Contemporary Classroom Vocabulary Assessment for Content Areas" by K.A.D. Stahl & M.A. Bravo, 2010, *The Reading Teacher, 63*(7), p. 573.

Magic Words Bookmark

(Inspired by *Donovan's Word Jar* by Monalisa DeGross)

Notice and collect different kinds of words while you read:

- **Big words that make you feel smart**

1.________________ from page ______
2.________________ from page ______

- **Tickle your tongue words**

1.________________ from page ______
2.________________ from page ______

- **Kind words that warm your heart**

1.________________ from page ______
2.________________ from page ______

- **Silly words that make you smile**

1.________________ from page ______
2.________________ from page ______

- **Soothing words that calm your fears**

1.________________ from page ______
2.________________ from page ______

- **Mysterious words that make you wonder**

1.________________ from page ______
2.________________ from page ______

- **Musical-sounding words**

1.________________ from page ______
2.________________ from page ______

Magic Words Bookmark

(Inspired by *Donovan's Word Jar* by Monalisa DeGross)

Notice and collect different kinds of words while you read:

- **Big words that make you feel smart**

1.________________ from page ______
2.________________ from page ______

- **Tickle your tongue words**

1.________________ from page ______
2.________________ from page ______

- **Kind words that warm your heart**

1.________________ from page ______
2.________________ from page ______

- **Silly words that make you smile**

1.________________ from page ______
2.________________ from page ______

- **Soothing words that calm your fears**

1.________________ from page ______
2.________________ from page ______

- **Mysterious words that make you wonder**

1.________________ from page ______
2.________________ from page ______

- **Musical-sounding words**

1.________________ from page ______
2.________________ from page ______

Best Ever Literacy Survival Tips: 72 Lessons You Can't Teach Without by Lori D. Oczkus.
© 2012 International Reading Association. May be copied for classroom use.

Wonderful Words Sorting Sheet

1. Collect interesting words as you read, and write one in each box. Or your teacher will give you words to write in the boxes. Make sure the words are spelled correctly.

2. Use scissors to cut apart the boxes to make your own word cards.

3. Sort the words into different groups. Move the words around and organize them by
   - Words that have the same beginning sound
   - Words that have the same ending sound
   - Words with the same word parts
   - Long words
   - Short words
   - Your own sort

Online Resources

List-Group-Label: www.readingrockets.org/strategies/list_group_label
Find tips and research for implementing the list-group-label strategy with your students and suggested books to use.

ReadWriteThink: www.readwritethink.org
Try these and many more free vocabulary lessons and tools:

- "Flip-a-Chip: Examining Affixes and Roots to Build Vocabulary" (Grades 3–5) by Lee Mountain
- "Interactive Flip-a-Chip"
- "Interactive Alphabet Organizer"

Vocabulary/Word Knowledge: Awesome Analogies: www.quia.com/cb/7146.html
Help students develop a deeper comprehension of the way words relate through this analogy game where they can play a solo game or challenge a friend.

Puzzle Soup: www.puzzlesoup.com
Inspire students with a new daily word puzzle.

Fun With Words: www.fun-with-words.com
Promote wordplay in your classroom to reinforce vocabulary knowledge.

"Researchers verify that vocabulary is one of the greatest predictors of reading comprehension (Baker, Simmons, & Kame'enui, 1998), and in order to learn any content area material, students need to be able to comprehend new vocabulary."

References

Anderson, R.C. (1996). Research foundations to support wide reading. In V. Greaney (Ed.), *Promoting reading in developing countries: Views on making reading materials accessible to increase literacy levels* (pp. 55–77). Newark, DE: International Reading Association.

Baker, S.K., Simmons, D.C., & Kame'enui, E.J. (1998). Vocabulary acquisition: Research bases. In D.C. Simmons & E.J. Kame'enui (Eds.), *What reading research tells us about children with diverse learning needs: Bases and basics* (pp. 183–218). Mahwah, NJ: Erlbaum.

Bear, D.R., Invernizzi, M.R., Templeton, S., & Johnston, F. (2012). *Words their way: Word study for phonics, vocabulary, and spelling instruction* (5th ed.). Boston: Allyn & Bacon.

Beck, I.L., & McKeown, M.G. (1983). Learning words well: A program to enhance vocabulary and comprehension. *The Reading Teacher, 36*(7), 622–625.

Beck, I.L., McKeown, M.G., & Kucan, L. (2002). *Bringing words to life: Robust vocabulary instruction*. New York: Guilford.

Beck, I.L., McKeown, M.G., & Omanson, R.C. (1987). The effects and uses of diverse vocabulary instructional techniques. In M.G. McKeown & M.E. Curtis (Eds.), *The nature of vocabulary acquisition* (pp. 147–163). Hillsdale, NJ: Erlbaum.

Beck, I.L., Perfetti, C.A., & McKeown, M.G. (1982). Effects of long-term vocabulary instruction on lexical access and reading comprehension. *Journal of Educational Psychology, 74*(4), 506–521.

Brassell, D. (2011). *Dare to differentiate: Vocabulary strategies for all students*. New York: Guilford.

Carlo, M.S., August, D., McLaughlin, B., Snow, C.E., Dressler, C., Lippman, D.N., et al. (2004). Closing the gap: Addressing the vocabulary needs of English-language learners in bilingual and mainstream classrooms. *Reading Research Quarterly, 39*(2), 188–215. doi:10.1598/RRQ.39.2.3

Cunningham, A.E., & Stanovich, K.E. (1998). What reading does for the mind. *American Educator, 22*(1-2), 8–15.

Cunningham, P.M. (2008). *Phonics they use: Words for reading and writing*. Upper Saddle River, NJ: Prentice Hall.

Editors of the American Heritage Dictionaries. (2006). *100 words to make you sound smart*. Boston: Houghton Mifflin.

Frey, N., & Fisher, D. (2007). *Reading for information in elementary school: Content literacy strategies to build comprehension*. Upper Saddle River, NJ: Prentice Hall.

Frey, N., & Fisher, D. (2009). *Learning words inside and out: Vocabulary instruction that boosts achievement in all subject areas*. Portsmouth, NH: Heinemann.

Gardner, H. (1983). *Frames of mind: The theory of multiple intelligences*. New York: Basic Books.

Goodman, L. (2004). Shades of meaning: Relating and expanding word knowledge. In G.E. Tompkins & C. Blanchfield (Eds.), *Teaching vocabulary: 50 creative strategies, grades 6–12* (pp. 85–87). Upper Saddle River, NJ: Prentice Hall.

Graves, M.F. (2006). *The vocabulary book: Learning and instruction*. New York: Teachers College Press; Newark, DE: International Reading Association; Urbana, IL: National Council of Teachers of English.

Graves, M.F., & Watts-Taffe, S.M. (2002). The place of word consciousness in a research-based vocabulary program. In A.E. Farstrup & S.J. Samuels (Eds.), *What research has to say about reading instruction* (3rd ed., pp. 140–165). Newark, DE: International Reading Association.

Haggard, M.R. (1986). The vocabulary self-collection strategy: An active approach to word learning. In E.K. Dishner, T.W. Bean, J.E. Readence, & D.W. Moore (Eds.), *Reading in the content areas: Improving classroom instruction* (2nd ed., pp. 179–182). Dubuque, IA: Kendall/Hunt.

Hart, B., & Risley, T.R. (1995). *Meaningful differences in the everyday experience of young American children*. Baltimore: Paul H. Brookes.

Hatt, C. (n.d.). *Better discussions in study groups*. Retrieved from www.choiceliteracy.com/public/796.cfm

Hoyt, L. (1999). *Revisit, reflect, retell: Strategies for improving reading comprehension*. Portsmouth, NJ: Heinemann.

Marzano, R.J. (2004). *Building background knowledge for academic achievement: Research on what works in schools*. Alexandria, VA: Association for Supervision and Curriculum Development.

Marzano, R.J. (2010). *Teaching basic and advanced vocabulary: A framework for direct instruction*. Boston: Heinle.

Nagy, W.E. (1988). *Teaching vocabulary to improve reading comprehension*. Newark, DE: International Reading Association.

Nagy, W.E., & Anderson, R.C. (1984). How many words are there in printed school English? *Reading Research Quarterly, 19*(3), 304-330.

Oczkus, L. (2004). *Super six comprehension strategies: 35 lessons and more for reading success*. Norwood, MA: Christopher-Gordon.

Oczkus, L. (2009). *Interactive think-aloud lessons: 25 surefire ways to engage students and improve comprehension*. New York: Scholastic.

Rasinski, T.V., Padak, N., Newton, J., & Newton, E. (2011). The Latin–Greek vocabulary connection: Building vocabulary through morphological study. *The Reading Teacher, 65*(2), 133–141.

Readence, J.E., Bean, T.W., & Baldwin, R.S. (2001). *Content area literacy: An integrated approach* (7th ed.). Dubuque, IA: Kendall/Hunt.

Ruddell, M. R. (1992). Integrated content and long-term vocabulary learning with the vocabulary self-collection strategy (VSS). In E.K. Dishner, T.W. Bean, J.E. Readence, & D.W. Moore (Eds.), *Reading in the content areas: Improving classroom instruction* (3rd ed., pp. 190–196). Dubuque, IA: Kendall/Hunt.

Scott, J.A., Jamieson-Noel, D., & Asselin, M. (2003). Vocabulary instruction throughout the school day in twenty-three Canadian upper-elementary classrooms. *The Elementary School Journal, 103*(3), 269–286.

Stahl, K.A.D. (2008). The effects of three instructional methods on the reading comprehension and content acquisition of novice readers. *Journal of Literacy Research, 40*(3), 359–393. doi:10.1080/10862960802520594

Stahl, K.A.D., & Bravo, M.A. (2010). Contemporary classroom vocabulary assessment for content areas. *The Reading Teacher, 63*(7), 566–578. doi:10.1598/RT.63.7.4

Vacca, R.D., & Vacca, J. (2002). *Content area reading: Literacy and learning across the curriculum* (7th ed.). Boston: Allyn & Bacon.

CHAPTER 10

Phonics and Phonemic Awareness: Classroom Guide to Best Practices and TOP 5 Phonics/Word Work Lessons

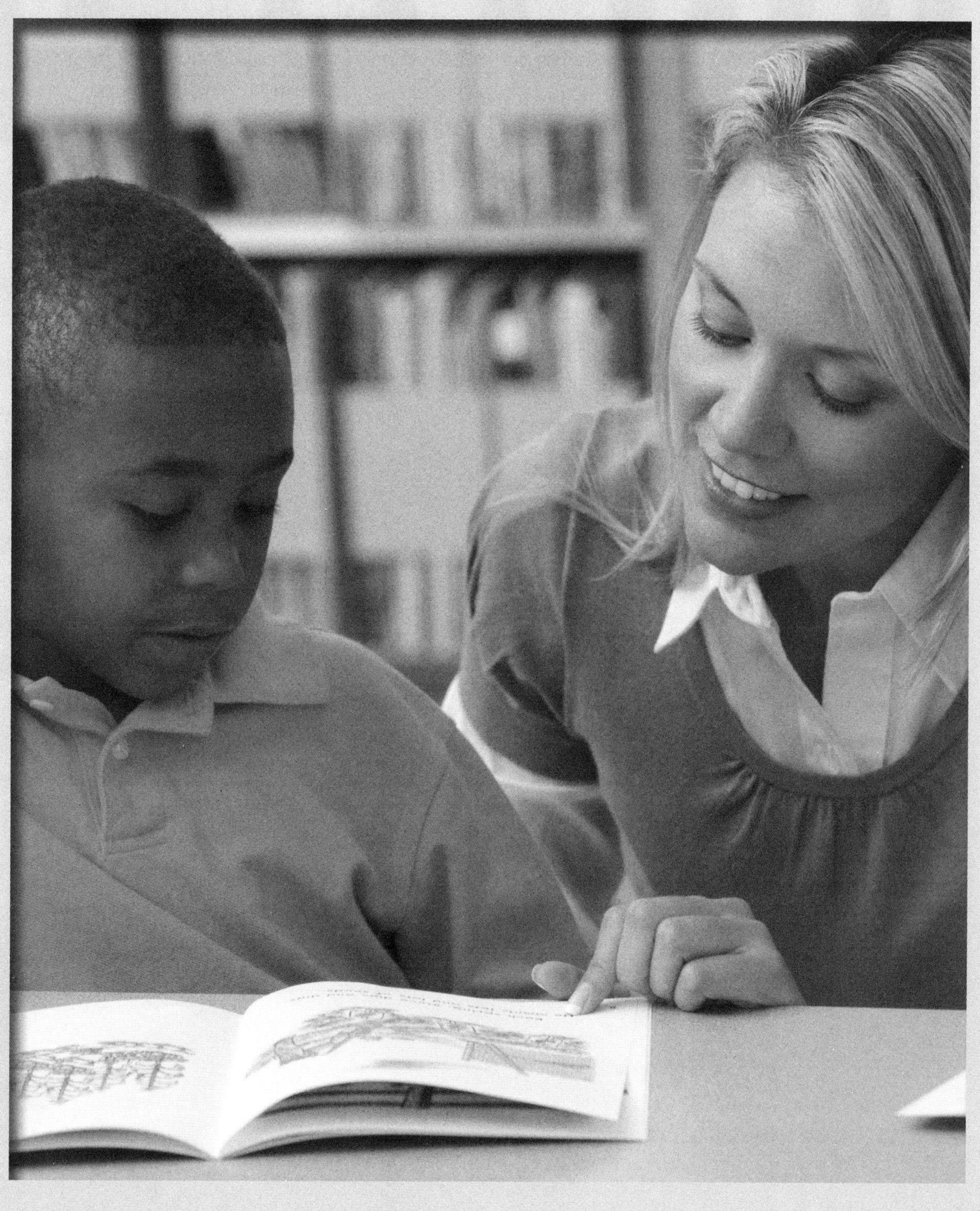

Best Ever Advice on… Phonics

My best idea for phonics is to teach kids about chunking a word. I put out my hands palms up and ask the kids to imagine chocolate in each hand. In my right hand is a teeny, tiny little bit and in my left hand is a big chunk. "Point to which one you want." Of course they point to the imaginary big chunk. I tell them that their brain likes chunks, too—but chunks or groups of letters in a word. Looking for larger units to decode in a word takes modeling and practice in many contexts but leads to reading multisyllabic words.

—Judy Lynch, Author of *Word Learning, Word Making, Word Sorting: 50 Lessons for Success* (Scholastic, 2002)

"How do you figure out a word you don't know when you are reading?"

I pose the question to the third graders seated on the floor during small-group instruction. The answers are telling:

"Reread it."

"Sound it out."

"Karate chop it into parts you know."

"Skip it!"

"Ask a friend."

James proudly offers his simple suggestion for word attack: "If I don't get a word, I just stare at it a little longer." Another child, Arianna, admits that she learned about phonics and figuring out unknown words by watching her favorite television show, *Wheel of Fortune.*

What Do You Remember About Learning to Read?

Do you recall phonics lessons from your elementary school days? Even now I can vividly picture my second-grade teacher, Mrs. Greene, with her rubber-tipped wooden pointer, as she pointed to letters, sounds, and various prefixes and suffixes on a phonics chart. Our job as good readers was to speak on cue the corresponding sounds as she pointed to each one. I can recall wondering what on earth all this noise and nonsense had to do with reading. Now we know from the research that programs that focus too much on teaching letter–sound relationships in isolation and not enough on putting phonics to work in meaningful contexts are not effective (Akhavan, 2008; National Institute of Child Health and Human Development, 2000). Today we teach phonics as a means to help children read well and enjoy reading in real books (Akhavan, 2008).

Phonics and Phonemic Awareness 101

Phonics is defined as knowing the connection between spoken sounds and the corresponding written letters or sound–symbol relationships (National Institute for Child Health and Human Development, 2000; Routman, 2000). Phonics begins with an understanding that each letter stands for a sound. Those letters and sounds are grouped into words. An effective way to teach phonics is using patterns and analogies to figure out unknown words (Cunningham & Cunningham, 2002).

Phonics should also be taught explicitly and systematically in the early grades (Burns, Griffin, & Snow, 1999) and then continued at upper grades as a more sophisticated word study where students consider vocabulary, roots, prefixes, suffixes, and the Greek and Latin origins of words (Rasinski, Padak, Newton, & Newton, 2008). Researchers suggest connecting phonics instruction to text rather than teaching phonics in isolation (National Institute of Child Health and Human Development, 2000).

Weighing in on the "P" Word

The goal of phonics instruction—or the relationship between sounds and letters—is to give students the tools they need to unlock words during reading. Children who have a strong awareness of phonemic structures are better readers (Adams, 1990).

Phonics is one of the critical pillars of a research-based reading program that also includes phonemic awareness, comprehension, fluency, and vocabulary (National Institute of Child Health and Human Development, 2000). Unfortunately, in the past, many debates have raged in the media, legislature, universities, and schools about how phonics should be taught. It seems that everyone has an opinion on the ever-popular "P" word! Perhaps parents at your school or even some of your non-educator friends have cornered you to ask if you believe in teaching phonics.

Most educators do agree that our students need phonics and phonemic awareness in order to read well, and 98% of primary-grade teachers regard phonics as a very important part of their reading program (Baumann, Hoffman, Duffy-Hester, & Ro, 2000). Researchers have also found that most primary-grade teachers do engage their students on a regular basis in some sort of lesson on phonics. The question then is when, how, and how much phonics should be taught and under what circumstances? The International Reading Association's (1997) position statement on phonics suggests that explicit instruction in phonics is an important aspect of reading instruction that is embedded in the context of a more complete reading and writing program.

Phonics Instruction in the Classroom

Do any of these situations sound familiar?

- The middle school students stumble over many of the words that are found in the history chapter such as *oligarchy*, *mediate*, and *mercenaries*, thus losing meaning as they read.
- First graders "guess" and skip words rather than attempting to figure them out.
- During fifth-grade small-group instruction, English language learners meet with their teacher to read the district's basal text. Several students in the group encounter difficulty figuring out the pronunciation and meaning of the selection vocabulary.

The purpose of phonics instruction is to provide students with the decoding skills so they can efficiently and quickly figure out unknown words as they read. There are many effective, research-based strategies to arm students with the phonics and decoding tools they need the most. Phonics instruction doesn't have to be dry. Today there are many meaningful and game-like ways to make the learning "stick" when you teach phonics lessons.

Common types of phonics instruction include:

Analogy Phonics: Teaching students to analyze unfamiliar words using known words and parts within words. Word families are helpful in teaching students to look for patterns. Word families are often called phonograms, rimes, or chunks and are composed of the vowel and sounds that follow it in the syllable, such as the phonogram, *all*. When a rime is combined with an onset, or beginning sound or sounds, many new words may be formed such as mall, call, stall, etc.

Example: If students know the rime *ump* and the word *jump*, they can figure out the words *stump*, *pump*, and *lump*.

Analytic Phonics: Teaching students to analyze letters and sounds learned in previous words to use in pronouncing new ones. This is often called moving from the known to the unknown.

Example: Students associate a particular word with a sound, such as *bat* for the letter *b*.

Then when students encounter other words that have *b* they can refer back to the word *bat*.

Embedded Phonics: An implicit approach where phonics lessons and skills are embedded in the text that is currently being read and the student relies somewhat on incidental learning as unfamiliar words occur in the literature.

> "The best way to develop fast accurate perception of word features is to engage in meaningful reading and writing, and to have multiple opportunities to examine those same words out of context, in isolation, in all their glory."
>
> —Bear, Invernizzi, Templeton, & Johnston (2000)

Example: During reading, the word *night* appears in the text so the teacher decides to pull that word out and teach it along with other words that have the same rime: *light*, *sight*, and *fight*.

Phonics Through Spelling: Using writing to teach students to segment words into phonemes and to then choose letters that go with those phonemes (invented or phonetic spelling).

Example: During writer's workshop the first graders slowly stretch the sounds in words as they write. One child, Jared, writes his story using "phonetic spelling": "The dog ran awa frm the grl." (The dog ran away from the girl.)

Synthetic Phonics: Teaching students how to change letters into sounds and blend sounds into words.

Example: Students segment the individual phonemes or sounds in a word such as *dog* by saying the sounds slowly—/d/ /o/ /g/—and then blending them together to make the word.

Phonemic Awareness Instruction in the Classroom

Phonemic awareness is the ability to hear, differentiate, and manipulate sounds, including segmenting and blending those sounds. Phonemic awareness involves the smallest units of sounds in spoken words only and is not about recognizing the written letters but rather the sounds. Phonemic awareness is the most powerful predictor of success in beginning reading. As many as 80–85% of our students acquire phonemic awareness easily with exposure to read-alouds, poetry, songs, tongue twisters, and nursery rhymes (Allington, 2002; Yopp, 1995) and some explicit instruction in the classroom. However, for the 15–20% who struggle, additional intervention and special training is needed. What does phonemic awareness look like? An example of phonemic awareness is when you are reading a poem aloud to students and you pause for the next rhyming word; students are using phonemic awareness to anticipate the next rhyming word.

Here are some ways to informally assess and provide practice for phonemic awareness. Notice students are not naming letters but making sounds only in their responses.

Rhyming Words: Read a poem. Pause so students can insert the rhyming words.

Example: One, two, buckle my _____.

Beginning Sound Substitution: Change the beginning sound.

graph paper and have students write individual letters on the squares to put together to "make" and then "break" up words!

Intermediate word work

Mr. Fen's sixth graders engage in active word-study activities as they study word origins, work on strategies for reading unfamiliar words, and study spelling patterns. Every week Mr. Fen involves students in lessons using a variety of word-learning activities that help students focus on phonics skills that are appropriate for sixth graders. The room is loaded with wall charts listing features of words (such as words using the same root word or prefix) the class has collected in lessons throughout the year.

Students work in pairs to sort words. Today students will analyze how words change when they go from a verb to a noun such as introduce–introduction, discuss–discussion, and donate–donation. The categories for the sort include words that don't change in spelling, words that drop the final *e*, and those with other changes. The room is lively with discussion, debate, and hands-on sorting of the words on cards. Later in the week, the students will create and act out skits for each of the words.

Practical Teaching Tip

Students save the words in envelopes in their word-study notebooks and periodically mix and match the categories of words to sort. Type up the words on a sheet that is divided into boxes, and have students cut apart the words.

Example: What rhymes with *dog* and starts with the sound /l/?

Sound Isolation: What does it start with? What does it end with? What sound is in the middle of the word?

Example: What sound does *cat* start with?

What sound do you hear in the middle of the word?

What sound does *cat* end with?

Syllable Segmentation: Clap for syllables.

Example: Clap as you say *valentine*.

Phonemic Segmentation: Say students' names and other words slowly.

Example: Say *Clifford* slowly, stretching the sounds out. Then say the word quickly.

Phonics and Word Work in Action

Primary phonics during small-group instruction

The first graders settle in around the kidney-shaped table and look eagerly at the front cover of a nonfiction book titled *The Fantastic Flying Squirrel* by Nic Bishop. After previewing the text to make predictions, the students begin to read silently. Miss Jimenez rotates to each student to have them read quietly to her. On page 6, Angela pauses to figure out the word *crunch*. Miss Jimenez coaches her using a variety of decoding strategies. After sounding out the *cr-*, Miss Jimenez asks Angela to look through the word for a part she knows by looking at the class word wall. Angela proudly spots *-unch* as a familiar "chunk" that the class worked on last week using the word *lunch*. She puts the *cr-* and *-unch* together and smiles proudly. "Great job!" praises her teacher. After all have read the book, Miss Jimenez teaches a quick minilesson to the entire group using individual dry-erase boards. The students work with the teacher to write *-unch* words: *lunch*, *bunch*, *hunch*, *crunch*. She hands out magnetic letters, and students build the words again.

Practical Teaching Tip

If you do not have magnetic letters handy, you can cut up large-square

Guidelines for Effective Phonics/Phonemic Awareness Instruction

Provide many opportunities for all students to read.

Studies show the amount of reading a child does affects decoding ability. Samuels, LaBerge, and Bremer (1978) discovered that struggling second graders used letter-by-letter decoding to figure out words. Eventually readers with higher literate capability in upper grades rely on word parts rather than individual letters to decode unknown words. Phonics instruction should be practiced as students read and enjoy real books. Struggling readers are often pulled to do more work in phonics worksheets and isolated drills when instead they need meaningful, explicit phonics instruction along with opportunities to read more (Adams, 1990; McGill-Franzen, Zmach, Solic, & Zeig, 2006). The goal of explicit phonics instruction is application to real texts.

Teach phonics and phonemic awareness skills in a logical sequence.

Your district most likely will provide you with an approved research-based sequence for explicitly teaching phonemic and phonics skills that comes from your district or state adopted curriculum. The Common Core State Standards (www.corestandards.org/) offer a logical scope sequence for phonics for each grade level. Phonics and phonemic awareness should be taught in the early grades and word study (prefixes, base words, suffixes, etc.) in grades 3–12.

Aa
Ee
Ii

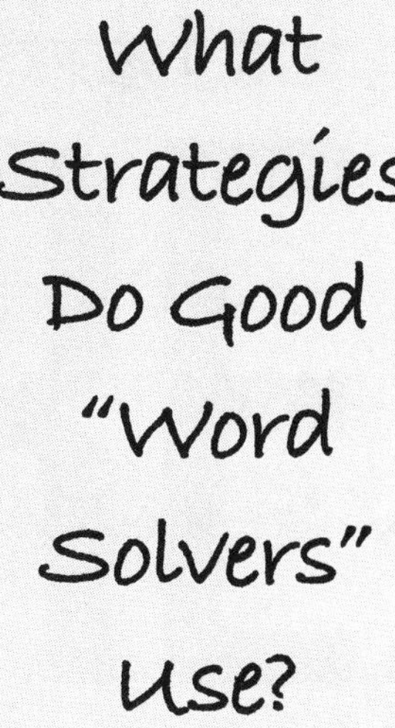
What Strategies Do Good "Word Solvers" Use?

- Discriminate letters in print quickly.
- Recognize whole words as units.
- Use word parts.
- Use known words to figure out unknown words.
- Sound out words by individual letters or letter clusters.
- Use base words to analyze parts.
- Analyze words left to right.
- Check attempts by using letter parts and word parts.
- Use context.
- Use references and resources such as dictionaries to look up meanings and pronunciations.
- Substitute words of similar meaning.

Adapted from Fountas and Pinnell (2001).

37 Rimes That Create 500 Commonly Used Words

ack, ain, ake, ale, all, ame an, ank, ap, ash, at, ate, aw, ay

eat, ell, est

ice, ick, ide, ight, ill, in, ine, ing, ink, ip, it

ock, oke, op, ore, ot

uck, ug, ump, unk

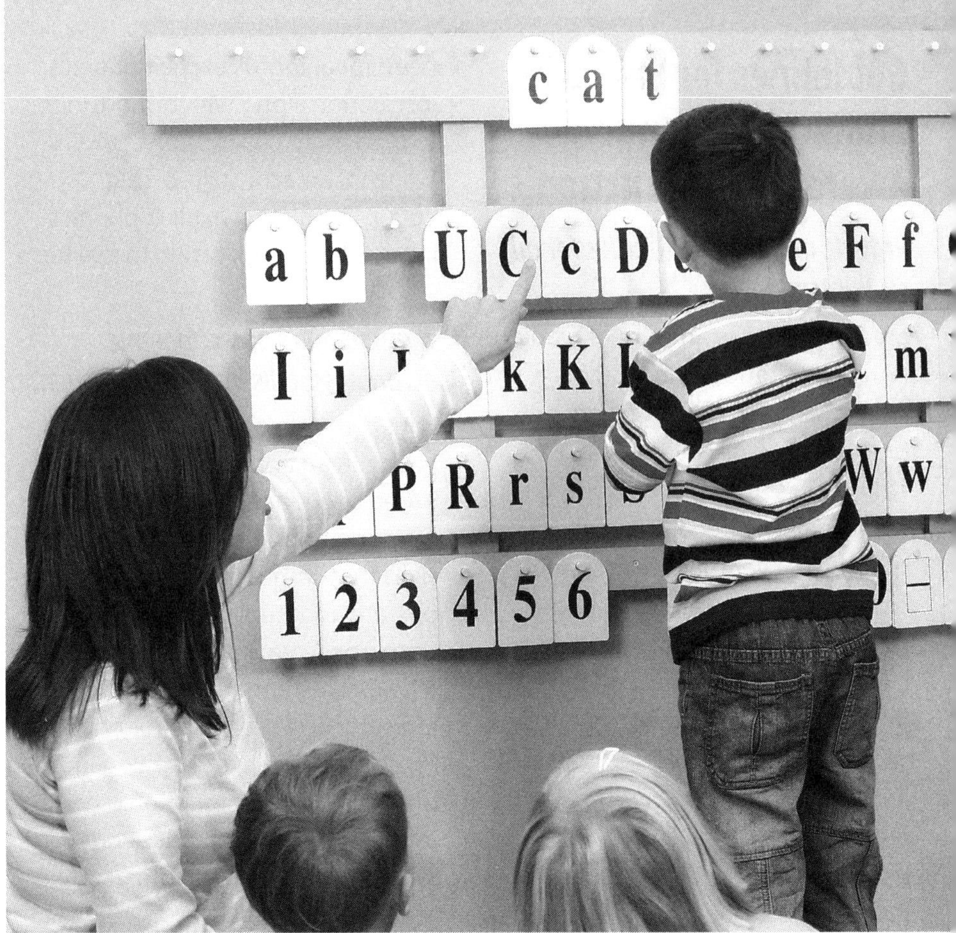

Base instruction on student needs.

Assess student needs often and teach word work and phonics in small-group settings so students' needs are targeted.

Provide explicit, scaffolded instruction and model strategy use for students.

Teach your phonics lessons using the gradual release of responsibility model (Pearson & Gallagher, 1983) where the teacher demonstrates, guides cooperative practice, and then has students try on their own. You can teach students the sounds that letters and words make but be sure to connect this learning with real texts. This sort of scaffolding is an example of what Routman (2011) calls "I do. We do. We do. You do."

Example: The teacher models how to read compound words while reading a text aloud. The teacher models how to figure out compound words found in the reading by breaking them into parts, rereading, and so on. Students hunt for compound words in teams or pairs. The cooperative practice may continue for another round. Then students practice on their own and keep track of the words and sounds in a notebook.

When modeling the use of phonics skills, the following techniques are options for showing students how to use decoding strategies to figure out unknown words.

Masking: When reading with any grade level, the teacher may use sticky notes to cover up or mask words while using a document camera, interactive whiteboard, or Big Book. You can cover the first letter leaving the remaining letters for students to guess what you have covered and then reveal the rest of the word letter by letter. Model how you figured out the word using the phonics and context of the sentence as well as to confirm the word.

Cloze: Cover a word every five words or so. You can leave the beginning sound out or cover it entirely. Students work together as the teacher models how to figure out the missing words.

Coach students during reading in the use of phonics/word strategies

During small-group or individual reading time, coach students as they read orally by asking them to use good-reader strategies to figure out words.

Encourage students to think about the following strategies:

- What does the word begin with?
- What would make sense here?
- Do you see any parts you know in the word?

- Look at the picture.
- Reread from the beginning of the sentence.
- Does that sound right?
- Does it look right?
- Change the vowel sound.
- What is another word that would make sense here?
- Read on.

Teach students to look for patterns.

The brain seeks patterns. Teach students to look for patterns so they can use those patterns to figure out related words. Teach rimes, such as the 37 rimes that make up 500 commonly read words. If a student can read *hill*, then he can also read *will*, *pill*, and *sill*. When you teach common prefixes, suffixes, and root words, students can use those patterns to read dozens of words.

Most Common Prefixes and Suffixes in Order of Frequency

Prefixes		
Highest frequency	**High frequency**	**Medium frequency**
un- (not, opposite of)	over- (too much)	trans- (across)
re- (again)	mis- (wrongly)	super- (above)
in-, im-, ir-, il- (not)	sub- (under)	semi- (half)
dis- (not, opposite of)	pre- (before)	anti- (against)
en-, em- (cause to)	inter- (between, among)	mid- (middle)
non- (not)		under- (too little)
in-, im- (in or into)		
Suffixes		
-s (plurals)	-ly (characteristic of)	-al, -ial (having characteristics of)
-ed (past tense)	-er, -or (person)	-y (characterized by)
-ing (present tense)	-ion, -tion (act, process)	-ness (state of, condition of)
	-ible, -able (can be done)	-ity, -ty (state of)
		-ment (action or process)
		-ic (having characteristics of)
		-ous, -eous, ious (possessing the qualities of)
		-en (made of)
		-ive, -ative, itive (adjective form of a noun)
		-ful (full of)
		-less (without)

Reprinted from Kieffer & Lesaux (2007); adapted from Blevins (2001).

Keep a visual record of classroom words.

While you read to and with the class from read-alouds, the district's basal text, or core literature, you can easily help students apply phonics and word-study skills. One way to do that is to model and keep running charts of the skills you are teaching. If students can see what they've been told orally, they are more likely to remember it. Akhavan (2008) says, "If you think it, ink it." Collect words from the texts you are reading with your class. For example, you might model how to figure out words using the *-tion* prefix and then create a chart of words that end in *-tion*. Or another chart might have words with the vowel sounds or with a silent *e*. It is helpful to use just one skill per chart.

A word wall is a place to put words in alphabetical order. You may include words from the books students are reading across the curriculum as well as spelling words and high-frequency words. You can color-code them and underline or outline the patterns in words that are on the wall. Play guessing games by giving word riddles for the words on the word wall.

Reinforce phonics and word work using game-like activities.

Students enjoy games. Play simple, easy-to-prepare games like Wordo (Cunningham, 2008), a game similar to Bingo, or concentration with word meanings or pictures on cards that students match to the words. Students may also draw five to seven words and write stories or make up a skit using the words. Or you might play Blend Baseball where students are divided into two teams. The pitcher says a word slowly in parts, and the student at bat blends the word to go to first base. Continue as in baseball with home runs

(Blevins, 2000). See the list of Online Resources at the end of this chapter for phonics-building activities.

Reinforce and teach phonemic awareness using silly word games, poetry, and songs.

There are many fun ways to allow students to develop an ear for phonemic awareness. When reading poetry, leave out the rhyming words and allow students to chime in with the words.

Reinforce phonics and word work during writing.

Reading and writing are reciprocal. When students use reference charts and word-study notebooks, they will often select words from those sources as they write. Or they may analyze the words and create new ones based on the rhyming patterns or word parts.

Provide manipulatives to use during lessons.

Be sure to allow students to reinforce the learning using a variety of hands-on tools including magnetic letters, letter and picture cards, word and letter cards, and individual dry-erase boards and markers.

Word Ladder

Example submitted by Timothy Rasinski

Work	change a letter to make what this article is about
Word	change a letter to make something you need to fish
Worm	change a letter to make the opposite of cool
Warm	subtract a letter to make the opposite of peace
War	rearrange the letters to make food that is uncooked
Raw	change a letter to make a male sheep
Ram	add a letter to make a word that means to stuff something inside a box
Cram	change a letter to make a mollusk that is used in chowder
Clam	add two letters to make a word that means a loud continuous noise or uproar
Clamor	subtract the first letter and change the M to make a word that means WORK
Labor	

(T. V. Rasinski, personal communication, 2011; see also Rasinski, 2005)

Lori's Top 5 Surefire Strategies for Phonics/ Word Work

For this chapter I have selected some commonly accepted "best practice" activities for engaging students in practicing phonics and word learning. These are some of the most effective activities that you can use to reinforce phonics skills. Hopefully, they will become familiar routines in your classroom!

1 *Win at Wordo (Cunningham, 2008)*

This game, similar to Bingo, can be played with students of any age. Students fill up a Wordo card by copying one word in each box from the class word wall.

For younger students you can make cards ahead of time, making sure the cards are different. To vary the game, try calling out the definition rather than the word.

2 *Score With Word Sorts (Cunningham, 2008; Fountas & Pinnell, 2001)*

Using a collection of words on cards, you can create ways for students to sort words. Although students could write the words as they sort them into categories, the learning is much more concrete and hands-on when they sort and manipulate cards. There are many meaningful ways to sort.

A closed sort means that the teacher assigns categories for sorting the words, such as words that start with /d/ or /c/ or words that end in the same suffix. An open sort means that the students create the categories for sorting the words. They analyze the words and come up with groupings for them. A speed sort is fun and gamelike, as students race one another and the clock to categorize all the words. A blind sort is when the teacher calls out the words in a given category and then the students figure out what the words have in common. Try using word sorts as group work, as a partner activity, as a center or independent activity, or as a teacher-led activity during whole-class or small-group reading.

Here are some sample ways to sort words:

- Length
- Syllables
- Words that start or end the same or that have the same vowel sound
- Words that start like names of students in the class
- Rhyming words
- Spelling patterns
- Word families
- Meaning

3 *Move It, Make It: Making Words (Cunningham, 2008)*

Making Words is a highly interactive manipulative activity where students move letter cards or magnetic letters around to form new words. The teacher or leader reads off the directions, and students listen to the words and select the letters needed to make the words. Students may also make a word then record it on a dry-erase board or paper. Making Words can be played in a center, at students' desks, or in a teacher-led small-group lesson. You can select a word from the text the students are reading or use the Online Resources listed at the end of this chapter.

Directions:

1. Select a word you want your students to make.
2. Make large individual letter cards for your copy of the word that you can use to demonstrate on a pocket chart.

Making Words Example

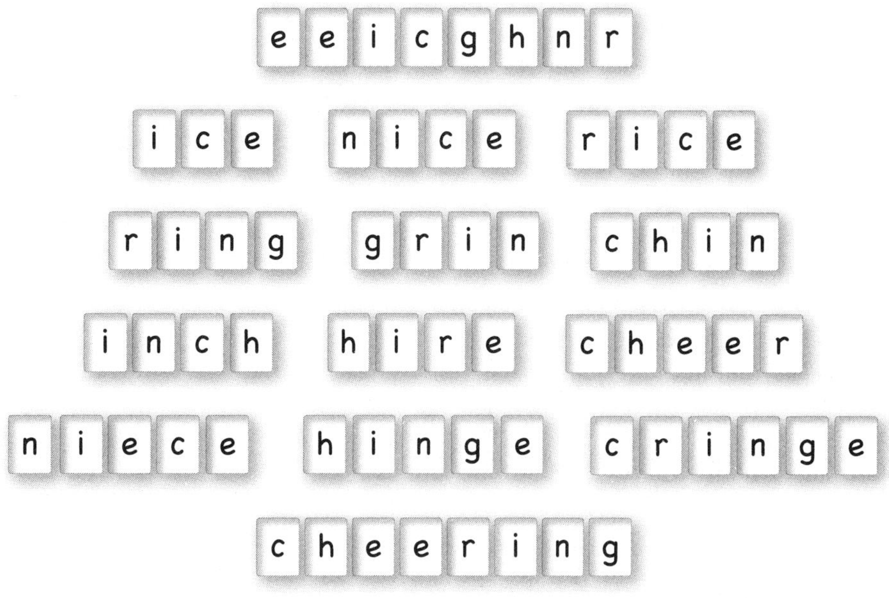

Adapted from Cunningham (2008).

3. Create as many smaller words as you can using the letters. Choose the words that will help you illustrate the spelling or phonics patterns you are teaching. Write the words on cards, one per card.
4. Pass out only the letters that students need for the word.
5. Name the letters with students.
6. Display the same letters on the pocket chart.
7. Next read aloud a short word you want students to make.
8. After students make the word, invite a student volunteer to make the word with your large letter cards so students can check their work.
9. Read aloud the next word and tell students to change the word and make it longer.
10. Continue by asking a volunteer to help make the words each time you provide one.
11. The last step is to ask students to use all the letters to make the word of the day.

4 *Build, Fix, Mix! (Fountas & Pinnell, 2001)*

This activity is a wonderful hands-on, partner study technique with a gamelike feel.

Directions:

1. After a lesson on a sound or spelling patterns, choose 3–4 words to study or allow students to choose the words.
2. In the Build stage, students make the words using magnetic letters or letter cards.
3. In the Mix stage, they mix up the letter cards.
4. In the Fix stage, they rebuild the words.
5. The activity continues as students mix up the letter cards again to rebuild.

Partners can take turns reading the words from the cards and doing the mixing and fixing. They may race to fix and mix as well.

5 *Let's Play the Name Game! (Diller, 2002; Cunningham, 2008)*

Younger students especially enjoy playing games related to their names.

Directions:

1. Create a sentence strip with each child's name and picture.
2. Ask students questions about the names, such as which name is longest, shortest, starts with ____, has chunks that you know, what do these names have in common, and so on.
3. Clap syllables in names, sort names, and alphabetize names.
4. Create one tongue twister per day using a student's name. Examples: Lori licks lollipops. Audrey actually acts audaciously! Tim tickles toes on Tuesdays!
5. Use the names on display to refer to when children are sounding out words. You can create analogies such as, "If you can read *Tracey*, you can read the word *truck*."

Q&A

How can I help my English language learners (ELLs) learn the phonics and phonemic awareness they need to succeed in English?

By playing up the strengths and helping shore up the areas of English that give ELLs problems, you can make learning to read in English easier for your students who speak another language. The good news is that second-language learners respond well to all the wonderful language games, word walls, poems, songs, and activities highlighted in this chapter. It is especially important to expose ELLs to a print-rich environment with lots of oral language and explicit phonics instruction. Developing vocabulary is of critical importance for ELLs. Reading instruction should not overemphasize phonics and phonemic awareness.

ELLs face some of the following challenges:

They may or may not be literate in their own language. If they are learning to read in English, phonics and phonemic instruction is easier. If they are not literate, they need to first understand print concepts.

Some of the sounds in the child's language may transfer to English, while other children come from languages that do not contain any of the sounds in English. Older children especially need to be taught the differences in sounds between languages.

Before Reading: Activate Prior Knowledge

- What do you think is important about teaching phonics to students?
- What difficulties do your students have with phonics?
- What are you doing now to teach phonics to students at your grade level? How is it working for them?
- What do you want to know about teaching phonics and phonemic awareness? (Skim the chapter to brainstorm.)

During Reading: Respond While Reading

- While reading this chapter, mark your text with self-stick notes. Use symbols to indicate questions (?), things you want to try (T), something you connect with (+), something interesting or surprising (!) (adapted from Hatt, n.d.).

After Reading: Think About and Discuss

- How should phonics be taught through the grades?
- What does instruction cover in primary and then intermediate grades?
- How would you define *phonics* and *phonemic awareness* to a parent?
- How can you connect phonics instruction to meaningful use in text?
- Discuss types of phonics instruction and practical applications for instruction, including analogy, analytic phonics, embedded phonics, phonics through spelling, and synthetic phonics.
- What is phonemic awareness? How can students learn about rhyming words, beginning sound substitution, sound isolation, syllable segmentation, and phonemic segmentation?
- Discuss the guidelines for teaching phonics and phonemic awareness. How do opportunities to read support students' use of phonics and phonemic awareness?
- What does explicit instruction and coaching look like at your grade level? What are some easy-to-prepare, appropriate, game-like activities you can use to reinforce phonics at your grade level?
- How can you help your English learners learn phonics and phonemic awareness in meaningful ways?

Putting Phonics and Phonemic Awareness Into Practice

Professional Development Breakout Groups

- For each grade level, work in teams to reread the chapter and make a list of useful lessons.
- Work on a team and try one of the Top 5 lessons with your group. Share with other groups. Discuss.
- Reread the section called "Keep a Visual Record of Classroom Words." Make a list of wall charts you will want to make with your class to reinforce phonics and phonemic awareness at your grade level.

Lesson Sharing

- Try one of Lori's Top 5 lessons with your class. Be prepared to share. On a scale of 1–5, how did the lesson go? Explain. What do you want to try next?
- Ask your students, "How do you figure out words when you are reading?" Make a chart to bring to a meeting to discuss with other teachers.

Teacher as Reader

- What do you remember about learning phonics as a child?
- How do you figure out words that present challenges to you?

Before the Next Meeting

Read: Select the next chapter your group will read. Mark the text during reading.
Try: Try one of the lessons from the next chapter, or try something new from this chapter.
Observe: Visit a colleague's classroom to observe a lesson on phonics and phonemic awareness, or record yourself teaching a lesson and share the video at a meeting.

Going Deeper With Phonics and Phonemic Awareness

- Try a book study using this practical resource loaded with great ideas for phonics instruction:

  Cunningham, P.M. (2008). *Phonics they use: Words for reading and writing* (6th ed.). Boston: Allyn & Bacon.

- Or consider studying the resources listed on page 152.

Clarifying Words Bookmark Lesson

Objective: To provide students with a reference tool to use during reading to help them figure out words.

Common Core Connections: Clarify words based on a variety of strategies including grade-level phonics and word analysis as well as clarifying words and phrases using context and part of words (sounds, prefixes, suffixes, root words, syllables).

Teacher Modeling: Ask students what good readers do to figure out words they don't know. Go over the strategies on the bookmark. Read aloud a portion of the text and model how to clarify a word. Have students put their fingers on the same word you are clarifying in their copy of the text. Think aloud as you share which strategies you are using to figure out the word. Use the starter "I didn't get the word, so I...."

Guided Practice: You can conduct the guided practice step with the whole class or in small groups. Invite students to work in pairs or groups and use self-stick notes to mark in their text the words to clarify. Create a two-column chart. Put words on one side, and on the other list the strategies from the bookmark or other resources that helped you to clarify. (Tip: When students say they don't have any words to clarify, tell them to think of a word a younger child would have trouble reading and understanding, or ask them to find the trickiest or longest word.)

Our Words to Clarify We didn't get...	Strategies to Clarify So we....

Independent Practice: Students continue to use the bookmark in pairs and on their own as they mark words they need to clarify.

Wrap Up: Ask students to think about which clarification strategies helped them the most and explain why those were useful.

Assessment Tips

Use formal and informal assessments to check phonics and phonemic awareness skill development. For a variety of practical classroom assessments, see Cooper, Robinson, and Kiger (2010) and Opitz, Ford, and Erekson (2011).

Assessing phonemic awareness

During phonemic awareness assessments, remember that students are not naming letters but making sounds! (See page 139 for examples.) Can the student do the following?

- isolate sounds
- blend sounds
- segment sounds
- segment syllables
- substitute sounds

Assessing letters and sounds

Cooper and colleagues (2010) recommend the following steps to help with letter recognition:

1. Use two sets of alphabet cards: one uppercase letters, the other lowercase letters.
2. Shuffle the cards in the uppercase set and ask the student to give you the name of each letter.
3. Do the same with the lowercase set.
4. Spread out all the cards and call out letters for the student to find.
5. Ask the student to match upper- and lowercase letters.
6. Keep track of letters each student knows and doesn't know.

Running Records are another useful tool for assessing letter sounds. (See page 140.) Watch for use of phonics or knowledge of letter sounds during guided reading lessons and write observations on self-stick notes. Check off and cite specific examples of student difficulty with the following:

- beginning sounds
- ending sounds
- medial sounds
- prefixes
- suffixes
- decoding one-syllable words
- decoding two-syllable words

Clarifying Words Bookmark

- What does the word begin with?

- What does the word end with?

- What would make sense here?

- Do you see any parts/chunks you know in the word?

- Look at the picture.

- Reread from the beginning of the sentence.

- Does that sound right?

- Does it look right?

- Change the vowel sound.

- What is another word that would make sense here?

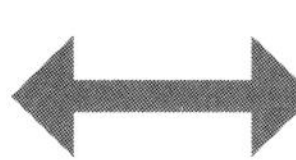

- Read on.

- Ask a friend.

Clarifying Words Bookmark

- What does the word begin with?

- What does the word end with?

- What would make sense here?

- Do you see any parts/chunks you know in the word?

- Look at the picture.

- Reread from the beginning of the sentence.

- Does that sound right?

- Does it look right?

- Change the vowel sound.

- What is another word that would make sense here?

- Read on.

- Ask a friend.

Best Ever Literacy Survival Tips: 72 Lessons You Can't Teach Without by Lori D. Oczkus.
© 2012 International Reading Association. May be copied for classroom use.

Clarifying Words Bookmark

1. Identify the difficult word.

The word ______________________
is tricky, because

a. I had trouble pronouncing it.

b. I didn't know what it meant.

c. I didn't know what it meant, and I couldn't pronounce it.

2. Try to clarify the difficult word.

I tried the following strategies to understand the difficult word:

___ I checked the parts of the word that I know (prefixes, suffixes, base words, and digraphs).

___ I tried blending the sounds of the word together.

___ I thought about where I have seen the word before.

___ I thought of another word that looks like this word.

___ I read on to find clues.

___ I tried another word that makes sense in the sentence.

___ I reread the sentence to see if the word I figured out made sense.

Clarifying Words Bookmark

1. Identify the difficult word.

The word ______________________
is tricky, because

a. I had trouble pronouncing it.

b. I didn't know what it meant.

c. I didn't know what it meant, and I couldn't pronounce it.

2. Try to clarify the difficult word.

I tried the following strategies to understand the difficult word:

___ I checked the parts of the word that I know (prefixes, suffixes, base words, and digraphs).

___ I tried blending the sounds of the word together.

___ I thought about where I have seen the word before.

___ I thought of another word that looks like this word.

___ I read on to find clues.

___ I tried another word that makes sense in the sentence.

___ I reread the sentence to see if the word I figured out made sense.

Online Resources

Timothy Rasinski's Word Ladders: www.timrasinski.com/?page=presentations
See samples of word ladders for grades 1–3 and 3–6, as well as other resources to use in your classroom to help build phonics knowledge.

Reading Rockets Reading Topics A–Z: www.readingrockets.org/article/341
Read "English Language Learners and the Five Essential Components of Reading Instruction" by Beth Antunez to find out how teachers can play to the strengths and shore up the weaknesses of English language learners in each of the Reading First components.

ReadWriteThink: www.readwritethink.org
Here are some lessons and interactive tools to help students with phonics and phonemic awareness:

- "The Big Green Monster Teaches Phonics in Reading and Writing" (Grades K–2) by Maureen Gerard
- "Building Phoneme Awareness With Phoneme Isolation" (Grades K–2) by Sarah Dennis-Shaw
- "Dr. Seuss's Sound Words: Playing With Phonics and Spelling" (Grades K–2) by Traci Gardner
- "Generating Rhymes: Developing Phonemic Awareness" (Grades K–2) by Sarah Dennis-Shaw
- "Interactive Word Family Sort" tool

SMART Exchange: exchange.smarttech.com
SMART Exchange has lots of really great interactive whiteboard activities for phonics and other areas of the curriculum.

References

Adams, M.J. (1990). *Beginning reading instruction in the United States*. Bloomington, IN: ERIC Clearinghouse on Reading and Communication Skills. (ERIC Document Reproduction Service No. ED321250)

Akhavan, N.L. (2008). *The Title I teacher's guide to teaching reading, K–3*. Portsmouth, NH: Heinemann.

Allington, R.L. (2002). Research on reading/learning disability interventions. In A.E. Farstrup & S.J. Samuels (Eds.), *What research has to say about reading instruction* (3rd ed., pp. 261–290). Newark, DE: International Reading Association.

Baumann, J.F., Hoffman, J.V., Duffy-Hester, A.M., & Ro, J.M. (2000). "The First R" yesterday and today: U.S. elementary reading instruction practices reported by teachers and administrators. *Reading Research Quarterly, 35*(3), 338–377.

Bear, D.R., Invernizzi, M., Templeton, S., Johnston, F. (2000). *Words their way: Word study for phonics, vocabulary, and spelling instruction*. Upper Saddle River, NJ: Merrill.

Blevins, W. (2000). Playing with sounds: Successful reading and spelling begin with phonemic awareness. *Instructor, 109*(6), 16–17.

Blevins, W. (2001). *Teaching phonics and word study in the intermediate grades: A complete sourcebook*. New York: Scholastic.

Burns, M.S., Griffin, P., & Snow, C.E. (Eds.). (1999). *Starting out right: A guide to promoting children's reading success*. Washington, DC: National Academy Press.

Cooper, J.D., Robinson, M.D., & Kiger, N.D. (2010). *Success with RTI: Research-based strategies for managing RTI and core reading instruction in your classroom*. New York: Scholastic.

Cunningham, P.M. (2008). *Phonics they use: Words for reading and writing*. Boston: Allyn & Bacon.

Cunningham, P.M., & Cunningham, J.W. (2002). What we know about how to teach phonics. In A.E. Farstrup & S.J. Samuels (Eds.), *What research has to say about reading instruction* (3rd ed., pp. 87–109). Newark, DE: International Reading Association.

Diller, D., & Starr, L. (2002). *Beyond the names chart: Using children's names for word study*. San Diego, CA: Teaching Resource Center.

Fountas, I.C., & Pinnell, G.S. (2001). *Guiding readers and writers, grades 3–6: Teaching comprehension, genre, and content literacy*. Portsmouth, NH: Heinemann.

Hatt, C. (n.d.). *Better discussions in study groups*. Retrieved from www.choiceliteracy.com/public/796.cfm

International Reading Association. (1997). *The role of phonics in reading instruction* [Position statement]. Newark, DE: Author. Retrieved July 18, 2011, from http://www.reading.org/General/AboutIRA/PositionStatements/PhonicsPosition.aspx

Kieffer, M.J., & Lesaux, N.K. (2007). Breaking down words to build meaning: Morphology, vocabulary, and reading comprehension in the urban classroom. *The Reading Teacher, 61*(2), 134–144.

Lynch, J. (2002). *Word learning, word making, word sorting: 50 lessons for success*. New York: Scholastic.

McGill-Franzen, A., Zmach, C., Solic, K., & Zeig, J.L. (2006). The confluence of two policy mandates: Core reading programs and third-grade retention in Florida. *The Elementary School Journal, 107*(1), 67–93.

National Institute of Child Health and Human Development. (2000). *Report of the National Reading Panel. Teaching children to read: An evidence-based assessment of the scientific research literature on reading and its implications for reading instruction* (NIH Publication No. 00-4769). Washington, DC: U.S. Government Printing Office.

Opitz, M.F., Ford, M.P., & Erekson, J.A. (2011). *Accessible assessment: How 9 sensible techniques can power data-driven reading instruction*. Portsmouth, NH: Heinemann.

Pearson, P.D., & Gallagher, M.C. (1983). The instruction of reading comprehension. *Contemporary Educational Psychology, 8*(3), 317–344.

Rasinski T.V. (2005). *Daily word ladders (grades 1–2, 2–3, 4–6)*. New York: Scholastic.

Rasinski, T.V., Padak, N.D., Newton, R.M., & Newton, E. (2008). *Greek and Latin roots: Keys to building vocabulary*. Huntington Beach, CA: Shell Education.

Routman, R. (2000). *Conversations: Strategies for teaching, learning, and evaluating*. Portsmouth, NH: Heinemann.

Routman, R. (2011, May). *"I do it." "We do it." "We do it." "We do it." "You do it."* [Teaching Edge Speaker Series]. Presented at the annual meeting of the International Reading Association, Orlando, FL.

Samuels, S.J., LaBerge, D., & Bremer, C. (1978). Units of word recognition: Evidence for developmental changes. *Journal of Verbal Learning and Verbal Behavior, 17*(6), 715–720.

Yopp, H.K. (1995). A test for assessing phonemic awareness in young children. *The Reading Teacher, 49*(1), 20–29..

"Phonics should also be taught explicitly and systematically in the early grades (Burns, Griffin, & Snow, 1999) and then continued at upper grades as a more sophisticated word study where students consider vocabulary, roots, prefixes, suffixes, and the Greek and Latin origins of words."

CHAPTER 11

Fluency Survival Tips: Guidelines and TOP 5 Strategies for Developing Fantastic Reading Fluency

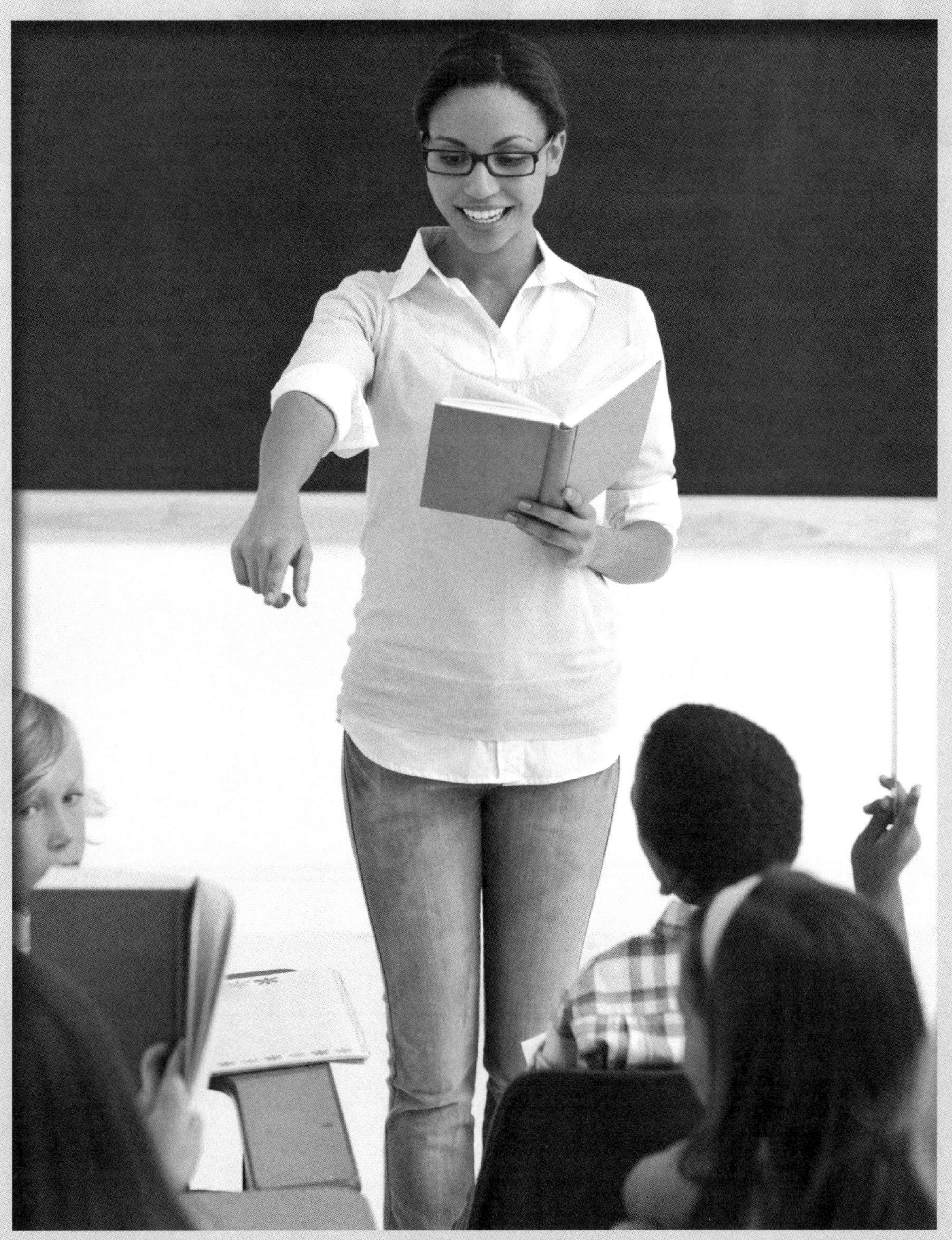

Best Ever Advice on… Fluency

The best way to develop fluency is through practice: reading widely and reading deeply. Deep reading involves having students rehearse (repeated reading) a brief passage for the purpose of reading it with expression and meaning. Poetry, song lyrics, Readers Theatre scripts, and excerpts from trade books are excellent texts for building fluency. Each week in second-grade teacher Chase Young's classroom, groups of students are assigned a Readers Theatre script that they rehearse all week. At the end of the week, the students perform their script for classmates and parents. Mr. Young's students love the opportunity to become stars, and Mr. Young loves the progress his students make in word recognition, fluency, and comprehension.

—Tim Rasinski, Author of *The Fluent Reader: Oral & Silent Reading Strategies for Building Fluency, Word Recognition & Comprehension* (2nd ed.; Scholastic, 2010)

Have you ever read with a student who plods along word by word in a choppy, halting, or monotonous manner? The robotic reading of some students sounds like this: "One... dddday...wh–when...he...w-e-n-t...o-u-tttt...." When students read slowly and with poor fluency, it is no wonder they lose meaning. It is estimated that more than 45% of U.S. fourth graders are not fluent readers and struggle with reading comprehension (National Center for Education Statistics, 2009).

Reading fluency is much more than reading quickly. Fluent readers sound smooth, graceful, and expressive. When students read fluently, they comprehend better, too.

Fluency is a bridge to comprehension. When your students practice fluency techniques, their silent reading comprehension dramatically improves (Pinnell et al., 1995; Rasinski, Rikli, & Johnston, 2009). The National Reading Panel (National Institute of Child Health and Human Development, 2000) identified fluency as one of the five pillars of essential research-based instruction, along with phonemic awareness, phonics, vocabulary, and comprehension.

Fluency involves three simple components (Rasinski & Griffith, 2010):

1. Rate: reading at a natural rate
2. Accuracy: decoding words accurately and effortlessly
3. Prosody: reading with appropriate expression using phrasing and intonation

Fortunately there are many practical, research-based ways to develop and boost the fluency of all our readers! This chapter covers essential guidelines to fluency success for your students, as well as simple lessons and fluency routines you can easily incorporate into your reading program.

What Effective Fluency Instruction Looks Like

Primary example

The first graders gather around the carpet with anticipation. Miss Lee selects a helper to point to the words in the Big Book of poems as the students reread their favorites from weeks past.

Miss Lee reads the new poem for the week once through, and students follow along. During a second exuberant read, she pauses after each natural break in the stanzas and asks her students to echo read, or repeat each line after she reads it. Throughout the week, students reread the poem with the teacher, partners, and at home.

Friday, the first graders read their weekly poem with expression to their fifth-grade big buddies. Then the cross-age pairs read chorally, using paired reading techniques (Topping, 1995), in a book that the little buddy has selected. Miss Lee ends the day by leading the class in a sing-along joyfully selected by the song monitor. The class reads the lyrics from the song chart. Afterward, students file out of the room, some still singing quietly under their breath.

Intermediate example

Giggles abound as the fifth graders complete their "passage a week" performances, acting out their parts while wearing hats or using props. Students work cooperatively throughout each week to figure out how they will perform their portion of a text.

Their teacher, Mr. Lewis, teaches a variety of lessons throughout the week (see, e.g., "Fluency Development Lesson" in Opitz & Rasinski, 1998). Monday, he introduces a poem or short text, reading the passage aloud and discussing its meaning. Tuesday, the students engage in a variety of repeated-reading methods, including echo reading and cumulative choral reading. Wednesday and Thursday, the students work in pairs to read and reread their assigned or chosen passages.

Mr. Lewis rotates around the room and coaches individuals and small groups, pointing out ways to make the reading sound more fluid and natural. By Friday, students are ready to perform their readings for the class. Mr. Lewis's students read a wide variety of texts together and independently to practice and build fluency and comprehension. The class also adapts one favorite reading per month and creates a Readers Theatre to perform for their little buddies.

Practical Guidelines for Fluency Instruction

Fluency is NOT just about speed!

Although reading rate is a predictor of reading fluency and fluency greatly affects comprehension, speed is not the only aspect of fluency instruction that improves overall reading. Unfortunately, in some school districts, fluency instruction is simplified to frequent measures of student reading rate in words per minute and to improving reading speed through rereadings. Fluency expert Timothy Rasinski warns that five minutes per day of

"NASCAR" or speed-reading won't do the trick (Rasinski & Griffith, 2010).

When students reread just to become faster, they don't think about meaning. Research indicates that students who practice only speed do not make the same gains as those who receive instruction in other important aspects of fluency, including phrasing and expression.

Try focusing on authentic reasons for rereading, such as performance. In Lorraine Griffith's intermediate classroom, students practice fluency in rich and purposeful performance activities such as Readers Theatre and weekly poetry. Her struggling readers make an average gain of 2.9 years per school year (Rasinski & Griffith, 2010).

Model fluent reading.

When you read aloud from a variety of texts, you are modeling fluent reading. Read aloud or play recordings of others reading aloud as you demonstrate and discuss fluent reading.

Project the text for the class to view and mark slashes between phrases so students can see that fluent readers group words together rather than reading word by word. You might circle or underline words to emphasize as you read aloud.

Draw students' attention to the different aspects of fluency by pointing out some of your fluent reading behaviors:

- "Why did I slow down or speed up during this part?"
- "Did you notice how I paused here? What were you thinking when I did that?"
- "Notice how I emphasized this word. How did that impact the reading?"
- "Did you notice how I read the dialogue in this part? How did that help you to know how the character felt?"
- "Did you see how I chunked the reading into meaningful phrases?"

Once in awhile, share a negative example: Read in a slow, staccato-like manner or too quickly without expression, and ask students what you should do to improve your fluency (Rasinski & Griffith, 2010). Your students will delight in correcting you!

Engage students in repeated readings and choral readings.

When asked how he learned to read, one first grader revealed proudly and matter-of-factly, "I learned to read by listening and following along to *Mike Mulligan and His Steam Shovel* seven times at the listening center!" When we reread the same text with students, we are providing a natural experience for developing fluency. Repeated readings are a motivating, supported, and easy way to improve reading fluency. Besides, chanting or singing together is fun—think how you feel singing in the shower or car with your favorite song blasting!

Focus on expression and prosody, not just speed. Provide many mini-performance opportunities for students to meaningfully practice fluency.

Meaningful Fluency Practice

Offer these mini-performance opportunities weekly at all grade levels:

- Read and sing songs together
- Choose a poem of the week to read and perform each day
- Conduct choral readings (students read with you in unison), antiphonal choral readings (groups of students take parts), and echo readings (students repeat a line after you read it)
- Engage in Readers Theatre, assigning students individual parts

Provide word study opportunities.

To read with expression and automaticity, students need to be able to decode words accurately. Make sure to incorporate a word study block into your reading instructional time. Word study includes sounding out words, spelling, learning word meanings, and the history of words. Word study can be game-like and fun. Try word ladders (Rasinski, 2005) or making and writing words (Rasinski & Heym, 2008).

Sample Word Ladder
(Provided by Timothy Rasinski)

Ask students to make and change words as you give clues. Students use paper, manipulative letters, or slates and change one letter at a time to make new words.

1. Start with *kin*.
2. Change one letter to make *sin*.
3. Change one letter to mean taking a drink: *sip*.
4. Change one letter to make gooey stuff: *sap*.
5. Change one letter to make something that helps find your way: *map*.
6. Change one letter to make a word that means sleep during the day: *nap*.
7. Change one letter to mean something you put on your head: *cap*.
8. Change one letter to make something you drink from: *cup*.
9. Change one letter to make a small dog: *pup*.
10. Add a letter to make *pump*.
11. Halloween word: *pumpkin*.

Provide coaching in fluency.

If you want to see a dramatic jump in the fluency of your students, provide specific coaching (Rasinski & Griffith, 2010). What does coaching in fluency look like? Make sure students are matched to text that is at their level (not too hard, not too easy). Listen as students read and provide them with specific feedback. Encourage them to read phrases rather than word by word and to use punctuation and expression. Model on the spot as individuals read for you. Praise approximations. Provide specific compliments and prompts such as

- "Good expression. I could feel the character's anger when you read...."
- "Great phrasing. You grouped those words and read them together so it sounded natural."
- "Read it again and group together the words to sound natural."
- "Read it again so it sounds like you are angry [or happy, etc.]."

Lori's Top 5 Surefire Strategies for Teaching Reading Fluency

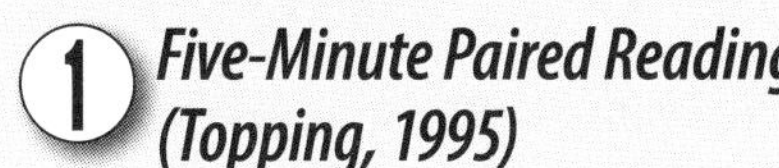

1 *Five-Minute Paired Reading (Topping, 1995)*

Paired reading is an extremely effective technique that can be used in the classroom and with cross-age tutors, adult tutors, or parents. Even in just five minutes per day, you will see results!

- Simply match a struggling reader with a more proficient reader.
- Select reading material at the instructional level of the less proficient reader. If possible, allow the less capable reader to select the text.
- The two readers sit side by side to read the text in unison.
- The less proficient reader holds a strip of paper or bookmark under each line of text. This reader moves the strip to the next line, helping control the reading speed. (The more proficient reader may need to slow down a bit so the partner can keep up.)
- After the reading, the partners discuss the selection.

2 *Lucky Listeners (Rasinski & Griffith, 2010)*

Students practice reading a passage in class and then at home read the same passage aloud to three willing audience members. That might require the student to get a bit creative and make a phone call to grandma (or hold a video chat!) or read aloud to a pet, a baby brother or sister, or a nice neighbor. Parents or other listeners sign a log and maybe even write a compliment or two. The Lucky Listener lesson can be conducted several times per week.

3 *Sing It Again, Sam!*

Download lyrics to popular songs that your students enjoy. Show music videos when possible. (Be sure to screen music videos and lyrics for appropriateness before sharing with your students.) Provide copies of the songs for students to mark up, underlining and circling words to emphasize and putting slash marks between phrases. Student groups may collaborate to respond to the song by

- Sketching a large mural or graphic

- Accompanying the lyrics with a dance or hand motions that demonstrate the meaning of vocabulary from the tune
- Writing a poem in response to the song
- Lip-syncing the song to perform for the class using a toy microphone

 *Poem a Week*

Select a poem to introduce each week. Students reread the poem all week and practice for a few minutes each day in pairs or groups to perform portions or all of the text on Friday. Keep the poetry in a class book or chart and provide copies for students to keep in their own poetry books. You might make the poem practice part of a work station during guided reading time.

Monday

- Model fluent, expressive reading.
- Invite the students to echo read: You read a line and students repeat it.
- Discuss what the poem means.
- Model how to figure out difficult words, figure out where to group words for phrasing, and what sort of expression or mood fits the piece.

Tuesday–Thursday

- Each day, begin the lesson by rereading the poem. Focus on some aspect of fluency by modeling how to figure out difficult words or how to emphasize certain vocabulary to emphasize meaning.
- Model accents or voices and emotions that fit the piece. Students are provided copies of the text to practice rereading in pairs or groups.
- Rotate to groups to coach students as they read. This is a critical step!

Friday

- Students perform the text in their pairs or groups. If you don't have time for each group to perform in front of the class, pair up groups to perform for one another.
- Performances might include drama, hand motions, or artwork to accompany the piece. Or groups can rotate to an area of the classroom and record their performance with an inexpensive video camera or make an audio recording.

 *Flash Mob Reading*

Mob reading, adapted from cumulative choral reading (Rasinski & Griffith, 2010), is a fun take on a popular Internet sensation: the mob dance. A mob dance takes place in a park, mall, or other public setting and begins with one person dancing alone to a song. Others gradually join in until a large group is dancing away. For a fantastic example, see Ocoee Middle School's "Gotta Keep Reading" spinoff on the Black Eyed Peas song "I Gotta Feeling," touted by the likes of Oprah!

Mob reading begins as one student or a group reads the first line, a few more students join in for the second line, and more students join in to read each line as the passage continues until everyone is reading together. This fun way to read and encourage repeated readings for an authentic purpose will surely end up as a class favorite. You may want to encourage students to add hand motions to go with each line of text to form a sort of dance (Oczkus, 2009).

Before Reading: Activate Prior Knowledge

- How would you define *reading fluency*?
- Explain what it sounds like to listen to a reading by a student who does not read fluently. What are the characteristics of nonfluent and fluent reading?
- Discuss problems your students experience with fluency and the texts they read at your grade level.
- What are some techniques you've found to be successful in developing reading fluency?

During Reading: Respond While Reading

- While reading this chapter, mark your text with self-stick notes. Use symbols to indicate questions (?), things you want to try (T), something you connect with (+), something interesting or surprising (!) (adapted from Hatt, n.d.).

After Reading: Think About and Discuss

- Why is fluency considered the bridge to comprehension?
- How does fluency impact silent reading?
- What are the three fluency components? Discuss students who might need help with one or more of the three fluency components.
- Why do you think many schools are equating fluency with words per minute and rereadings?
- What other components of fluency are also critical, and what does research say about those aspects of fluency?
- What is the impact of meaningful practice and performance on fluency? How can you model fluent reading and conduct fluency think-alouds?
- Discuss repeated and choral readings and their role in developing fluency.
- How does word study develop fluency?
- Discuss possible coaching prompts you can use to develop fluency. Why is coaching fluency important?
- How can you make fluency work an integral part of your week?

Putting Fluency Into Practice

Professional Development Breakout Groups

- Break into five groups and study each of Lori's Top 5 Reading Fluency lessons. Discuss and share ideas.
- Work in teams to brainstorm ways you can use performance as a vehicle for developing fluency.
- Create lesson plans. Refer to ideas in the chapter.

Lesson Sharing

- Try one of Lori's Top 5 lessons with your class. Be prepared to share. On a scale of 1–5, how did the lesson go? Explain. What do you want to try next?
- Try two or more of the Top 5 lessons and share results.
- Try assessing several students using the Fluency Recording Sheet and the Directions for Administering a One-Minute Fluency Assessment. Bring to a meeting and discuss.

Teacher as Reader

- With a partner, try the paired reading technique. How does it help develop fluency? What might be the best way to partner students for this activity? How is paired reading helpful to the struggling reader? How is it like singing to the radio in the shower?
- What do you remember about your level of fluency in oral reading as a child?

Before the Next Meeting

Read: Select the next chapter your group will read. Mark the text during reading.
Try: Try one of the lessons from the next chapter, or try something new from this chapter.
Observe: Visit a colleague's classroom to observe a lesson on fluency, or record yourself teaching a lesson and share the video at a meeting.

Going Deeper With Fluency

- Try a book study using this practical resource loaded with everything you need to know about fluency:

  Rasinski, T.V. (2010). *The fluent reader: Oral & silent reading strategies for building fluency, word recognition & comprehension* (2nd ed.). New York: Scholastic.

- Or consider studying the resources listed on page 166.

Paired Reading Bookmark Lesson

Objective: To provide students with a bookmark with prompts they can use with a partner while participating in paired reading. With just five minutes per day of paired reading with a more proficient reader, a struggling reader can make great gains in fluency. Tutors may also be trained in this effective technique.

Common Core Connections: Students follow agreed-upon procedures and roles for discussion with partners. Students read with accuracy and fluency to support comprehension.

Teacher Modeling: To model the paired reading procedure, call up a student to model with you or a pair of students to model for the class. You may wish to partner struggling readers with stronger readers or even partner cross-age tutors.

1. The students select a text to read together (or you can assign one).
2. Two students share one copy of the reading and hold the text between them on their laps, a table, or the floor.
3. Give one of the students a clear acetate marker or a bookmark that extends the width of the page so it will fit under a line of text. The purpose of the bookmark is to move it down the lines of text to help students read with fluency. The bookmark aids in keeping the pair at the same place in the text and promotes a nice steady pace.
4. First, model with the pair how to predict what the text is about. Then they count to three and begin reading aloud in unison.
5. If they come to a word they do not know, tell them to have one of the participants read the word and go on. If they are both stumped by the word, tell them to skip it for the moment. Remember, the emphasis is on reading fluidly.
6. Reading together at the same pace often requires one partner to slow down to match the other's reading speed.
7. Model with the pair how to discuss the questions at the end of the bookmark.

Variation: The method often includes another component (Topping, 1995) with the following steps: (1) Indicate to the pairs which child is partner A and which is partner B. They begin reading in unison. (2) When it is partner A's turn, he taps partner B on the arm to indicate he is ready to read alone orally, and partner B ceases reading aloud but follows along silently and continues moving the marker. (3) When partner A gets stuck on a word, partner B again joins in orally to continue the fluid reading until partner A taps her arm to indicate she wants to read alone again.

Guided Practice: Keep modeling often by calling on partners to model for the class. Circulate and monitor the pairs' progress and coach as necessary.

Independent Practice: Put the Paired Reading Bookmark in a reading station or center (see "Paired Reading" poster). Students may also practice reading at home with parents or siblings.

Wrap Up: Ask students to reflect on what they liked about the paired reading session and what they learned from it. Ask them to share problems and brainstorm ways to solve them.

Assessment Tips

Quick Fluency Check Bookmarks

Objectives: These two bookmarks are handy reference tools to help when you administer one-minute fluency checks as students read to you.

Administering a One-Minute Fluency Assessment

As a student reads to you for one minute, monitor for rate, accuracy, and prosody:

Rate—Watch for halting reading, with many pauses, or natural, conversational, fluid reading. Be sure to note what type of book the student is reading: an independently selected book, just-right leveled text, content-area grade-level reading, or grade-level basal or novel.

Accuracy—Does the student make many errors? Look for patterns in the types of errors. Watch for and record substitutions, mispronunciations, and omissions. Does the student always make one kind of error or a mix of several? This information is valuable when planning follow-up word work with your class and small groups of students. Do not count the following as errors: self-corrections (these are a positive sign of self-monitoring!), repeated words (also a positive behavior for self-checking), and inserted extra words (just call the student's attention to it). The formula for calculating the accuracy percentage is found on the bookmark.

Prosody—Does the student read word for word or by phrasing the material to make it sound natural? Watch for smoothness, expression, tone, and mood. Emphasis on key words is another great reading behavior students need to demonstrate and learn as part of prosody in fluency.

Coaching Prompts for Fluency (Rasinski & Griffith, 2010)

Don't forget to give praise and to coach! Be sure to praise the student and provide specific compliments for each of the aspects of fluency, not just speed! Sample compliments are as follows:

Rate

- "Great job reading in a loud voice."
- "I like the way you slowed down when the character ________ was talking. I knew what he was feeling."
- "The way you read the setting paragraph really made me feel like I was there at the ________. You set a ________ mood."

Accuracy

- "Great self-correcting! You knew that the word ________ didn't sound right the first time you read it."
- "You read the sentence ________ twice to check what it said. Good job!"

Prosody

- "Great phrasing. You grouped those words and read them together so it sounded natural."
- "Read it again and group the words to sound natural."
- "Read it again so it sounds like you are angry [or happy, etc.]."

Paired Reading Bookmark

Materials: partners, a book, a bookmark (clear acetate)

1. **Choose a Book**—Choose a book with your partner. Share one copy.
2. **Sit Side by Side**—Place the book between you where you can both see it.

3. **Predict**—Look at the text illustrations and headings. What do you think the text is about?
4. **Put the Marker in Place**—One reader holds the bookmark under the text and will pull it down the text as you read together.
5. **Begin Reading Aloud**—Count to three and begin reading aloud at the same time. The student holding the marker moves it down the text under each line.
6. **Stay Together**—Try to read together at the same speed.
7. **Keep Going**—Try to stay together. It's OK for just one partner to read the hard words aloud and go on. If neither of you knows a hard word, skip it and go on.
8. **Discuss**—When you are done reading, discuss:
   - What was your favorite part?
   - This was mostly about....
   - I agree/disagree with...because....
   - Why do you think...?
   - What are you wondering?

Paired Reading Bookmark

Materials: partners, a book, a bookmark (clear acetate)

1. **Choose a Book**—Choose a book with your partner. Share one copy.
2. **Sit Side by Side**—Place the book between you where you can both see it.

3. **Predict**—Look at the text illustrations and headings. What do you think the text is about?
4. **Put the Marker in Place**—One reader holds the bookmark under the text and will pull it down the text as you read together.
5. **Begin Reading Aloud**—Count to three and begin reading aloud at the same time. The student holding the marker moves it down the text under each line.
6. **Stay Together**—Try to read together at the same speed.
7. **Keep Going**—Try to stay together. It's OK for just one partner to read the hard words aloud and go on. If neither of you knows a hard word, skip it and go on.
8. **Discuss**—When you are done reading, discuss:
   - What was your favorite part?
   - This was mostly about....
   - I agree/disagree with...because....
   - Why do you think...?
   - What are you wondering?

Best Ever Literacy Survival Tips: 72 Lessons You Can't Teach Without by Lori D. Oczkus.
© 2012 International Reading Association. May be copied for classroom use.

Paired Reading Poster

Materials: partners, a book, a bookmark (clear acetate)

1. **Choose a Book**—Choose a book with your partner. Share one copy.

2. **Sit Side by Side**—Place the book between you where you can both see it.

3. **Predict**—Look at the text illustrations and headings. What do you think the text is about?

4. **Put the Marker in Place**—One reader holds the bookmark under the text and will pull it down the text as you read together.

5. **Begin Reading Aloud**—Count to three and begin reading aloud at the same time. The student holding the marker moves it down the text under each line.

6. **Stay Together**—Try to read together at the same speed.

7. **Keep Going**—Try to stay together. It's OK for just one partner to read the hard words aloud and go on. If neither of you knows a hard word, skip it and go on.

8. **Discuss**—When you are done reading, discuss:
   - What was your favorite part?
   - This was mostly about....
   - I agree/disagree with...because....
   - Why do you think...?
   - What are you wondering?

Quick Fluency Check Bookmarks

Administering a One-Minute Fluency Assessment

Date ______ Name of Student _________

- Time student reading for one minute.
- Ask the student to pause only briefly on words he or she doesn't know and to keep going if he or she can't figure them out.
- After three seconds, tell the student the word and count it as an error.

What did you notice?

- **Rate—**Does the student read
  __at a conversational pace
  __with expression
  __with good volume
- **Accuracy—**How many words did the student read correctly in one minute?

  ____

  Count these as errors
  - mispronunciations
  - substitutions
  - omissions

  Do *not* count these as errors:
  - self-corrections
  - repeated words
  - inserted words (ignore these)

Calculate the accuracy percentage: # of words read in a minute – # of errors = # of words read correctly

- **Prosody—**Does the student read
  __in phrases and groups of words, not word by word
  __with expression and feeling
  __ dialogue with expression
  __important words with more emphasis
  __using punctuation properly when reading

Fluency Recording Sheet

Date ______ Name of Student _________

Student will read (name of book/text):

____

Circle level of the reading material:

at grade level

below grade level

above grade level

Notes during one-minute reading (record mispronunciations, substitutions, omissions):

Words-per-minute calculation:
# of words read in a minute – # of errors = # of words read correctly

Fluency score in grade-level material:
Excellent = above 98%
Good–Acceptable = 92–98%
Frustration Level = below 92%

Fluency Observations (mark with a +, ✓, –):

- **Rate—**Does the student read
  __at a conversational pace throughout
  __with good volume
- **Accuracy—**Does the student read words and
  ____mispronounce __omit __substitute
- **Prosody—**Does the student read
  __in phrases and groups of words, not word by word
  __with expression and feeling
  __dialogue with expression
  __important words with more emphasis
  __using punctuation properly when reading

Q&A

How do I assess reading fluency? I want to measure speed but also the other important aspects of fluency.

Fluency, or the ability to read a text automatically and with expression, can be assessed by observing students' reading rate, accuracy, and oral prosody in reading of grade-level materials. As students read a passage, note whether it is grade-level material or material that is at the student's actual reading level and look for the following:

- Rate: Students read aloud for one minute from an unrehearsed passage. To calculate words per minute, subtract the total number of errors from the total number of words read in the first minute.
- Accuracy: Calculate the percentage of words read accurately in the passage. (Look for 92–98% on grade-level passages; below 92% is frustration level and above 98% is independent level.)
- Prosody: Listen for expression, volume, phrasing, smoothness, and pace that is conversational. See Tim Rasinski's Fluency Rubric: at www.timrasinski.com/presentations/multidimensional_fluency_rubric_4_factors.pdf.

For details on scoring fluency, refer to Jan Hasbrouck's articles "Understanding and Assessing Fluency" and "Screening, Diagnosing, and Progress Monitoring for Fluency: The Details" at the Reading Rockets website.

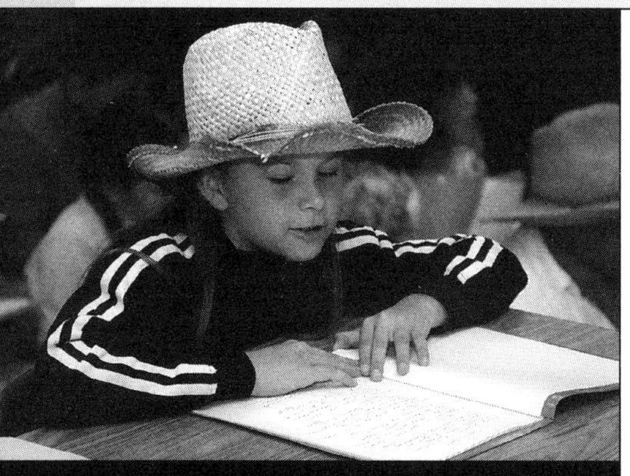

"Fluency is a bridge to comprehension. When your students practice fluency techniques, their silent reading comprehension dramatically improves (Pinnell et al., 1995; Rasinski, Rikli, & Johnston, 2009)."

Resources

Online

ReadWriteThink: www.readwritethink.org

ReadWriteThink is a great resource for hundreds of free downloadable lessons in all aspects of reading. Here are some fluency lessons to try:

- "History Comes Alive: Using Fluency and Comprehension Using Social Studies" by Veronica Montes
- "Improving Fluency Through Group Literary Performance" by Devon Hamner
- "Poetry: A Feast to Form Fluent Readers" by Sheila K. Seitz

Reading Rockets Fluency: www.readingrockets.org/atoz/fluency

Reading Rockets offers a collection of research-based articles on fluency, including Jan Hasbrouck's articles mentioned in the Q&A section of this chapter.

Great Professional Books

Essential Readings on Fluency, compiled and introduced by Timothy V. Rasinski

Fluency: Differentiated Interventions and Progress-Monitoring Assessments (4th ed.) by Jerry L. Johns and Roberta L. Berglund

The Fluent Reader: Oral & Silent Reading Strategies for Building Fluency, Word Recognition & Comprehension (2nd ed.), including DVD showing strategies in action, by Timothy V. Rasinski

Great Poetry Collections

The Random House Book of Poetry for Children: A Treasury of 572 Poems for Today's Child, selected by Jack Prelutsky and illustrated by Arnold Lobel

Sing a Song of Popcorn: Every Child's Book of Poems, selected by Beatrice Schenk de Regniers, Eva Moore, Mary Michaels White, and Jan Carr, and illustrated by nine Caldecott Medal artists

References

Hatt, C. (n.d.). *Better discussions in study groups*. Retrieved from www.choiceliteracy.com/public/796.cfm

National Center for Education Statistics. (2009). *The nation's report card. Reading 2009: National Assessment of Educational Progress at grades 4 and 8* (NCES 2010–458). Washington, DC: Institute of Education Sciences, U.S. Department of Education. Retrieved February 4, 2011, from nces.ed.gov/nationsreportcard/reading

National Institute of Child Health and Human Development. (2000). *Report of the National Reading Panel. Teaching children to read: An evidence-based assessment of the scientific research literature on reading and its implications for reading instruction* (NIH Publication No. 00-4769). Washington, DC: U.S. Government Printing Office.

Oczkus, L.D. (2009). *Interactive think-aloud lessons: 25 surefire ways to engage students and improve comprehension*. New York: Scholastic; Newark, DE: International Reading Association.

Opitz, M.F., & Rasinski, T.V. (1998). *Good-bye round robin: 25 effective oral reading strategies*. Portsmouth, NH: Heinemann.

Pinnell, G.S., Pikulski, J.J., Wixson, K.K., Campbell, J.R., Gough, P.B., & Beatty, A.S. (1995). *Listening to children read aloud: Data from NAEP's integrated reading performance record (IRPR) at grade 4*. Washington, DC: U.S. Department of Education, Office of Educational Research and Improvement.

Rasinski, T.V. (2005). *Daily word ladders: 100 reproducible word study lessons that help kids boost reading, vocabulary, spelling & phonics skills—independently!* New York: Scholastic.

Rasinski, T.V. (2010). *The fluent reader: Oral & silent reading strategies for building fluency, word recognition & comprehension* (2nd ed.). New York: Scholastic.

Rasinski, T.V., & Griffith, L. (2010). *Fluency through practice & performance*. Huntington Beach, CA: Shell Education.

Rasinski, T.V., & Heym, R. (2008). *Making & writing words: Essential word families*. Huntington Beach, CA: Shell Education.

Rasinski, T.V., Rikli, A., & Johnston, S. (2009). Reading fluency: More than automaticity? More than a concern for the primary grades? *Literacy Research and Instruction, 48*(4), 350–361. doi:10.1080/19388070802468715

Topping, K. (1995). *Paired reading, spelling and writing: The handbook for teachers and parents*. New York: Cassell.

CHAPTER 12

Guided Writing—The Missing Middle Piece! TOP 5 Powerful Lessons for Improving Writing

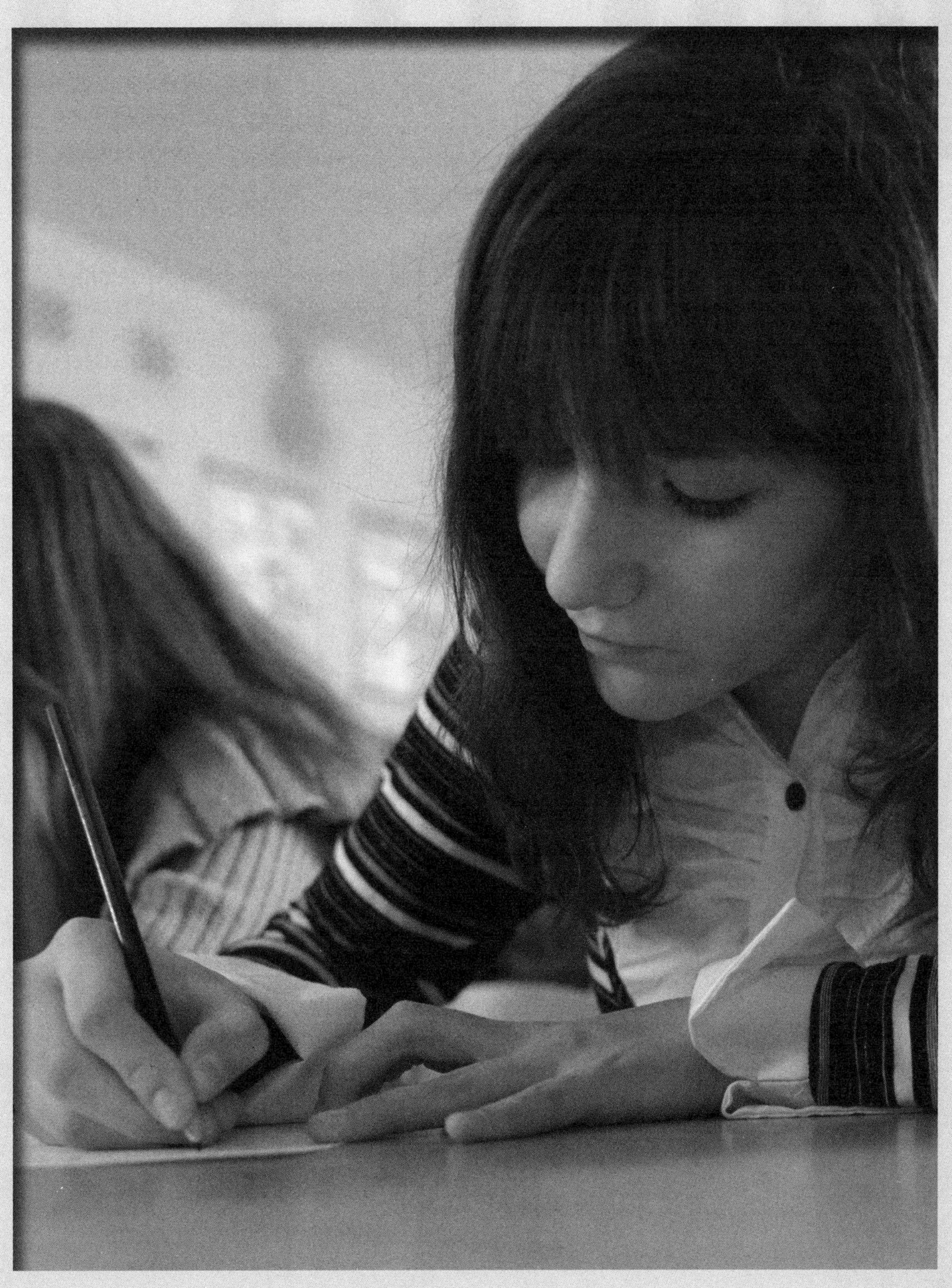

Best Ever Advice on... Guided Writing

For English learners and struggling writers, guided writing is an essential step in the writing process. I have found that these students benefit greatly from sharing a writing task, especially if you use "cool tools." This extra support and the added fun of using a cool tool help students see themselves as creative, successful writers.

Writing an essay can be overwhelming for many students. I break them into teams for at least the introductory paragraph. Each member has to write only one sentence on a colored strip of paper. One writes the hook, another the conclusion/transition, and the rest write one of the "sneak preview" sentences. They put them on pieces of construction paper, decide how to order them, and tape them down. We post them around the room and do a gallery walk, giving feedback to one another. Now everyone has a paragraph they are proud of. They either continue on their own or work together to finish the essay. This scaffolding builds students' confidence in their own abilities as writers, gives them the opportunity to see and discuss their peers' writing, and provides a framework to use when writing other essays. In other words, instructional time well spent.

—Kathy Langham, Sixth-Grade Teacher

If you ask students to define writing, their answers reveal how they feel about putting the pen to paper (or their fingers to the keyboard). You may hear:

"Writing is magical."

"Writing is using your imagination."

"Writing is a way of sharing your ideas."

Unfortunately, not enough students share positive comments about writing. Many openly admit that they do not enjoy writing. Others add to the anti-writing sentiment by explaining their reasons for hating the process of putting pen to paper:

"I have trouble getting ideas."

"Teachers always want you to rewrite."

"It is boring!"

One fifth grader expressed concern about testing in her definition of writing:

"Writing is what teachers and students do to torture students. Then every once in a while we take a district writing test and I really hate that!"

Motivating students of any age to write often presents a challenge.

Does this scenario sound familiar to you? You teach a complete writing lesson that includes showing students examples from literature, modeling the writing for the class, and possibly even engaging students in a shared writing activity. Then you ask students to begin writing a draft, only to find that at least five to seven of them (or more!) expertly begin to avoid writing by sharpening pencils, asking to go to the restroom, coughing, doodling, looking around the room, or digging around in their desks. As you rotate around the room to confer with each one of the lost writers, most of them ask, "What are we supposed to do?" or reluctantly admit, "I don't know what to write!"

Problems Students and Teachers Experience With Writing

Test results confirm that there is a growing concern about student writing. The National Assessment of Educational Progress (NAEP; National Center for Education Statistics, 2008) reports that many of our students, sometimes up to two-thirds, are performing below proficient standards.

Teachers everywhere express concerns about teaching students to write:

- *My students write listy, dull, lifeless pieces that don't include details.*
- *The students find it difficult to think of ideas to write about.*
- *Students can't organize their thoughts.*
- *Voice is seriously missing from student writing.*
- *Report writing is getting harder for them.*
- *I have trouble getting around to all the students during writers workshop.*
- *I have to give so many writing assessments. No wonder students hate to write!*
- *Our district doesn't have a formal writing program, just the one embedded in the district adopted reading program. It is not enough!*

The good news is that even though some of the test results appear dismal, over the past twenty years we *have* come a long way in the teaching of writing. We know from research in best practices that we should support our writers through prewriting, drafting, editing and sharing copies in meaningful ways. We model how to write by thinking aloud and drawing examples from quality literature (Routman, 2005). During writers workshop writers explore topics of their choice and work with peers to hone their craft (Calkins, 1994). Rubrics with clear expectations guide our teaching. Traits of good writing include ideas, organization, voice, sentence fluency, and conventions, guide our lessons and assessments (Culham, 2003; Spandel, 2001). In many of the classrooms I work in around the country we have added guided writing as a practical way to improve writing for all students, especially those who struggle! (Oczkus, 2007).

In this chapter, we will explore a practical and effective tool you can add to your bag of effective writing "tricks." Add it to your writing lessons any time you feel students need more supported practice to really "get" the genre or skill you are teaching.

Take a Peek Into Classrooms

Here are some examples of writing that include rich modeling, cooperative practice, and supported independent practice.

Primary example—yummy descriptions!

The first and second graders in Mrs. Sims' combination class are working on writing descriptive paragraphs. Mrs. Sims is frustrated with the students' first attempts to write descriptions, which include lots of "I likes" and sentences that start with "The," such as "The lemon looks like...," "The lemon smells like…," and "The lemon tastes like...." I am coaching in her classroom and we decide together to model for students how to write descriptions using more interesting sentence structures. I use a chart and bring in a banana to use in one of my favorite modeled writing lessons that students enjoy (Oczkus, 2007). I write a series of sentences that start with "The banana smells like…" and "The banana looks like…" and read them in a monotone.

"What is wrong with my description of the banana?" I ask the class.

"Too many '*thes*,'" observes Sondro, and the other children nod in agreement.

With a show of hands, I ask the students if I should start over with more interesting beginnings. The class agrees that I need to scrap my efforts and begin again. So, I invite volunteers to come up and cross out all the "*thes*" on the chart. Then I rewrite the piece with more varied sentences such as, "My little yellow banana is like a bright yellow moon shining at me. When I grab the tasty snack, its smooth skin feels like a rubber ball against my hand. It squishes between my teeth and smells so sweet. I love bananas!" The class agrees my second attempt is better.

To practice descriptive writing, I hand a piece of fruit to each table team, and give each individual student one sentence strip with either a hand, an eye, a nose, or a tongue on it to cue the sense that student will be writing about. I make my way to each group to guide the sentence writing. Students may refer to the chart from my modeling for their sentence beginnings (Oczkus, 2007; Mariconda, 1999).

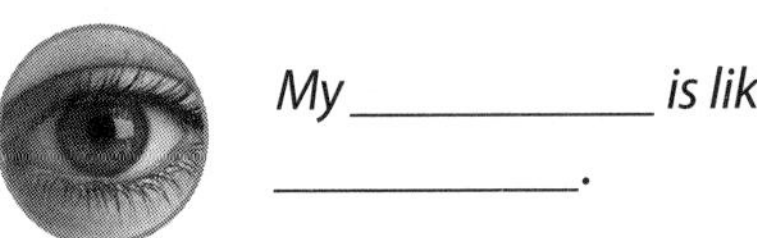

My ___________ is like a ___________.

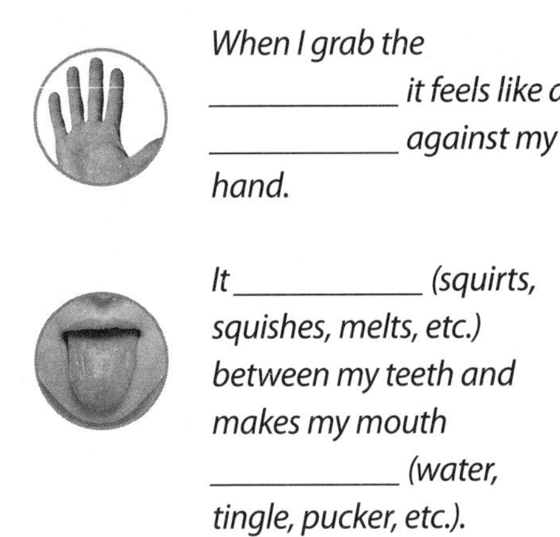

When I grab the ___________ it feels like a ___________ against my hand.

It ___________ (squirts, squishes, melts, etc.) between my teeth and makes my mouth ___________ (water, tingle, pucker, etc.).

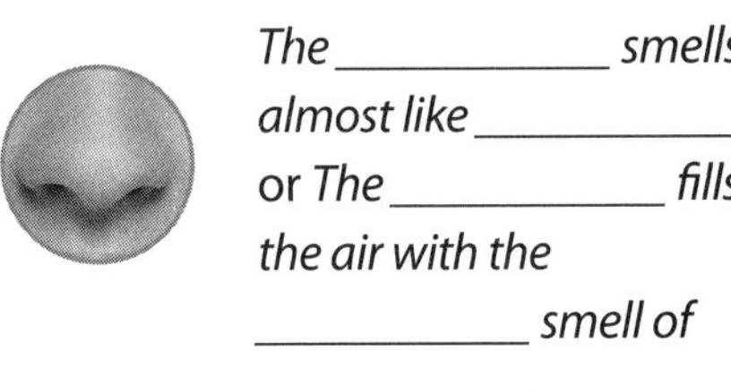

The ___________ smells almost like ___________. or *The ___________ fills the air with the ___________ smell of ___________.*

After each child writes his or her strip, their teams read their strips, assemble them in any order, and glue them onto a poster. The group reads and acts out their descriptions. In the days to follow, individual students write descriptions of the school lunch menu items which are displayed in the cafeteria and read them over the morning announcements. The students suggest that maybe teams could write descriptions for local restaurants! A letter-writing lesson is now in order and the students are hooked!

Intermediate example—acting out narrative beginnings

The district requires that students write personal narratives and stories at every grade level. I am visiting fourth grade for three weeks to work on the development of narratives. Yesterday, I wrote a modeled story in front of the class and told students about the time my daughters rode a roller coaster that broke down. I invited students to act out my story by pretending to be my daughters and myself. I opted for a dialogue beginning.

"Rebecca, where are you?" I screamed in a not so calm voice as I squinted upwards trying to peer into the roller coaster cars to find my six year old. I couldn't see her against the bright blue spring sky, so I repeated the panicked cry, "Rebecca, where are you?" Just moments earlier the rickety coaster suddenly stopped with the cars perched on various points on the ride.

Today I invite the class to help act out another narrative. Afterwards teams of students will help write possible beginnings for the story. The students eagerly raise their hands to volunteer to be the "actors" as I narrate a made-up story that *could* have happened in our neighborhood when a coyote openly roamed the streets of our town! Early morning and late evening sightings of the wild creature kept everyone on edge. I make up a narration while the volunteer actors ad lib as I go. Jack tip-toes across the classroom pretending to empty the kitchen trash in the dark when he freezes in his tracks to listen to a branch snap. Enrique hides behind a chair posing as the nervous coyote. I instruct the actors to freeze and pull out a chart to brainstorm some possible story beginnings that include:

A noise: "Crack! Jack's heart skipped a beat as he froze in place."

A thought: "Was that the coyote?" Jack nervously thought as he listened to the branch cracking in the night air."

A quote: "'Jack, I don't care if you are afraid to empty the trash in the dark. You forgot to do it after school. Do it NOW! ,' screamed his mom."

After writing each of the scenarios I ask table teams to act out the beginnings. The class is spellbound and engaged as the makeshift actors ham it up! Then I give each table team strips of paper and ask them to select a way to begin the story they just witnessed. I assign tables different types of beginnings (a noise, a thought, or a quote). I cover my chart and ask students to come up with NEW beginnings. Students have five minutes to write out their sentence strip beginnings. All groups then act out their beginnings while one group member reads from their strip. We post the strips and reflect on what we learned about beginnings. The next day each student brainstorms a possible narrative and writes a few beginning sentences choosing to start with a noise, thought, or piece of dialogue.

Middle school example—persuasive graphic organizers for success

"I think students should be allowed to use their cell phones at school," Jenny says during our debate about cell phone usage during class hours.

"It would be distracting," chimes in Peter.

"Yeah, but there are many apps that we can use for educational purposes including an agenda," adds Jaime.

The sixth graders are working on persuasive writing pieces. Yesterday I modeled persuasive writing by first showing some examples of advertisements and an essay written by my own daughter on "Why Our Family Needs a Dog." (Her essay worked, we eventually got one!) I used a graphic organizer to model how to write an essay persuading parents to allow a student to stay up later. As I wrote, I filled in the persuasive paragraph format that included the following components:

- A peppy opening sentence
- A thesis
- A sneak preview to my three supporting reasons

Today, students are working in teams and using the same graphic

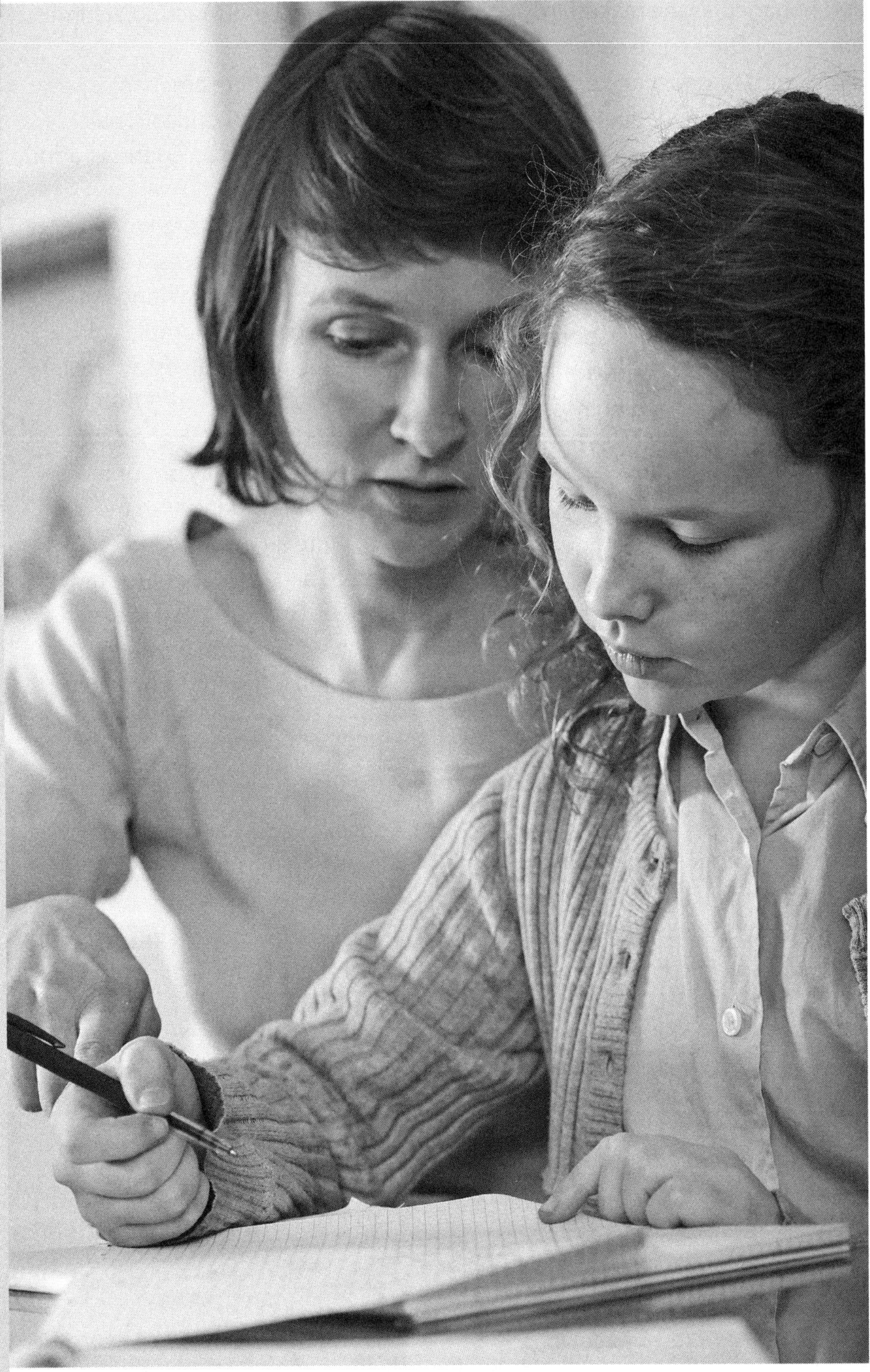

while still motivating students to enjoy writing? What practices will yield the best results when applied on a regular basis? What can you do to improve student writing without adding to your workload? By improving our scaffolding, or support, during lessons we can dramatically improve our students' writing. Scaffolding writing for students gives students the support they need from the fledgling idea stage to writing and publishing full-blown writing assignments in a variety of genres. Scaffolding is just good teaching and is often called the gradual release of responsibility (Pearson & Gallagher, 1983).

The scaffolding model applies to learning just about anything, from cooking, to academics, to sports. Teaching writing is much like teaching a child to ride a two-wheeler bike. Every child is different in the need for support. I remember my son, the oldest child, taking off the first day without training wheels. My middle daughter made us hold onto the seat for several weeks as she leaned into us to stop. My little one peddled a few feet between her parents in a sort of catch-and-release game. The same goes for writing. Students vary in their need for support. Some need more examples before they can write. Some require more practice in groups, or teacher guidance, in order to really understand the writing genre your class is studying. When you understand the steps to scaffolding writing you can weave in and out of them as you differentiate instruction for your students.

Here are the scaffolding steps that make a difference in supporting students as they write. Note that each of the scaffolding steps includes what I like to call "Cool Tools," or ways to engage students. Consider that not every lesson includes *all* the pieces, but over the course of a week or a unit of study you will want to

organizer to construct their group pieces. Each student is "in charge" of one portion of the organizer and fills out a colored sentence strip to paste onto the organizer. Each group shares their initial paragraph. Later in the week, I continue to model and guide the class in writing a five paragraph persuasive essay that in the weeks to come turns into a class letter to the principal requesting limited use of cell phones for educational uses during school.

Scaffolding Writing: Guided Writing—The Missing Middle Piece!

So, what are the next steps we need to take to meet the demand for better writing and improved test scores,

Steps to Excellent Writing!

Scaffolding Step	Definition
Identify the genre/ skill in mentor texts	Students find and study examples of the writing strategy, skill, or technique in literature, often called mentor texts. **Lori's Cool Tools:** *Make copies of pages from the text and highlight or circle examples of good writing. Act out portions of the text to study good writing, such as dialogue, description, or action.*
Teacher modeling	The teacher writes a quick example in front of the students, thinking aloud as he or she writes. **Lori's Cool Tools**: *Engage students as you write by asking them to show a thumbs up/ down for ideas, punctuation, or any teaching point. Students may also write on slates for feedback, or act out portions of the writing so the class can "see" how the story is developing and "see" why you are adding the next portion of action or dialogue.*
Shared writing	The teacher still holds the pen but the students contribute verbally to the discussion. A child may also serve as a volunteer and write in front of the class as the teacher and class help the student writer. **Lori's Cool Tools:** *Same as above.*
Guided writing— The missing middle piece!!!	Students write portions of a group-negotiated text. The teacher frames the assignment and works with the teams. **Example:** Students write descriptions and each student writes one sentence on a strip. The team assembles their paragraph and shares. Guided writing may occur during writers workshop with just one group based on need or in whole-class lessons with cooperative teams. **Lori's Cool Tools**: *Use interesting and varied papers for students to write their portion of text on such as strips, self-stick notes, index cards, transparencies, large construction paper, or large posters. Students connect their papers together for a completed cooperative piece.*
Independent writing	Students write on their own with teacher assistance as needed. **Lori's Cool Tools**: *Students use a rubric for the assignment that gives the criteria for a well-done piece.*
Reflection wrap-up	At the end of a lesson, a student may share writing with the class. Students give compliments and suggestions. Students discuss in teams what they learned and examples from their writing. **Lori's Cool Tools**: *Students use sticky notes to comment on each other's writing or on their own.*

Adapted from Lori Oczkus workshops based on *Guided Writing: Practical Lessons, Powerful Results*, by L.D. Oczkus, 2007, Portsmouth, NH: Heinemann.

include all the types of scaffolding to give students the support they need to write well.

Important Guidelines for Improving Student Writing

To make your writing lessons "stick," and to fully engage students along the way so they enjoy writing and improve their writing skills, try the following. These easy-to-implement guidelines can make a dramatic difference in your students' writing.

Help students see strong models using mentor texts.

Many teachers find that the best writing students do is often *after* they have read a powerful piece of literature that inspires them to write something on their own. The first step in a writing lesson is not to write at all but to read a well-written text and analyze it! Your minilesson and modeling may begin with a strong mentor text (Hoyt & Stead, 2011; Dorfman & Cappelli, 2007, 2009). A mentor text is any text that you use in your lesson as a model of whatever skill or strategy you are teaching. It can be from an article, book, nonfiction text, poem, or even another student. When using a particular piece of literature, you might select it to model genre, voice, word choice, or just about any aspect of author's craft or writing skills—even punctuation! There are many great professional books, as well as online bibliographical resources, for both fiction and nonfiction mentor texts (Dorfman, & Cappelli, 2007, 2009; Hoyt & Stead, 2011).

Using a mentor text to launch your lessons is easy. After reading a text, select your teaching point(s) using examples from the literature. For example, students of all ages love it when I bring in *Come On, Rain!* by Karen Hesse, a picture book dripping with descriptions of a warm summer rain on a sweltering hot day in the city. The senses come alive as we hear, smell, feel, and see the story through rich, descriptive language.

After simply reading the text, we then hunt for sensory descriptions to analyze. We discuss examples from the text including "squinting into the endless heat," "stuffy cave of her room," and "sizzling like a hot potato," which we record on a chart. Students are encouraged to use the same sort of writing technique in their own pieces.

Read aloud from mentor texts to model examples of author's craft, techniques, and skills that students may wish to try in their own writing.

Look to mentor texts to show

- *Text organization (fiction, or nonfiction!)*
- *Use of adjectives, metaphors, similes*
- *Plot or story line*
- *Sequence of events*
- *Use of dialogue, action, emotions*
- *Nonfiction text features*
- *Peppy vocabulary*
- *Commas and other conventions*

Model by writing in front of students.

Actually writing in front of students is an extremely critical step in helping them to become writers. Be careful not to simply "explain" the writing assignment, but rather use a pen or computer and *physically* write and compose in front of students (Oczkus, 2007). When modeling, I use the document camera or computer and compose a narrative beginning in front of my students as I write and spell each word. For example, when writing a story about my daughter slipping in the kitchen I wrote out in front of students:

"MOM!" screamed Rachael as she crashed to the floor, "My ankle is sore and I can't get up." I ran into the room and spotted Charley, our maltipoo with her tail between her legs hiding under a chair.

Although modeling takes a bit longer, students actually "get" the teaching points, so the extra time is worth it! After you write, ask students to turn to partners and share what they liked about your writing (Routman, 2005).

Some teachers tell me they are intimidated by writing in front of students. One way around that fear is to write out your example ahead of time. However, when you conduct your lesson, always make it look like you are composing on spot, struggling and writing the example for the first time. To make your modeled writing more authentic you can think aloud questions (Oczkus, 2007) such as:

- *What should I say next?*
- *Let me think.... What word might I write here?*
- *I am stuck on how to spell this word.*
- *Oops, I left out a detail.*
- *Maybe I will add....*

Modeling writing for your students is worth the effort. Besides, writing expert Nancie Atwell says, "You only have to write a little bit better than your students for them to take away something from your writing" (as cited in Routman, 2005).

Try using drama during writing lessons.

Drama is a really wonderful, hands-on way to help students find "holes" in their writing. When I asked sixth graders to read aloud their narrative drafts by inviting a few "actors" to listen to the reading, and act it out as they go, Liam found out that his story about his dog eating the family goldfish contained a constant string of dialogue and not enough action to set the stage for the conversations. The one-pager lacked in paragraphs describing details, and students in the class looked puzzled as the actors simply repeated the dialogue he'd created. The impromptu reading and drama provided the writer with powerful revision feedback.

Down the hall, first graders read aloud their stories from sketches they drew as a team. One child narrates while the others act out the collaborative piece. The narrator naturally "fills in" dialogue and descriptions. Students work with the teacher to write out their creation.

Drama is a great tool for either revising writing, or a means of planning writing. Try having students read aloud their pieces while other students act out the reading on the spot. Students enjoy the concrete feedback to their writing.

Provide time for daily writing.

To build up their writing muscle, students should write some every day (Routman, 2005; Calkins, 1994). Writing takes discipline, stamina, and endurance which, like anything

else, becomes easier with practice! Provide quiet time for students to work on their writing daily. Let students know not all of their efforts will be stellar, but that the practice along the way will improve their ability to write.

Lead students through the writing process.

Be sure to include in your writing instruction the basic writing process steps:

1. **Brainstorming or prewriting** (discussing, reading a book, sharing an experience)

2. **Writing a first draft** (explaining that getting thoughts down quickly might be messy, encouraging students to cross out as they write)

3. **Revising** (reading to a peer or teacher, looking for places to add details, improve word usage, or cut material)

4. **Editing** (reviewing conventions, spelling, etc.)

5. **Publishing** (typing the piece up in a presentation format, report, booklet, online booklet, etc.)

Encourage authentic purposes for writing.

Surely you recall in school writing papers just for the sake of writing and then receiving a grade. Whenever possible try to tie your writing units to authentic writing purposes such as

- An editorial
- Posters for the school hallway
- Your class newsletter or the school website
- School announcements
- Reviews of restaurants, movies, or books
- Letters
- Sharing information with parents or the public in some way

Teach students to self-assess.

If you think about it, when we write we are assessing ourselves constantly. As we reread and compose along the way, we ask, "Where am I going with this? Is this a good word to use? Does this make sense?" When you give students the tools to self-assess during every step of the writing process, they grow as writers. By modeling first and providing mentor texts, you can set up simple criteria or even rubrics to write with. Many schools use the Traits of Writing to teach and assess writing. The Traits (Culham, 2003; Spandel, 2001) include:

Ideas
Do I have ideas that fit together?
Have I included details that make sense?

Organization
How is my writing organized? (Does it have a beginning, middle, end, or other organization for the genre?)
Is it in an order that makes sense?

Word Choice
What word is the best fit?
Is this word strong enough, or is there a better one?

Voice
Does the writing show my personality, feelings, and/or enthusiasm?
Is the writing interesting for my reader?

Sentence Fluency
Are my sentences varied (some long, others short)?
Do my sentences all begin the same or differently?

Conventions
Have I checked my spelling?
Do I have the right punctuation?

Lori's Top 5 Surefire Strategies for Writing Instruction

1 *Wonderful Weekend Webs: Write in Detail! (Oczkus, 2007)*

As part of weekly writing, I like to have students elaborate on a topic or zero in on a small moment to write about in detail. When we ask students to write about their weekend, we often get a string of "bed to bed" activities in a "listy," sort of dull piece:

"I went to my grandma's. We had my cousin over. I played video games. We ate pizza. I went to bed."

For a number of years, I have shared a very practical technique I call "Weekend Webs" (Oczkus, 2007). Students still have the opportunity to list their activities, but then we take it one step further and encourage writers to focus on just one event or topic to write about. The Weekend Web journal is a collection of short practice paragraphs and peppy sentences that we do not necessarily bring to a full piece of writing or publication. Weekend Webs are super easy to implement and you don't need any special materials!

Steps to Writing a Weekend Web

- Model your weekend web by creating a web on the board. Think aloud about your weekend activities as you draw your circles and fill them in.
- Select just ONE of the circle topics on your Weekend Web and elaborate on it by writing words and spokes from it (see Weekend Web Example). On my web, I elaborated on the colorful fall leaf I spotted on my walk.
- Write a few sentences about your selected topic in front of students.

  Example: *"The warm September sunshine beats down on me as I amble along on my daily walk with Charley, my dog. She pulls on the leash as she darts after a maple leaf frolicking around in the gentle warm wind. That's when I notice its warm autumn colors, yellow and red, a lone leaf, the first messenger of fall."*
- Lead students to quickly web their own weekends as they include activities and things they noticed. (Give them a limited time, such as two to three minutes, and encourage them to keep their pencils on the paper as they brainstorm. Circulate to prompt reluctant students.)
- Ask students to select just one of their items on their web to elaborate on and to add detail to. (Time this detail brainstorm for one to two minutes.)
- Encourage students to discuss their web topics of choice with a partner and then begin writing just a few sentences on their own.

Weekend Web Example

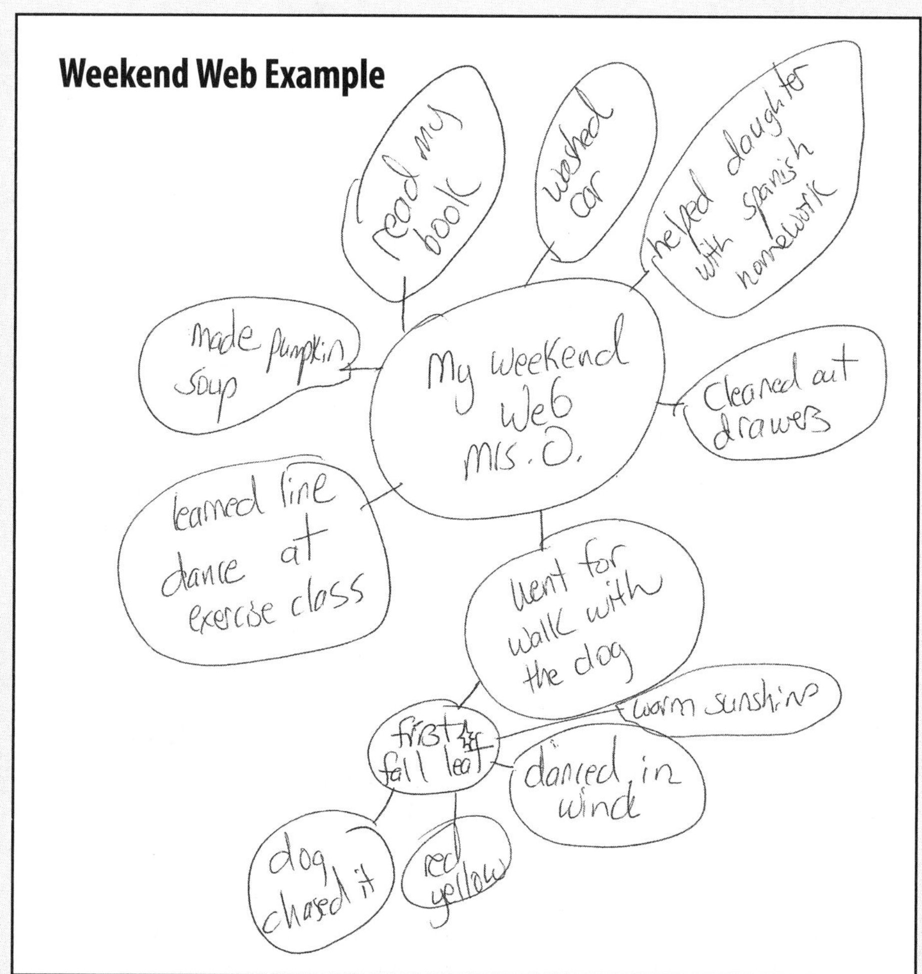

2 *Live Rubrics (adapted from Oczkus, 2007)*

With all the game show and reality shows on television, students "get" scoring more than ever, and this game-like activity makes assessment fun.

Live Rubric Procedure

- Select three to four skills or strategies to teach and assess as students write. For example, when writing stories you might teach students to include the following elements over the course of your minilessons in a unit on narrative writing:

Action
Description
Dialogue
Character's Feelings/Thoughts
(Mariconda, 1999; adapted by Oczkus, 2007)

- Make large posters or cue cards for each of the four elements of writing (action, description, dialogue, character's feelings/thoughts). Students may even illustrate.
- Select four students to hold up the cue cards. While a (willing) volunteer reads his or her writing, the cue card holders hold up their cards every time they hear their particular skill or strategy being utilized.
- Ask the writer to evaluate whether he/she used all the required elements. Ask the cue card holders and the class to discuss and offer suggestions to the writer.
- Students may work in small teams and take turns being in charge of one of the elements—action, description, dialogue, character's feelings/thoughts—as the group members take turns reading their pieces and evaluating each other's writing.

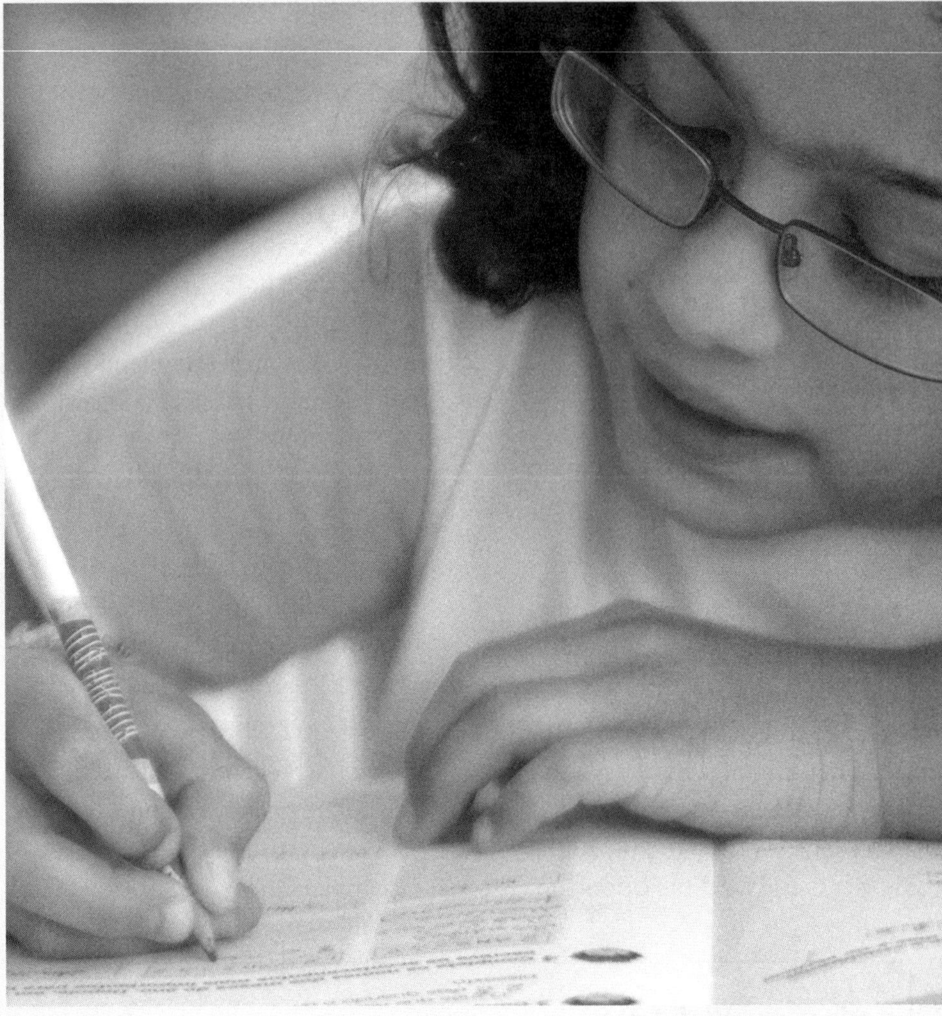

3 Daily Sentence "Make Overs" (adapted from Oczkus, 2007)

Students need practice in adding detail to their work and in deeply understanding what the phrase "add detail" means for each piece of writing. In this exercise, students begin with a daily simple sentence and add to it. For example, if the starter says, "He cried," students have just a few minutes to elaborate and "grow" the sentence into something like, "The boy, Sammy, a spoiled brat, became so frustrated when his toy airplane broke, that he cried a bucket of tears." When students work in teams, Daily Sentence Elaboration becomes a game-like competition.

Daily Sentence "Make Overs" Procedure

- Provide students (or invite a volunteer to suggest) a brief, dull sentence such as:

  Her room is dirty.
  The seat was sticky.
  The ice cream was good.
  Her head ached.
  She ran.

- Give teams "fun" paper on which to write the dull sentence and the elaboration. Try colorful self-stick notes, index cards, or giant poster paper and markers. Students may also use computers and create bold, colorful sentences using word art programs. You may want to time students as they race to elaborate and grow interesting sentences.
- You can give points for the number or quality of words used, such as issuing points for using active verbs.
- Students may also illustrate their peppy sentences.
- Ask students to select one sentence from their work to share with their partner or group. The group works as a team to "make over" the writer's selected sentence.

4 Stroll Line: Sharing Writing

A stroll line is a way for students to share their writing with peers for feedback and to create a built-in audience! A stroll line works during any phase of the writing process from sharing ideas prior to writing, to editing and reading final copies aloud.

Procedure for Stroll Line Sharing

- Students line up in two lines across from one another. They bring either their writing or ideas and brainstorms to discuss and share.
- Signal for students to take turns sharing writing. Tell them which line shares with their partners first.
- Encourage positive comments and questions only. Suggestions should be constructive.
- Signal for students to switch partners by asking one of the lines of students to remain stationary while the other line takes a step to the right. The student at the head of the line rotates to the space left at the end of the line.
- The rotating and sharing continues with the teacher cueing the movement of the lines.
- For a fun variation, you may play music and have students rotate past the other line, stopping with the music to read their piece to the partner across from them.
- Students sit at their desks and make changes to their writing based on comments from classmates.

5 *Colorful Writing*

Using color-coded paper strips, have students code the parts of their writing. I like to call this popular practice "that strippy (rhymes with hippie!) thing" (Auman, 2003).

Color Coded Paragraphs Procedure

- Take whatever you are teaching in writing—poetry, paragraphs, essays, stories, etc.—and assign color-coded strips to each part of the writing. For example, when we write essays, we use the following colored strips:

  Lavender: Catchy beginning sentence

  Green: Topic/thesis sentence

  Red: Main points

  Yellow: Details

  Green: Wrap up that restates topic

- Color-coding works really well with guided writing teams. Each student in a team of four to six is in charge of one colored strip as the team constructs a practice piece of writing to share with the class.
- Guided writing teams glue down their strips in an order that makes sense.
- Teams share writing in creative ways, including a "tour" as they rotate around the room to read or as groups stand up and share.

Before Reading: Activate Prior Knowledge

- Do your students like to write? Why or why not?
- What stalling behaviors do they exhibit when writing?
- What problems do students have when writing?

During Reading: Respond While Reading

- While reading this chapter, mark your text with self-stick notes. Use symbols to indicate questions (?), things you want to try (T), something you connect with (+), something interesting or surprising (!) (adapted from Hatt, n.d.).

After Reading: Think About and Discuss

- Study the Peek Into Classrooms. What do you like about the lessons? How does guided writing fit into any writing program? How would you define it?
- What are the scaffolding steps to writing? Which of these do you already teach?
- How does guided writing add extra support? Would you use guided writing with every lesson?
- What is the role of mentor texts and what can you teach with such a text?
- Discuss modeled writing. What is easy and hard about writing in front of students?
- How might drama help scaffolding writing for students?
- How much time should be spent daily on writing?
- Review and discuss the steps to the writing process and the Six Traits of Writing. How do they look at your grade level?
- How can you actively involve struggling readers in the lessons?
- What does guided writing look like in a writers' workshop model?

Putting Guided Writing Into Practice

Professional Development Breakout Groups

- Study the scaffolding steps to writing. Break into groups and discuss specific steps.
- Choose mentor texts to discuss and brainstorm possible lessons. What would you use them for: six traits, writer's craft? Why?
- Choose a lesson you always teach or need to teach at your grade level, such as persuasive essay or narrative story. Work as a team to develop a guided writing lesson that you can use immediately. How will the guided writing steps help your students succeed?

Lesson Sharing

- Try one of Lori's Top 5 lessons with your class. Be prepared to share. On a scale of 1–5, how did the lesson go? Explain. What do you want to try next?
- Ask your students to define writing. How do their definitions reflect their attitudes about writing?

Teacher as Reader

- As you read, notice the writing. Bring in well-written paragraphs from your own readings that are appropriate to share with your class. Discuss how reading sets a model for writing.
- Write in front of students and conduct a think-aloud as you write. Share the results with other teachers.

Before the Next Meeting

Read: Select the next chapter your group will read. Mark the text during reading.
Try: Try one of the lessons from the next chapter, or try something new from this chapter.
Observe: Visit a colleague's classroom to observe a guided writing lesson, or record yourself teaching a lesson and share the video at a meeting.

Going Deeper With Guided Writing

- Try a book study using this practical resource loaded with everything you need to know about guided writing:
  Oczkus, L. (2007). *Guided writing: Practical lessons, powerful results*. Portsmouth, NH: Heinemann.
- Or consider studying the resources listed on page 185.

A Reading Lesson: Read Like a Writer Fiction Mark Lesson

Objective: To share with students the elements of fiction writing by having them watch for fiction elements of action, description, dialogue, and feelings while reading so that they can begin to use these elements in their own writing.

Common Core Connections: Students identify in literature the following narrative techniques: actions, thoughts, feelings, dialogue to show character responses.

Teacher Modeling: Select a text to read aloud from which to model the four fiction elements. You might use a book the class is already reading or select a special mentor text that will help you demonstrate one or all of the story elements. As you read, pause and select one of the elements to share. Sketch and or write your response. Read another page or two and pause to model another of the elements.

Guided Practice: After you model each element in your read-aloud, allow partners to discuss and find another example to share with each other. Circulate to offer support and prompts.

Independent Practice: Encourage students to collect good examples from all kinds of books to share with the class and their partners.

Wrap Up: Ask students to reflect on which of the elements the author used the most in the pages read that day. Ask students to reflect on how these elements strengthen their writing.

A Writing Lesson: Read Like a Writer Fiction Mark Lesson

Objective: To encourage students to use the same bookmark on which they collected examples from stories as a template for creating their own narratives.

Common Core Connections: Students write using narrative techniques: actions, thoughts, feelings, dialogue to show character responses.

Teacher Modeling: Discuss examples from the literature that students have been reading or bring in a mentor text. Select just one of the elements or choose a little of each (action, dialogue, feelings, or description) to use in your modeling as you write a quick little narrative. Maybe select something that happened in your home in the past week (the dog got out, you stubbed your toe in your salsa class, your cake burned). As you write your story, use the bookmark to help plan your writing and as you rotate through each element. Or select just one of the elements and write a few brief sentences, for example, the description of a setting.

Guided Practice: Students work in groups of four, with each group member selecting a different element of fiction. The group decides on a common narrative to write about from a list the class brainstormed together. Students write the story together, with each one focusing on an element. Or each writes a few sentences on a strip focusing on one element, then the group combines their sentences. Assist groups as they work or call one group at a time to guide story writing.

Independent Practice: After practicing in teams, students use the information they've learned about the elements of fiction to write their own pieces or just one of the elements.

Wrap Up: Lead the students in a brief discussion about which elements helped them the most when writing. Discuss what was helpful or not helpful.

Assessment Tips

Formative Assessments During Lessons

While moving through the steps of a scaffolded lesson, you can create opportunities for students to demonstrate their understanding along the way. If you observe the formative assessments, and students miss something in the lesson, you can

- Reteach difficult points to the entire group
- Provide more practice
- Group students for small-group instruction
- Coach individuals

Scaffolding Step	Formative Assessment
Identify the skill in mentor texts	Observe discussions. Students turn in examples they've found, recorded on self-stick notes or as part of a writer's notebook page. Or students underline points in a text.
Teacher modeling	Observe students during their response time in the lesson. If students turn and talk to a partner or write briefly on a slate or in a journal during your lesson, study responses.
Shared writing	Same as for teacher modeling.
Guided writing	Each student takes a piece of the writing to complete. Study individual as well as group or partner compositions for teaching points.
Independent writing	Before students write on their own, create a class rubric for the writing based on what you taught in the lesson. Include just a few points for students to include. Observe samples for those points. Make piles of student work: got it, sort of got it, missed it. Coach small groups/individuals.
Reflection wrap-up	Observe students' comments on their writing. Adjust next steps.

Six Traits for Teaching and Assessment

When designing your own rubrics with your class, or when designing a quick grading system for writing, use the Six Traits of Writing as a guide for assessment and instruction (Culham, 2003; Spandel, 2001):

1. Ideas: Does the writing have a well-developed idea? Are enough details included?
2. Organization: How is the writing organized? Does the order make sense for the genre?
3. Word Choice: Is there variety in word choice?
4. Voice: Does the writing show personality, feelings, enthusiasm? Is it interesting to read?
5. Sentence Fluency: Are sentences varied in length, complexity, and variety?
6. Conventions: Is spelling, punctuation, and grammar appropriate for the grade level?

Share the rubric with students throughout the process. For detailed rubrics for assessment in various genres, see Oczkus (2007).

Read Like a Writer Fiction Mark

When you read, be on the lookout for how the author writes a story and includes…

Action

Draw an action from the reading.

Description

How did the author describe the setting or a character? Write or sketch.

Dialogue

What did the characters say?

Character Feelings

How did the author let us know how the character felt? Write or sketch.

Circle the one the author included more of:

Action

Description

Dialogue

Feelings

Why do you think the author did that? Discuss.

Read Like a Writer Fiction Mark

When you read, be on the lookout for how the author writes a story and includes…

Action

Draw an action from the reading.

Description

How did the author describe the setting or a character? Write or sketch.

Dialogue

What did the characters say?

Character Feelings

How did the author let us know how the character felt? Write or sketch.

Circle the one the author included more of:

Action

Description

Dialogue

Feelings

Why do you think the author did that? Discuss.

Best Ever Literacy Survival Tips: 72 Lessons You Can't Teach Without by Lori D. Oczkus. © 2012 International Reading Association. Adapted from *The Most Wonderful Writing Lessons Ever: Everything You Need to Teach the Essential Elements—and the Magic—of Good Writing* by B. Mariconda, 1999, New York: Scholastic, and from *Guided Writing: Practical Lessons, Powerful Results* by L.D. Oczkus, 2007, Portsmouth, NH: Heinemann. May be copied for classroom use.

Online Resources

Activities for Demonstrating the Traits of Writing: www2.scholastic.com/browse/article.jsp?id=3749243
Practical ideas for introducing the Traits in grades 6–8, but can be used in an elementary classroom, too.

Elaborating and Expanding Sentences Lesson Idea: myenglishpages.com/blog/elaborating-expanding-sentences
Students sketch sentences before and after rewriting them.

The Writing Fix: writingfix.com/index.htm
The Writing Fix, sponsored by the Northern Nevada Writing Project, is a wonderful source for writing ideas.

Chart Chums: chartchums.wordpress.com
Chart Chums is a wonderful blog on creating writing charts for your lessons.

ReadWriteThink: www.readwritethink.org
ReadWriteThink is a great resource for hundreds of free downloadable lessons in all aspects of reading, including poetry writing lessons and rich writing resources. Try "Sentence Quest: Using Parts of Speech to Write Descriptive Sentences" (Grades K–2) by Renee Goularte.

Q&A

How can I engage students, especially my struggling students, more actively in their writing conferences?

I find that when I am conferring with students during writers workshop, students are more engaged if they are in control of their work. I sit or kneel next to each student and ask, "What would you like me to help you with? What are you doing well? What do you like about your piece so far? What is your plan?" (Calkins, 1994). I ask the student to select their favorite sentence or part to read aloud to me. If we are editing, I find it helpful to always give the student the pen or pencil to mark, add, or change as we read the draft together. If we are at the computer, then the student is the one moving the cursor, reading aloud, and making all changes (this works well with my high schoolers at home too!). By simply giving the child the control of the conference, they stay more engaged!

References

Auman, M. (2003). *Step up to writing* (2nd ed.). Longmont, CO: Sopris West.
Calkins, L.M. (1994). *The art of teaching writing*. Portsmouth, NH: Heinemann.
Culham, R. (2003). *6+1 traits of writing: The complete guide (grades 3 and up)*. New York: Scholastic.
Dorfman, L.R., & Cappelli, R. (2007). *Mentor texts: Teaching writing through children's literature, K–6*. York, ME: Stenhouse.
Dorfman, L.R., & Cappelli, R. (2009). *Nonfiction mentor texts: Teaching informational writing through children's literature, K-8*. York, ME: Stenhouse.
Hatt, C. (n.d.). *Better discussions in study groups*. Retrieved from www.choiceliteracy.com/public/796.cfm
Hoyt, L., & Stead, T. (2011). *Explorations in nonfiction writing, grade 2*. Portsmouth, NH: Heinemann.
Mariconda, B. (1999). *The most wonderful writing lessons ever: Everything you need to teach the essential elements—and the magic—of good writing*. New York: Scholastic.
National Center for Education Statistics. (2008, April 3). *The nation's report card: writing 2007*. Retrieved October 14, 2011, from nces.ed.gov/pubsearch/pubsinfo.asp?pubid=2008468
Oczkus, L.D. (2007). *Guided writing: Practical lessons, powerful results*. Portsmouth, NH: Heinemann.
Pearson, P.D., & Gallagher, M.C. (1983). The instruction of reading comprehension. *Contemporary Educational Psychology, 8*, 317–344.
Routman, R. (2005). *Writing essentials: Raising expectations and results while simplifying teaching*. Portsmouth; NH: Heinemann.
Spandel, V. (2001). *Books, lessons, ideas for teaching the six traits: Writing in the elementary and middle grades*. Wilmington, MA: Great Source.

"By improving our scaffolding, or support, during lessons we can dramatically improve our students' writing. Scaffolding writing for students gives students the support they need from the fledgling idea stage to writing and publishing full-blown writing assignments in a variety of genres."

Bibliography of Children's Literature

This bibliography of children's literature, provided by the experts at Booksource.com, is organized by teaching topic for use with your students.

Motivation

Carlson, N. (2007). *I don't like to read!* New York: Viking.

Ernst, L.C. (1998). *Stella Louella's runaway book.* New York: Simon & Schuster.

Greenwald, T. (2011). *Charlie Joe Jackson's guide to not reading.* New York: Roaring Brook.

Gutman, D. (2008). *Nightmare at the bookfair.* New York: Simon & Schuster.

Hopkins, L.B. (Ed.). (2011). *I am the book.* New York: Holiday House.

Kirk, D. (2007). *Library mouse.* New York: Abrams.

Parr, T. (2005). *Reading makes you feel good.* New York: Little, Brown.

Sierra, J. (2004). *Wild about books.* New York: Knopf.

Sturm, J., Arnold, A., & Frederick-Frost, A. (2009). *Adventures in cartooning.* New York: First Second.

Tashjian, J. (2010). *My life as a book.* New York: Henry Holt.

Willems, M. (2010). *We are in a book!* New York: Hyperion.

Winter, J. (2004). *The librarian of Basra: A true story from Iraq.* Orlando, FL: Harcourt.

Reading Aloud

Boelts, M. (2007). *Those shoes.* Cambridge, MA: Candlewick.

Deedy, C.A., & Wright, R. (2011). *The Cheshire cheese cat: A Dickens of a tale.* Atlanta, GA: Peachtree.

Katz, A. (2010). *Poems I wrote when no one was looking.* New York: Margaret K. McElderry.

Laminack, L.L. (2011). *Three hens and a peacock.* Atlanta, GA: Peachtree.

Tavares, M. (2005). *Mudball.* Cambridge, MA: Candlewick.

Willems, M. (2011). *Hooray for Amanda and her alligator!* New York: Balzer & Bray.

Comprehension

Predicting

Abbott, T. (2008). *The postcard.* New York: Little, Brown.

Avi. (2008). *The seer of shadows.* New York: HarperCollins.

Jenkins, S., & Page, R. (2003). *What do you do with a tail like this?* Boston: Houghton Mifflin.

Kasza, K. (2005). *The dog who cried wolf.* New York: Putnam.

Pilkey, D. (1994). *Dog breath: The horrible trouble with Hally Tosis.* New York: Blue Sky.

Polacco, P. (2008). *For the love of autumn.* New York: Philomel.

Questioning

Bunting, E. (1994). *Smoky night.* Orlando, FL: Harcourt.

Hatkoff, I., Hatkoff, C., & Kahumbu, P. (2006). *Owen and Mzee: The true story of a remarkable friendship.* New York: Scholastic.

Hatkoff, J., Hatkoff, I., & Hatkoff, C. (2009). *Winter's tail: How one little dolphin learned to swim again.* New York: Scholastic.

Hatkoff, J., Hatkoff, I., Hatkoff, C., & Kahumbu, P. (2008). *Looking for Miza: The true story of the mountain gorilla family who rescued one of their own.* New York: Scholastic.

Shea, P.D. (1995). *The whispering cloth: A refugee's story.* Honesdale, PA: Boyds Mills.

Simon, S. (1989). *Whales.* New York: HarperCollins.

Clarifying

Bunting, E. (2001). *Gleam and glow.* San Diego, CA: Harcourt.

Greenfield, E. (1978). *Honey, I love.* New York: HarperCollins.

Hesse, K. (1998). *Come on, rain!* New York: Scholastic.

Rylant, C. (1995). *The Van Gogh cafe.* San Diego, CA: Harcourt.

Schachner, J.B. (2003). *Skippyjon Jones.* New York: Dutton.

Van Allsburg, C. (1981). *Jumanji.* Boston: Houghton Mifflin.

Summarizing

Grifalconi, A. (2002). *The village that vanished.* New York: Dial.

Hoffman, M. (1991). *Amazing Grace.* New York: Dial.

Mortenson, G., & Roth, S. (2009). *Listen to the wind: The story of Dr. Greg and* Three cups of tea. New York: Dial.

Scieszka, J. (1989). *The true story of the 3 little pigs.* New York: Penguin.

Simon, S. (2002). *Animals nobody loves.* San Francisco: Chronicle.

Yolen, J. (1992). *Encounter.* Orlando, FL: Harcourt.

Connecting

Clements, A. (1988). *Big Al.* New York: Simon & Schuster.

Freedman, R. (1980). *Immigrant kids.* New York: Dutton.

McLerran, A. (1991). *Roxaboxen.* New York: HarperCollins.

Moss, M. (1999). *Emma's journal: The story of a Colonial girl.* San Diego, CA: Harcourt.

Simon, C. (1998). *Milton Hershey: Chocolate king, town builder.* New York: Children's.

Underwood, D. (2010). *The quiet book.* Boston: Houghton Mifflin.

Inferring

Farris, C.K. (2003). *My brother Martin: A sister remembers growing up with the Rev. Dr. Martin Luther King, Jr.* New York: Simon & Schuster.

Garland, S. (1993). *The lotus seed.* San Diego, CA: Harcourt.

Jenkins, S. (1998). *Hottest, coldest, highest, deepest.* Boston: Houghton Mifflin.

Kramer, S. (1992). *Lightning.* Minneapolis, MN: Lerner.

Soto, G. (1992). *Too many tamales.* New York: G.P. Putnam's Sons.

Winnick, K.B. (1996). *Mr. Lincoln's whiskers.* Honesdale, PA: Boyds Mills.

Evaluating

Bridges, R. (1999). *Through my eyes.* New York: Scholastic.

Karas, G.B. (2005). *On Earth.* New York: Putnam.

Madrigal, A.H. (1999). *Erandi's braids.* New York: Putnam.

Polacco, P. (1994). *Pink and Say.* New York: Philomel.

Smight, L. (2006). *John, Paul, George and Ben.* New York: Hyperion.

Yolen, J. (1998). *Snow, snow: Winter poems for children.* Honesdale, PA: Boyds Mills.

Nonfiction

Jenkins, S. (2010). *Bones: Skeletons and how they work.* New York: Scholastic.

Jenkins, S., & Page, R. (2006). *Move!* Boston: Houghton Mifflin.

Manning, P.L. (2007). *Dinomummy: The life, death, and discovery of Dakota, a dinosaur from Hell Creek.* Boston: Kingfisher.

McDonnell, P. (2011). *Me...Jane.* New York: Little, Brown.

Preus, M. (2010). *Celebritrees: Historic and famous trees of the world.* New York: Henry Holt.

Smith, D.J. (2002). *If the world were a village: A book about the world's people.* Toronto, ON, Canada: Kids Can.

Assessment

Cohen, M. (1980). *First grade takes a test.* New York: Greenwillow.

Finchler, J. (2000). *Testing Miss Malarkey.* New York: Walker.

Finchler, J., & O'Malley, K. (2006). *Miss Malarkey leaves no reader behind.* New York: Walker.

Klise, K. (2007). *Regarding the bees: A lesson, in letters, on honey, dating, and other sticky subjects.* Orlando, FL: Harcourt.

Marshall, E. (1983). *Fox at school.* New York: Puffin.

Rathmann, P. (2006). *Ruby the copycat.* New York: Scholastic.

Rylant, C. (1991). *Henry and Mudge take the big test.* New York: Simon & Schuster.

Winkler, H., & Oliver, L. (2007). *The curtain went up, my pants fell down.* New York: Grosset & Dunlap.

Vocabulary

Banks, K. (2006). *Max's words.* New York: Farrar, Straus and Giroux.

DeGross, M. (1994). *Donavan's word jar.* New York: HarperTrophy.

Frasier, D. (2000). *Miss Alaineus: A vocabulary disaster.* San Diego, CA: Harcourt.

Ringgold, F. (2002). *Cassie's word quilt.* New York: Knopf.

Schotter, R. (2006). *The boy who loved words.* New York: Schwartz & Wade.

Fluency

Brinckloe, J. (1985). *Fireflies!* New York: Macmillan.

Fleischman, P. (1988). *Joyful noise: Poems for two voices.* Harper & Row.

Fleischman, P. (2000). *Big talk: Poems for four voices.* Cambridge, MA: Candlewick.

Fox, M. (2002). *The magic hat.* San Diego, CA: Harcourt.

Hoberman, M.A. (2001). *You read to me, I'll read to you: Very short stories to read together.* Boston: Little, Brown.

Laminack, L.L. (2004). *Saturdays and teacakes.* Atlanta, GA: Peachtree.

Lionni, L. (1968). *The alphabet tree.* New York: Knopf.

Locker, T. (2000). *Cloud dance.* San Diego, CA: Harcourt.

Writing

Ideas

Fleischman, P. (1998). *Weslandia*. Cambridge, MA: Candlewick.

Frasier, D. (1997). *Out of the ocean*. San Diego, CA: Harcourt.

Muth, J.J. (2002). *The three questions*. New York: Scholastic.

Muth, J.J. (2003). *Stone soup*. New York: Scholastic.

Noble, T.H. (2007). *The orange shoes*. Chelsea, MI: Sleeping Bear.

Schotter, R. (1996). *Nothing ever happens on 90th Street*. New York: Orchard.

Sierra, J. (1998). *Antarctic antics: A book of penguin poems*. San Diego, CA: Harcourt.

Wisniewski, D. (1998). *The secret knowledge of grown-ups*. New York: HarperTrophy.

Organization

Colfer, E. (2004). *The legend of Spud Murphy*. New York: Hyperion.

McLeod, B. (2006). *SuperHero ABC*. New York: HarperCollins.

Nolen, J. (1998). *Raising dragons*. San Diego, CA: Harcourt Brace.

Pérez, L.K. (2002). *First day in grapes*. New York: Lee & Low.

Shannon, D. (2000). *The rain came down*. New York: Scholastic.

Singer, M. (2000). *On the same day in March: A tour of the world's weather*. New York: HarperCollins.

Smith, C.R., Jr. (1999). *Rimshots: Basketball pix, rolls, and rhythms*. New York: Penguin.

Spier, P. (1980). *People*. New York: Doubleday.

Teague, M. (2002). *Dear Mrs. LaRue: Letters from obedience school*. New York: Scholastic.

Waber, B. (2002). *Courage*. Boston: Houghton Mifflin.

Word Choice

Aston, D.H. (2007). *A seed is sleepy*. San Francisco: Chronicle.

Gray, L.M. (1995). *My mama had a dancing heart*. New York: Orchard.

Hartman, B. (2002). *The wolf who cried boy*. New York: Putnam.

Horvath, P. (2001). *Everything on a waffle*. New York: Farrar, Straus and Giroux.

Palatini, M. (1995). *Piggie pie!* New York: Clarion.

Sentence Fluency

Baker, K. (1991). *Hide and snake*. Orlando, FL: Harcourt.

Baylor, B. (1994). *The table where rich people sit*. New York: Atheneum.

Burleigh, R. (1998). *Home run: The story of Babe Ruth*. Orlando, FL: Harcourt.

Davies, N. (2001). *Bat loves the night*, Cambridge, MA: Candlewick.

Davies, N. (2001). *One tiny turtle*. Cambridge, MA: Candlewick.

Fletcher, R. (1997). *Twilight comes twice*. New York: Clarion.

Fox, M. (2000). *Harriet, you'll drive me wild!* Orlando, FL: Harcourt.

Graham, J.B. (1999). *Flicker flash*. Boston: Houghton Mifflin.

O'Malley, K. (2005). *Once upon a cool motorcycle dude*. New York: Walker.

Peters, L.W. (2003). *Our family tree: An evolution story*. San Diego, CA: Harcourt.

Waboose, J.B. (1997). *Morning on the lake*. Buffalo, NY: Kids Can.

Voice

Cronin, D. (2011). *The trouble with chickens: A J.J. Tully mystery*. New York: Balzer & Bray.

Freymann, S., & Elffers, J. (1999). *How are you peeling? Foods with moods*. New York: Scholastic.

Hall, D. (1994). *I am the dog, I am the cat*. New York: Dial.

Hopkins, J. (2002). *The three armadillies Tuff*. Atlanta, GA: Peachtree.

Lawrence, C. (2011). *The case of the deadly desperados*. New York: Putnam.

MacLachlan, P. (2010). *Word after word after word*. New York: Katherine Tegen.

O'Malley, K. (2010). *Once upon a royal superbaby*. New York: Walker.

Stadler, A. (2003). *Beverly Billingsly takes a bow*. San Diego, CA: Harcourt.

Sturges, P. (1999). *The little red hen (makes a pizza)*. New York: Puffin.

Weeks, S. (2009). *Sophie Peterman tells the truth!* New York: Beach Lane.

Winter, J. (2009). *The fabulous feud of Gilbert and Sullivan*. New York: Arthur A. Levine.

Conventions

Carr, J. (2007). *Greedy apostrophe: A cautionary tale*. New York: Holiday House.

Dahl, M. (2006). *If you were an adverb*. Minneapolis, MN: Picture Window.

Dahl, M. (2006). *If you were a synonym*. Minneapolis, MN: Picture Window.

Loewen, N. (2007). *If you were a conjunction*. Minneapolis, MN: Picture Window.

Pulver, R. (2003). *Punctuation takes a vacation*. New York: Holiday House.

Raschka, C. (1993). *Yo! Yes?* New York: Orchard.

Truss, L. (2008). *Twenty-odd ducks: Why, every punctuation mark counts*. New York: Putnam.

Prewrite

Fletcher, R. (1996). *A writer's notebook: Unlocking the writer within you*. New York: HarperTrophy.

Hopkins, L.B. (1993). *The writing bug*. Katonah, NY: Richard C. Owen.

Reynolds, P. (2004). *Ish*. Cambridge, MA: Candlewick.

Spinelli, E. (2008). *The best story*. New York: Dial.

Wong, J.S. (2002). *You have to write*. New York: Margaret K. McElderry.

Write

Frazee, M. (2003). *Roller coaster.* San Diego, CA: Harcourt.

Gibbons, G. (2000). *Apples.* New York: Holiday House.

Keats, E.J. (1967). *Peter's chair.* New York: Harper & Row.

Myers, W.D. (1993). *Brown angels: An album of pictures and verse.* New York: HarperCollins.

Nixon, J.L. (1988). *If you were a writer.* New York: Simon & Schuster.

Ryder, J. (1994). *My father's hands.* New York: William Morrow.

White, E.B. (1952). *Charlotte's web.* New York: HarperCollins.

Revise

Barnett, M. (2012). *Chloe and the lion.* New York: Hyperion.

Burleigh, R. (2011). *The adventures of Mark Twain by Huckleberry Finn.* New York: Atheneum.

Burton, V.L. (1939). *Mike Mulligan and his steam shovel.* Boston: Houghton Mifflin.

Fox, M. (1988). *Koala Lou.* Orlando, FL: Harcourt.

Lester, H. (1997). *Author: A true story.* Boston: Houghton Mifflin.

Edit

Heller, R. (1987). *A cache of jewels and other collective nouns.* New York: PaperStar.

Heller, R. (1988). *Kites sail high: A book about verbs.* New York: Grosset & Dunlap.

Heller, R. (1989). *Many luscious lollipops: A book about adjectives.* New York: Sandcastle.

Heller, R. (1991). *Up, up, and away: A book about adverbs.* New York: Grosset & Dunlap.

Heller, R. (1995). *Behind the mask: A book about prepositions.* New York: Grosset & Dunlap.

Heller, R. (1997). *Mine, all mine: A book about pronouns.* New York: Grosset & Dunlap.

Heller, R. (1998). *Fantastic! Wow! and Unreal! A book about interjections and conjunctions.* New York: Grosset & Dunlap.

Publish

Aliki. (1986). *How a book is made.* New York: HarperCollins.

Christelow, E. (1995). *What do authors do?* New York: Clarion.

Christelow, E. (1999). *What do illustrators do?* New York: Clarion.